Proverbs

AMPLIFIED AND APPLIED

———

DICK BROGDEN

Copyright © 2022 Live Dead
ALL RIGHTS RESERVED.

Published by Abide Publishers
1600 N. Boonville, Suite B&C, Springfield, MO 65803

Cover design, typesetting, and interior design by Lucent Digital (www.lucentdigital.co).

No portion of this book may be reproduced, stored in a retrieval system, or transmitted in any form or by any means—electronic, mechanical, photocopy, recording, or any other—except for brief quotations in printed reviews, without the prior written permission of the publisher.

Scripture quotations used in this book are from the New King James Version®. Copyright © 1982 by Thomas Nelson. Used by permission. All rights reserved.

ISBN: 978-1-952562-08-2

Printed in the United States of America

For Mom and Dad Chapman

Whose daily practical wisdom has made all their children glad

Contents

1	Introduction
3	Chapter 1
23	Chapter 2
37	Chapter 3
57	Chapter 4
73	Chapter 5
85	Chapter 6
101	Chapter 7
113	Chapter 8
129	Chapter 9
137	Chapter 10
151	Chapter 11
163	Chapter 12
173	Chapter 13
183	Chapter 14
201	Chapter 15

217	Chapter 16
233	Chapter 17
247	Chapter 18
259	Chapter 19
275	Chapter 20
293	Chapter 21
309	Chapter 22
325	Chapter 23
343	Chapter 24
361	Chapter 25
375	Chapter 26
389	Chapter 27
403	Chapter 28
417	Chapter 29
431	Chapter 30
447	Chapter 31
463	Endnotes

Introduction

This book approaches each verse in Proverbs uniquely, paraphrasing and expanding application to multiple meanings. It took three years to write as I plodded through the book line by line, precept by precept. The result is not an exposition of each proverb; rather, each verse served as a launching point for my own thoughts and perspective as I amplified and applied them. My hope is that my musings on the wisdom laid out for us in the book of Proverbs will inspire your own.

DICK BROGDEN
LIVE DEAD MOVEMENT CO-FOUNDER
JEDDAH, SAUDI ARABIA

PROVERBS

Chapter 1

1.1

It bothers me that both David and Solomon (father and son, great kings of Israel) did not end well. It bothers me that inappropriate behavior with women led to disaster for both men. David's adultery led to murder and family tragedy, and Solomon's unrestrained lust led to idolatry. The Bible does not hide the flaws of its characters lest we deceive ourselves. Forced to wrestle with the tragic sins of those we admire, we are likewise forced to confront our own deadly sins and passions. Wincing at the poor choices of the great helps us in facing our own idiotic and self-destructive tendencies more honestly. David and Solomon have much to teach us concerning living life skillfully (a definition of wisdom), but we can also learn from their folly, if we will. Perhaps their pain can save us from ours, and their wisdom can lead us to joy.

1.2

We know because God reveals. We discern because the Holy Spirit nudges us. Wisdom and discernment exceed intelligence. You can be a foolish genius or a wise simpleton. God's intention for us is that we be wise and discerning—but not professional critics. We need to be as astute in seeing the good as we are quick to notice the bad. Wisdom can be gleaned by reading and observation—especially from those who have gone before us and learned the hard way. Old dead guys[1] are a precious resource, and their wisdom can be mined from the pages they leave behind. Discernment comes from attentive listening to Jesus in the moment. He doesn't usually shout. He just quietly, subtly, and gently elbows us—nodding with His head, pointing with His eyes. The perceptive and the discerning listen and watch well—and their obedient observance makes them wise.

1.3

Wise men listen and obey, doing what is right no matter the cost. To consistently do what is right will make you unpopular, for you must treat all men unequally. Equity does not apportion equally, but according to need, context, and worthiness. Justice and judgment are learned, not memorized, for they are active living truths, not formulas or codes. The purest form of leadership and the truest judgment stands on the principle that all men and situations must be treated differently. Only the Holy Spirit can grant us the wisdom to do this well and the strength to bear the misunderstanding that will inevitably follow.

1.4

There is nothing wrong with being simple. This world lauds the complex, the dashing, the worldly-wise, but Jesus honors those without guile. In an age that increasingly speeds up, loses patience, and demands quick decisions, the wise young man will slow things down. Time is the friend of the righteous and rush is his enemy. Prudence is simply slowing things down to ensure you take the time to listen to the Lord—the wisest of all. Very few decisions in life are improved by making them with alacrity. When a young man can incorporate the patience of an old man into his decision-making process, he may frustrate and disappoint his peers, but he will better honor His heavenly Father. In the long run slowing down to check with the Lord of time will speed you up. Taking the time that good decisions require is the shorter route to health, peace, and happiness.

1.5

What puts you in the camp of the wise is not how much you know, but how you continually learn. The foolish plateau in desire and humility. They lose the desire to learn, and they lose the humility to learn from everyone. A man of understanding intentionally acquires wise counsel; he seeks it out even from unusual sources. Wise counsel can be gained from our failures and from our critics, from our enemies and from adversity. The ones who like us least can serve us best, for there is often a kernel of truth in their accusations. Don't be too proud to glean wisdom from every person, every day, in every situation.

1.6

It's good to struggle to understand. While there is a place for didactic teaching, there is also a reason that Jesus sometimes used parables, why Solomon used proverbs, and why prophets and seers sometimes used riddles and enigmas. Wisdom, therefore, is not something that can be bought or transferred. In a sense it has to be earned by participatory struggle, by wrestling through to make the knowledge personal. By the same token, sometimes it's wise not to spoon feed truth to our disciples. Sometimes the kindest thing we can do is to leave them to struggle through alone—alone, that is, with Jesus, who is the fount of all wisdom. The wise learn to embrace the struggle to understand truth, for on the other side of that struggle is real ownership of and participation in that very truth.

1.7

Knowledge begins with reverence, reverence for God. Knowledge does not begin with intelligence, effort, discipline, or even revelation. It begins with acknowledging there is an all-wise God, and you are not Him, and neither is the collective wisdom of man. The first step in being smart is the refusal to put God on trial. C. S. Lewis referred to man's arrogant and disrespectful questioning of God as "putting God in the dock"—the "dock" being the British term for where the accused sat or stood during his trial. Don't be the fool who despises wisdom by starting from the vantage point that God is wrong or unjust, and thus you should question Him. The starting place for wisdom is to acknowledge and respect that God is both good and wise, and that He will reveal to you His reasons when He feels it best to reveal them.

1.8

God appoints all authorities. Fathers and mothers are authorities, and they were chosen by God to impact your life. Your parents may have been neurotic, controlling, insecure, Muslim, poor, wise, godly, kind, distant, generous, demanding, or a thousand other things—it does not matter. They were God-appointed so that you might learn from them. We can learn from every authority figure, good or bad. To think we can only learn from the good or the ones we agree with is arrogant. We can learn from everyone that God sets over us. The wise will eagerly submit to their parents wherever and whenever they can (the only exception being if the parents' law contradicts God's law), for they will not only learn, but they will also receive the blessing from honoring the first commandment that promises God's blessing. Do not thoughtlessly or quickly abandon the tradition and customs of your parents. What irritates or embarrasses you now might comfort, guide, and protect your own children in the future.

1.9

Riches and grace come from obeying our authorities. The first line of authority in our lives is our parents, but in the course of our days we will have the opportunity to submit to many different people. Every time we listen, obey, honor, and submit, we not only practically benefit (make good choices and avoid disastrous ones), but we are also spiritually adorned with riches and grace. Think of it in terms of being honored in Hawaii or India with a garland of flowers. Every time we respect our authorities by cherishing and enacting the wisdom they give us, it's as if we have another wreath of beauty, of riches placed around our spiritual neck. It is then in our best interest to submit to the wisdom of our elders. The humility of listening and obeying makes us spiritually and emotionally both wealthy and beautiful.

1.10

A central part of wisdom is the "happy no!" Many sinful things will waft their siren songs in our direction. Enticement will come from people, places, and pleasures, but the wise learn how to say "no" firmly, graciously, sometimes fiercely, but always happily. The "happy no" is derived not from the sadness of missing out on something you want to do yet avoid because it is bad for you, but from the joy of staying pure, free, and fulfilled by obedience to Jesus. When we live conscious that we are most fulfilled when we do what Jesus wants in unbroken obedient fellowship with Him, we happily say "no" to the enticements of this world. The joy of being right with Jesus is a pleasure no fleeting sin can rival. We do not consent to the silly ideas of sinners, for we know the highest joy of making Jesus happy, a happiness that fills our soul with delight.

1.11

There are many ways to murder; the most common of which is to assassinate character by malicious words. Jesus talks about heart anger and the malicious tongue in no uncertain terms, how they are poisonous and murderous, defiling the one who carries them as much as the one against which they are launched. In the course of life, there will be others who encourage you to kill with your words by their attitude, posture, cynicism, jealousy, and critical attitude. Wisdom refuses to associate with that killing spirit; it refuses to malign, gossip, slander, or assassinate others with words. Why? Because wisdom recognizes that murder always boomerangs. Every time you "murder" another (even with your words), you kill a little bit of yourself. Murder is but a subtle form of suicide.

1.12

God made men to love battle, conquest, difficulty, and challenge. Men are motivated by competition, and this is, in essence, a good thing. Yet, when competition shifts from fighting evil to removing our brother or fellow man, a good passion is bent toward evil purposes. The fallen manifestation of competition tries to eliminate competitors, and it seeks to overcome others rather than to overcome challenges. There is a godly ambition which seeks to take territory for the King, but this ambition is so easily twisted towards striving for notoriety, even if that means we drag brothers and sisters down, stepping on them in order to be noticed. The wise know that we are not in competition against men and women; thus, it is folly to think their removal is our advancement. Let God make the assignments, give the promotions, and shuffle the troops. Let us recruit to the good King's army. Let us not remove the very ones who could help turn the tide of war.

1.13

Don't led greed and ambition cause you to run over people. If we peel away the layers of self-justification, which so adroitly cloak our real motives, we find that the heart of our slander and criticism of others is jealousy. We covet the respect others have earned; we lust after the affirmation we see others receive; and we long for the recognition others deserve. Our wicked and evil hearts want to pull others down so that we can be lifted up. We would rather step on others and be noticed than humbly get down on our hands and knees so that others can stand on us. Wisdom is content to rejoice in the strength and advance of others, content to do the hard work required of any legitimate honor, and content even not to be noticed by man and to live solely for the approval of the God who sees all. The all-seeing and all-knowing One will one day reward justly and fairly. There is no need to be jealous or greedy for the praise and possessions of men if we live constantly for the commendation of God.

1.14

Not all unity is sanctioned by God. There is a form of unity that would link us with evil people and causes, a unity that God warns us to avoid. While it is true that we can be friendly to most and merciful to all, there are certain people with whom we should carefully avoid intimacy. Disciples of Jesus are equipped and prepared to reach out to all kinds of people only when their core group of friends is godly and Christ-minded. There are enticing invitations and opportunities to spend time with those who do not glory in Christ nor worship Him. These invitations can be enticing for a range of reasons: the inviters are winsome, they are the power brokers of the community, they are affluent and resourceful, they are intelligent and witty, or even they are lost and needing the Savior. This last category can be the most compelling of all, but even then, we are only safely able to reach the lost if we ourselves are surrounded by and accountable to others of "like precious" faith. Be friendly to all and be best friends with those who follow Jesus with equal (or more) passion to yours.

1.15

Some people are to be avoided. It seems counter intuitive when we are told to befriend enemies, eat with sinners, go to the most unreached places and resistant peoples, and forgive 490 times, yet the same Lord who commands us to go the second mile and bear others' burdens commands us to shun some and turn others over to Satan. Wise sons reach out to the wicked from the firm ground of being surrounded by the righteous. When Jesus saves us from sin, He pulls us from an evil river disgusting in its vileness. Friends and family, colleagues and neighbors may still be floundering in that putrid river, drowning in filth. We need to stand far enough away from the unstable banks of that river so that the ground does not erode beneath us, collapse and tumble us back in, yet close enough to reach into that slime to offer a helping hand. We can only genuinely help others if we stand on solid ground. Solid ground is a circle of godly friends. Stand with them on the Solid Rock that they hold you up (and back) when you reach out into the path of the drowning.

1.16

Peace is something to which we run. Bureaucracy, injustice, traffic, insults, delays, and frustrations all tend to speed us to anger, which does not result in the righteousness of God. There are many ways to be improperly violent—the crowning one being physical force—but we can also attack with our eyes, our words, our posture, our attitude, or even by withholding appropriate affection, response, or engagement. Sometimes we most painfully attack others by avoiding or starving them. Do not speed your way to violence; rather, run to make peace. Be the anger swallower. Be the diffuser of tension. Be the cheek turner. Let your calm response deescalate arguments. With gentle words, looks, and touches, be the one who brokers peace. The wise pour water on flames, not gasoline.

1.17

Little birds see and easily escape the simple snares of the hunter. How much more will God assist humans to escape vain attempts to hunt with sneaky words. In our brokenness and insecurity, we usually hunt those who threaten us. We look for fault in their words (as hunters of Jesus did) by asking them questions that would entrap, hoping to latch on to an inconsistency. In our vanity we think we look better by making the other look bad. In reality no one wins in assassination; murder and murderer alike are despoiled. The persuasion of Jesus is to lift up and liberate not tear down and bind. Jesus likes simple, open truth—not sneaky and disingenuous plots to capture. Wisdom puts energy into setting others free, not tripping them into prison. If a fight needs to be waged (and on rare occasions it does), then battle on a level plane, person to person, wielding only words of truth in the bright light of day. Do not snare with the weapons of slander and the cowardly assistance of a gang of assassins who shoot poisoned arrows from the dark of night.

1.18

Plotting the demise of others is really just waiting for your own decline and fall. Counter to the "dog eat dog" philosophy of the world, a philosophy that demands competition with others in order to advance, Christianity shockingly charts that the way to advancement is promoting the strengths of those around you. In the world, you step on the backs of others, biting them as you climb in order to achieve. In the body of Christ, you get down on your hands and knees and let others stand on your back. It's self-evident that the most stable stance is that which has hands and knees planted on the firm ground of humility. Those that try to perch on the backs of the unwilling stand on unsteady ground indeed. One twitch of unhappy shoulders sends oppressors tumbling down. Be the wise one who plots and empowers the success of others. Do not be the fool who schemes for others to fall—the blood spilt will ultimately be your own.

1.19

Greed starves you. Satisfaction is a choice. When Paul said, "I can do all things through Christ who strengthens me," he did so while writing about money. He could live with plenty or paucity; in both cases he would choose to be satisfied. The hunger for food is but the first revelation of greed, obvious because it is both daily and observable. I can see a fat man and know with some certainty that greed has mastered him, but a skinny man's frame and the presence of an unearned and un-stewarded high metabolism does not immediately reveal whether he is greedy for gold or acclaim. The problem with greed is that it is insatiable. The antidote for greed is choosing to be satisfied with less than you want. This starts at the dining table, but must extend to acclaim, affirmation, finances, success, opportunity, and even friends. It is not the attaining of our full hopes that satisfies us; it is choosing to be glad and grateful whether or not all our desires materialize.

1.20

Fools tend to be hard of hearing. Wisdom is out there in the streets and marketplaces yelling at the top of her voice. Unashamedly and unreservedly, wisdom bangs on every door, rattles every window, interrupts every conversation, cold-calls at supper, junk-mails herself to your inbox, subtitles every movie, harmonizes with every song, and ubiquitously seeks an audience. The lie of Gnosticism is that wisdom is for the few. The reality of truth is that it is freely offered to all and that God in His generosity employs a multitude of delivery mechanisms. Wisdom can be heard calling through nature; wisdom can be gleaned through reading a biography; and wisdom can be downloaded from pagan, godless friends. God can teach us what not to do by observing the disobedience of the rebellious and what to do by recalling the piety of the saints. Babes, sages, and even teenagers can all be our teachers. Wisdom is sourced in God Himself, most clearly revealed through the Bible, and it courses freely through a thousand other channels and mediums. If you meet or become a fool, you need not extend pity, nor demand it. Fools are those who refuse the free, public offering of wisdom by consciously stopping up their own ears.

1.21

Wisdom is aggressive and insistent, vocal and public. We should make it a point to learn from every single person we meet. You don't have to respect someone in order to learn from them. Enemies are faithful teachers, and critics are capable coaches. We grow in wisdom through interaction with both supporters and those who oppose us. Watching poor leadership teaches us how not to live. Observing the consequences of immoral choices motivates us to biblical morality. Living with difficult people spurs us to resolve to treat others kindly. Working under abusive authority helps us determine not to subject others to the pain we have traversed. It is prudent to be well read in history and civic affairs, for much wisdom is gleaned just by listening to the public discourse. We are meant to engage with and learn from the broken people and structures of the world, to be in the middle of the conversation without being of it.

1.22

Pure humor is the most difficult of all of comedy. Late night humor is funny because it is mean. It is relatively easy to be crude, cynical, and sarcastic. It comes naturally to our fallen natures to criticize, tease, mock, and scoff. It's much harder to make people laugh by lifting others up. Scoffing and scorning may make you feel witty and intelligent, but it actually makes you stupid. It is difficult to scorn someone and learn from them at the same time. The wise learn from all men and women. When we stop scorning, we start learning. We don't get wiser by demeaning others; we actually get more foolish. Fools hate knowledge because they prefer to demean others and by doing so cement their ignorance. The baby steps of wisdom include forsaking scoffing so that you can learn from others, all others.

1.23

Repentance is both a confession and a lifestyle. When we live repentant, God pours out His Spirit on us. Repentance has two incredible blessings. First, God so loves a perpetually contrite heart that when He finds one, He lavishes His wisdom, counsel, strength, comfort, and power upon it. Second, repentance leads to fresh revelation. When we live contrite, God makes His words known to us, and through His words we learn of His character. If we do not turn (repent), we will not receive fresh fillings of the Spirit and we will not have the words of God revealed to us. God's rebuke (discipline that often is channeled to us through our disappointments) is an invitation to turn toward His blessings because repentance does not just return us to former status, it can actually elevate us past where we used to stand to fresh outpourings of the Spirit, fresh revelations of God. However, much as it costs us in shame to repent, it is much more expensive not to.

1.24

There has never been a problem with God's voice. There has never been a problem with God's initiative. What distinguishes the God of the Bible from all other gods is His steady calling and seeking of the lost. All other religions vainly search for a transcendent or remote or mysterious deity who makes himself difficult to find. But the one true God never stops seeking, calling, searching, or agonizing over His lost children. In mercy, our God calls. He stretches out His hands in invitation—even when we stop up our ears and shrug off His embrace. Do not believe the internal or external lie that the fault in our separation or estrangement from God is God's fault. He ever calls, He ever reaches. Let us have the wisdom to receive His embrace and to take His call.

1.25

The rebuke of God is the vanguard of His wisdom. When we disdain rebuke—from God or man, from friend or foe—we forfeit a wealth of learning. Rebukes are the slaps that stun us and arrest us, intended to shut us up and silence our nonsense so that we might listen. All too often we miss the benefit of the rebuke because the slap intended to silence us (in order that we listen) instead makes us cry in self-pity or howl in self-righteous indignation. We can't learn if we are reacting viscerally to rebuke. Fools lash out when rebuke shames and stuns them, missing the follow-up lesson. The wise shut up when rebuked, for they know some precious insight is heading their way.

1.26

Man's emotions are sourced in God. God is not a dispassionate being. He is emotionally real and forceful, and not just in what we consider the "pleasant" emotions of joy, happiness, peace, and contentment. God also laughs at the calamity of the stubborn and mocks those who are terrified because they disobeyed. God gets angry and hates. He is so emotionally against evil things and people that He will destroy them in a blaze of fury. God's wrath is balanced with but not absorbed by His love. We were created to be passionately emotional. We should laugh, dance, and celebrate with both soul and body. And we should grieve, cry, shout, and zealously attack evil wherever we find it. God is passionate in opposite directions (wrath and mercy), and thus should we likewise be. God is an emotional being and He created us to bear that emotional image. Whole people enjoy and exhibit a range of emotions. God is not inhibited in a full range of emotional expression; neither should His highest creation—humankind—be.

1.27

The effects of sin appear sudden, but in reality they are the result of a series of accumulated disobediences. Terror and destruction seem to appear out of nowhere, but the sovereignty of God is too mercifully patient to allow random disaster. Distress and anguish are not accidents, not if we believe that God is sovereignly good in all He ordains and all He allows. A good God will punish evil, even when that evil is found in His children—especially when it is found in His children. Good parents get the cavities in their children's teeth fixed before they do benevolent dentistry among the poor. God is glorified just as much when a person goes to hell as when a person goes to heaven. A merciful God grants eternal life with Himself as a reward to all who repent. A just God sentences the unrepentant and rebellious to eternal death and punishment. Both acts deserve awe and worship. The foolish are surprised when the effects of their sin catch up with them. The wise ever know they deserve terror and destruction and are ever thankful that God in grace does not unleash it upon them.

1.28

God is not our genie. Contrary to perception, God does not wait around silently like our butler waiting for us to summon Him and give Him an assignment. Just because we ask, God will not necessarily leap to attention. Just because we cry, God will not necessarily sprint to us like a nanny to her charge. The Bible expressly says that sometimes God will not answer, that we will seek Him and not find Him. We cannot expect to disobey, scorn, ignore, and abuse the Lord of majesty for large periods and then expect Him to grant our every selfish demand. He is not ours to command; we are His to obey. God is at work in the earth and in eternity, He is not waiting around for us to think up something for Him to do. If He answers us, it is out of His great condescension, mercy, and patience. How foolish the woman who thinks God is her genie, and how wise the woman ever thankful that Almighty God is gracious enough to listen to—and often grant—her very small scheme petitions.

1.29

Knowledge of God follows respect. We have to want to learn about God on God's terms. We cannot dictate the terms of our learning; the knowledge of God is not a self-guided study. In hubris, man tries to dictate to God how God should reveal Himself. I have had men ask me to make a case for God, with the stipulation that I could not do that using God's Word, as if God is their puppet to come and play self-muted charades for their amusement. To disrespectfully demand from God your preferences for His means of revelation is foolish. E. Stanley Jones refers to it as "a blind man searching in a dark room for a black cat that isn't there." If we want to know God, we have to start with respect. He is the teacher. He dictates the terms. He sets the lesson plans, and He determines the assignment. We cannot presume to learn from God and teach Him at the same time.

1.30

God gives us multiple chances to learn wisdom. Over and over, He offers us His counsel and mercies us with His rebukes. Fools earn that dubious status the hard way—by repeated disobediences and multiple intentional refusals of God's offered wisdom. Do not pity the foolish man, nor expect pity for your folly. Fools become foolish over time as a consequence of multiple refusals of God's help. The fool constantly and repeatedly says no to God's instruction; the wise one constantly and repeatedly says yes. Wisdom, like folly, is earned over time. It is the multiple acceptances of God's teaching, counsel, and rebukes that make us wise —no matter the surprising places or people they issue from. To be with Christ in the school of wisdom is to recognize a slow, long process of daily learning. To graduate with a degree in folly is likewise earned over time.

1.31

There is an aching emptiness to getting your own way. Be wary of getting what you insist on. It could very well send leanness to your soul. God in His wisdom withholds from us the things we think we want, for He knows what will destroy or harm us. If we persist in pursuing the things for which we lust, eventually God allows us to have them, and we eat of that fruit, finding it pleasant to our mouth but bitter to our stomach and spirit. The pleasures of getting our own way last for a moment, but the consequences must be digested in full. A friend puts it crudely but succinctly: "Choosing to sin is like taking a crap in your pants. It feels good for a second, and then you have to live with your own filthy mess."

1.32

Lazy, wayward complacency is not neutral or harmless; it's actually death. To turn away from God's laws, principles, and commands is not to choose an equally opportune path. God's path is the only one without poisonous landmines. God's path is not easy. In fact, it is brutally hard and involves a cross. But it is safe to the soul. If you turn away from the wisdom of God, you will die a long, slow, agonized death. It's just not worth it. But there's more. God's path is so counter-cultural, and sin so ubiquitous, lodged in our heart and DNA, that walking with Jesus is like going up the down escalator. You can't just stand complacently. You can't even walk idly. You have to put your head down and bite into the climb. Both the turning from God's ways and complacency in them will destroy you.

1.33

Safety is not in our self-designed fortresses, but in our obedience. Listening to Jesus keeps us safe. Because our primary problem is ourselves (not the devil, not our critics, not our persecutors), we can't actually go anywhere to escape evil. An evil heart, mind, and will accompanies us to all locations and into all places of rest, refuge, or renewal, for it is inextricably within us. The only possible place of escape from evil is not a physical location. It is a state of listening obedience. Because our safety is in listening to

Jesus, we can be fearless. We can go anywhere and face any foe, for we have overcome the myth that safety is a place. Obedience is our only security.

PROVERBS

Chapter 2

2.1

Wisdom is preserved by appreciating and applying it. Similar to learning a new language, we need to use it or lose it. We appreciate wisdom. We treasure wisdom by accumulating it, not in a storehouse or stockpile ahead of us, but in a legacy of actions that trail behind us. We are not disconnected from our deeds of the past. Godly treasure is mercy and love wisely spent on others. We only actually retain wisdom by giving it away, and we give it away by living it out to the benefit and blessing of others. When we hear truth and then act on it habitually, we have actually possessed it eternally. We don't memorize truth or wisdom; we live it. No one is considered wise for their potential in the future; rather, the wise are known by their truth acts in the most recent past. You are only wise if the last thing you did was wise.

2.2

Wisdom is a discipline, a posture, an inclination. In order to grow in wisdom, and to become and stay wise, we must incline (discipline) ourselves towards it. We must be intentional about actively listening for wisdom. In other words, we go searching for it. The wise posture themselves in such a way that their ears are finely tuned towards wisdom's subtle broadcast. We do not accidentally become wise, nor do we stumble across wisdom haphazardly. We sit poised and attentive in front of wisdom's radio, slowly and carefully spinning the dial of choice. We move past rhetoric and foolish talk, clever lies and brash perversion, we fine tune the receptors of our soul so that distracting static is minimized. And we search out that clear channel where wisdom is simply broadcast. We let it flood into our ears and we apply it by acting wisdom out with our bodies.

2.3

Finding wisdom not only demands we use our ears, but also our voice. We must lift up our voice and cry out for it. Wisdom is a marketplace commodity; it both seeks you and demands, insists that you seek it. Think of it like a choice item for which you long with which you will adorn your spiritual house. You must enter the crowded and noisy bazaar of life, knowing that in that pulsating throng there are many aggressive vendors all trying to sell their wares. Some of them cry out in a seller's voice: "WISDOM! WISDOM!" You must lift your buyer's voice and quest with equal vigor: "WISDOM? WISDOM?" In the mutual yelling, buyer and seller will find one another, association will be made, friendship engaged. We do not wait for wisdom to find us. We seek it out aggressively, encouraged that the seeking is mutual.

2.4

Those who mine silver and gold eagerly seek the precious minerals clutched inside the earth. Occasionally, the earth releases its tight stewardship of what is precious and distributes these hidden treasures via a rippling, gentle stream, or a sudden and violent geological act. When we realize just how precious wisdom is, we are not content to wait for its beneficial bestowal; instead, we don our mining gear and go digging. We don't dig for material gain, increased intelligence, or theoretical amusement. We dig because we seek the treasure of the knowledge of God—a prize indestructible, impossible to lose or have stolen. We are not mining a mountain. We are digging into deity, and the God we mine is an inexhaustible treasure. Thus, we dig reverently, awed at the size and scope of Who we seek.

2.5

Knowledge of how God is to be reverenced keys open the knowledge of His character. Respectful and appropriate fear of the Lord is where our journey to understanding Him begins. In the New Testament, our loving God is revealed as Father. We revel in our sonship and the boldness with which we can approach our heavenly Dad. As we grow from childhood to maturity, we realize the Old Testament revelation as well: our intimate Daddy was a holy and glorious King before we were born. We first knew His smile and embrace, but now we notice His throne, His judgments, His authority, and His awesomeness. We don't shudder in fear of Him—His joy in us is still our first thought—but we do stand still in awe wanting even more strongly to honor and please Him, to be worthy of His joy. We hide in the curtains at the back of His throne room, peek out and marvel as the kings of the earth, all nations, the elements, demons and devil, and all the cosmos grovel at the feet of our Daddy. When we understand that God wants to be both enjoyed as loving Father and reverenced as glorious King, we have opened the door to wisdom.

2.6

Wisdom is given by revelation, and revelation is given by the Word of God. Wisdom comes from the self-disclosure of Jehovah, and Jehovah has chosen the primary vehicle of His self-disclosure to be through speaking, through verbal inspiration. Yes, God speaks through nature. Yes, God speaks through His actions. Yes, God speaks through science. Yes, God can speak through art and images and a hundred other means. But the primary way God communicates is through His speech: God talks to us with words. We do not worship the Bible. The Bible is but the faithfully written down spoken words and acts of God. The acts of God are made purposeful through His verbal explanation of them. Jesus demonstrates His love by dying for us then reveals the meaning of that act by verbally explaining it to us. We may not like this. We may demand otherwise. But the wise woman realizes that God chooses to give knowledge and understanding by issuing it out of His mouth. This is why God incarnated as the living Word. This is why the wise then spend a lot of time in the written Word. This is why the wise constantly listen to God the Holy Spirit. Because God, wonderful Counselor, still speaks through words.

2.7

Wisdom is a supply and a defense. Wisdom gained now provides in the present and protects in the future. God in His benevolence stockpiles wisdom for us. He gives neither Spirit nor wisdom by measure. He delights to flood, saturate, fill, overwhelm, and lavish the spirit of wisdom, counsel, discernment, and understanding upon us. When we walk in the light, in integrity, it is as if we have a library card that allows us free checkout of heaven's daily living manuals. Our integrity is what gives us access to all the stored-up wisdom of God. Integrity also shields us from the attacks of folly. The grandest folly comes wrapped in deceptive intelligence. The devil is able (cunning angel of light that he is) to make foolish things seem wise. We are able to see through his disguises and be shielded from his traps when we have a legacy of continually checking out, reading, and applying God's insight. It is the familiarity with the feel of the true that helps us recognize the false.

2.8

God is the source and defender of justice. God sits enthroned on the highest appellate court of the universe. God ensures justice at the personal, communal, and national levels. There is always recourse for the innocent, even when all human systems have faltered. The seeming final dominance of human systems and leaders is an illusion. Timeless in majesty, towering over the wrecks of our justice system, is the unchanging, all knowing wisdom of God. When our courts and arbitrators fail us, we are not worried or dismayed. We just take our concern right to the top. We appeal to Jehovah, the Judge of all the earth who shall surely do right. We are ultimately guarded and preserved by the Eternal, so wise that no false accusation tricks Him, so discerning that no slick accuser befuddles Him, and so all knowing that no hidden truth escapes Him. The innocent never worry in court. We stand tall and confident in the dock, and we lift our eyes up to the Judge.

2.9

Wisdom treats people differently. Equity and equality are not synonymous, even as they are complementary truths. As parents, we give different portions, even different foods to our children depending on their age. As leaders, we release different levels of information to our followers depending on their maturity. As shepherds, we give different liberties to our flock depending on their experience. The lowest and most insecure form of leadership is to fall back on rules (rather than principles) and to demand the same things of all people. Justice is neither communism nor democratic capitalism. Justice apportions what is right to each one, even if the wages are different. The righteous empower all to ascend the difficult mountain, even if that means assigning different paths (times, levels of difficulty) to different climbers. Justice and righteousness are wise enough to treat people uniquely and strong enough to bear the inevitable false accusation of partiality.

2.10

Wisdom is not synonymous with intelligence, nor does it lodge solely in our brains. Wisdom certainly has an intelligence component, just as it has emotional and spiritual elements. Wisdom has to enter our hearts and be pleasant to our souls. Wisdom is not solely mechanical or clinical; it is also relational and includes discernment. It is just as necessary to note the prick of conscience or the disquiet of spirit as it is to review and analyze facts. The wise take into account logic, facts, data, and evidence. These cognitive aspects are brought before the Lord and laid out before Him, and added to them, is an examination of spirit. The wise weigh both the objective details and the subjective promptings of the Spirit (often communicated through emotion, sense, peace or disquiet, joy or caution) before they make a decision. It is not wise to remove the subjective, spirit-prompted aspects from our decision-making process. Wisdom acknowledges that our intellect is limited and that God speaks to us through both our minds and our spirits.

2.11

If discretion is indeed the better part of valor, then understanding is its constant companion. Both discretion and understanding are preservatives. They preserve both the knower and the one known about. There is a common misconception that knowledge is power. Those who are privy to the most information testify that knowledge is often pain. Broken lives in this broken world endure terrible things, and over time (and as our responsibility increasingly grows) we must see and hear things that are difficult to bear. While we certainly can use privately known facts to hurt or abuse, we can also protect and preserve others by swallowing them, by being the final terminus for that painful reality. It is the preservation of others' dignity that in the end maintains our own. Understanding reminds us we always reap what we sow, and if we protect others by our discretion, we will in due course be protected. Discretion is a loving investment in both the future of our friends and our own.

2.12

Perversity is the opposite of wisdom. Any sexual act outside of a marriage between one man and one woman is perverse. This includes pornography and masturbation. This includes adultery and fornication. This includes homosexuality and bestiality. This includes rape and child abuse. This includes sexual jokes and innuendo. Yes, all these are perverse, and none of them should have any place among the wise. Crass, crude inferences and smirks and language are not morally neutral. They are evil, they are folly. Immoral behavior wears the thin cloak of adventure and is scented with the alluring perfume of the exotic, but behind that flimsy robe and cheap scent is stupidity. Perversity pretends to be enlightened but is actually foolishly blind. Perversity is not enlightened; it is not open; it is not liberating; and in the end, it is not even pleasurable. Perversity wounds, deceives, betrays, poisons, and ultimately kills—not just the victims, but also the perpetrators. It may seem funny or fancy in the moment to be perverse, but it's actually stupid.

2.13

It is possible to leave the faith. Right relationship with God is a well-lit path with Jesus Himself being the light. To walk with Him is to have a clear way in front of us. It's such obvious illumination that to leave it requires great intentionality. You cannot accidentally lose your salvation. To walk in darkness, you must choose to leave the light and press further and further into blindness. Whoever wants to stay in the light can turn towards the light or can return back to the light. Those who have lost their salvation chose to forfeit it. They were not expelled—they deserted. They clawed, kicked, screamed, bit, and thrashed their way out of the loving embrace of their heavenly Father. We can have great confidence. We can be eternally secure. No one can pluck us from the Father's hand. The only one who can take us away from our safety is ourselves.

2.14

The celebration of evil is a long, deliberate choice, a choice that started with small concessions. When we see the shocking delight in perversity around us, we wonder how something so obviously wicked and dark can be celebrated as wise and enlightened. Evil is now ubiquitously called "good," and when the good call out evil as "wicked," they are labeled hateful and ignorant in turn. How did we get here? How does society become so confused about what is right and what is wrong? By tiny accommodations. Do you smile at an off-color joke? You are beginning to celebrate evil. Do you watch a sensual program or performance? You are beginning to celebrate evil. Do your eyes undress another in the public square? You are beginning to celebrate evil. Let us direct our primary attention to the evil within our own hearts. Let us be vigilant. Let us not make any concession or accommodation to the mildly perverse in our own heads and hearts. If we do, we are no better than those who call what is shockingly bad good. We are on the road to the celebration of evil.

2.15

Evil is birthed in good. In creation, there was good first, and when good was bent, evil was born. In other words, evil does not start out as obviously wrong. Evil is initially a slight aberration of the good, a slight divergence, a one-degree course alteration that steadily progresses away from what is straight. The distance between full-grown evil and good is immense. The distance between newborn evil and good is miniscule. Evil does not tend to be a right-angle departure from what is good. It is a slow, steady parting, and for much of the initial journey eye contact is retained. Wisdom is the crucial ability to discern small aberrations from truth early on. Much early evil seems insignificant, trivial, and inconsequential. God's wisdom will alert our spirits to evil before our human wisdom can detect it. Do not despise the promptings, the disquiet, the leadings of the Spirit of God within you. Often that inner witness is an alarm, and God is warning you that good is about to be bent.

2.16

Flattery is the first step in the seduction process. Immorality first appeals to our weakness, not our strength. When there is a latent brokenness within us, the immoral person or process seek to deceive us in that area. When we don't feel manly, immorality tells us we are powerful. Where we don't feel respected, immorality tells us we are wise. If we are not confident, immorality insinuates we are brave to taste her fruit. When we don't feel desired, immorality winks and beckons. Our initial defense against seduction is to become flattery proof, to become deaf to flattery. We close our ears to flattery through two primary disciplines: first, receiving and believing what our heavenly Father thinks about us, and second, coming to terms with our weaknesses, accepting them, and going to our Father for help. When we believe all the good things the Father speaks over us, the whispers of the immoral person sound hollow and unattractive. When we acknowledge our weaknesses and take them to God in humble contrition, He perfects His strength in them, and no shade-tree seductress can improve on the manufacturer's repairs.

2.17

Wisdom decides to make a life-long covenantal friendship with truth. We are more susceptible to lying, stealing, pride, hypocrisy, sexual deviance, and all other sins when we get away from our truest friends and the simple commands of God. True friends tell you the truth even when you don't want to hear it. In fact, when you don't want to hear truth is when you need to listen the closest. True friends are true because they know your truth. They know your follies, sins, and misadventures as well as your gifts, accomplishments, and valor. If a friend tells you something that makes you angry, wisdom suggests there must be something in that barb you need to heed. When we move away from (close our ears and hearts to) intimate friends who are unimpressed with us—yet love us fiercely—we fight with one arm disabled. If we compound that handicap by ignoring the simple commands of God, then we go to war armless, and it is easy for any foe, even the smallest, to strike us down. Obey the ten commandments and listen to your truest friends—that's essential biblical wisdom.

2.18

Sexual sin of any kind slowly kills you. Sexual sin has more dire consequences than most any other sin, for it is a triple assault against the image of God. Sexual sin aggrieves all parties involved including the protagonist. If you rape or molest another, you not only horrifically attack the image of God in them, but you also mar the image of God in yourself. If you view pornography, you're not only trafficking the one you lust over, but you pimp out and un-dignify yourself. If you have sex with anyone besides your spouse or engage in any sexual act outside loving intimacy with your spouse, you actually strike a murderous, suicidal, and idolatrous blow—murderous because you assault the image of God in the other, suicidal because you mar the image of God in yourself, and idolatrous because you insult and offend God Himself. Sexual sin leads to death—your own.

2.19

You never fully recover from egregious sexual sin, even when you repent. This sober reality is intended to help us flee sexual sin, to hate it with a vengeance. God unhesitatingly offers forgiveness to all who sincerely repent, but forgiveness should never be confused with the obliteration of consequences. The consequences of sexual sin are far reaching and stretch across families, communities, and ministries. A minister may repent and be restored from sexual sin, but he or she will never regain the authority to tell the young struggler that they can live in victory, that they will never fall sexually. At best they can offer God's mercy (which is so thankfully true), but they cannot fully say, "Follow me as I have followed Christ." They are reduced to saying, "Don't do what I did; it's not worth it." An adult may receive forgiveness for breaking up their family, but this does not guarantee that family will ever be reunited, and if it is, there will always be the scar of painful memories even if there is no scab. There is a pure, bright, joyous way to eternal life. If you chose to leave it, you can still repent and return to the journey, but you will never regain that original path. Something precious is lost forever, and you will have to live with the consequences, painful as they are to all.

2.20

William Carey, missionary to India, said: "I can plod, to this I owe everything." Wisdom is a long, slow, purposeful walk. It is neither a meander nor a sprint; it is a determined, unrelenting march. To walk in the way of goodness, to keep the path of righteousness requires daily, steady effort. We rise from our beds each morning to fall on our knees and plea: "Heavenly Father, let me steadily march on today!" Good, wise, righteous living is not always exciting, and it is hardly ever easy. It is a daily dedication, an ongoing discipline, a covenant with ourselves that today we will intentionally do what is good, what is right. We approach each day with the mentality, "As God gives me strength, I am going to keep plodding. I won't necessarily walk very fast, but I'll never stop moving. Relentless, with no shadow of turning, I will pursue what is right and what is good."

2.21

Right choices and right living are rewarded in the long term. We don't always immediately see the consequences of our choices. Sometimes the initial result of making a wise choice is pain and trouble, loss and grief. But short-term trouble is always better than long-term problems and pain. Wisdom refuses to be enamored with short-term success or fooled by easy wins and quick gains. Wisdom always considers the long-term consequences of a decision, for at the end of the day the upright will be the last ones standing, the ones who remain and abide in the land. To be wise is to see into the future and to be willing to struggle and even suffer in the present for the enduring good of what lies ahead. To be foolish is to scorn future enduring benefits for the brief and passing pleasures of the now.

2.22

Wickedness and evil are ultimately self-defeating. There are two enemies that evil can never defeat: One is Jehovah, and the second is itself. God will always eventually judge, uproot, and destroy evil. In His serene wisdom God allows evil for moments in time, but evil is not by nature eternal—it is not outside of time. There was no evil in eternity past, and there will be no evil in eternity future. Thanks be to God, evil has a determined shelf life, limited, time bound, and brief when eternity is kept in view. The second overwhelming enemy of evil is evil itself. Inherent to good is unity, while inherent to evil is division. The wicked slay the wicked. Evil self-cannibalizes. A house divided indeed cannot stand, and evil has always been and will ever be (in its short life) a divided house. Wisdom attacks evil in three ways—one of them active, two passive. Actively, we oppose evil wherever we find it; we stand against it in the name of the Lord. Passively, we step back and allow the God of time to judge and uproot evil, and we wait soberly for evil to destroy itself.

PROVERBS
Chapter 3

3.1

Wisdom is an active remembrance, not a relaxed assumption. God's laws are like guardrails on the edge of a precipice. They simply remind us not to hurt ourselves. Due to our intrinsic folly (expressed as rebellion because we resent being reminded of boundaries), we willfully forget. We have the unusual ability to push what we know to be true (that there are painful consequences to breaking through God's loving barriers) into the recesses of our awareness, willfully climb past the helpful protection of God's limits, and then be shocked, offended, defensive, and accusatory when our choices lead us to difficulty and trouble. We keep God's commands with our hearts before we keep them with our bodies. We look at those barriers of His law with thanks and joy, not with scorn and resentment. When our heart looks at law with grace and gladness, we are well on our way to wisdom and freedom.

3.2

Long life without peace is torment. Long life with peace brings joy to yourself and to all around you. When we not only obey but appreciate the boundaries of God, we are actually happier and freer. The clever lie of the devil is that God's restrictions make us grumpy, that His limitations make us sad, that His laws deny us material and present happiness. The eternal truth of the loving Father is that all things are done for His glory and our good and that the "no" of God is as kind and helpful as His "yes." Peace comes from accepting and believing that God is sovereignly good in all He ordains and all He allows. When we have wrestled our doubting spirits to that truth, we have entered the path of peace and we will find joy in God, in ourselves, in long life, and in one another over the long term. It is a losing and frustrating battle to constantly war against God's goodness. Peace comes from surrendering to the blessed assertion that God really is good (all the time, for that is His nature) and that *all* He does deserves our praises.

3.3

Mercy and truth are the two legs with which we run the race of life. We can certainly hop along on one leg, but that leads to no medals. We can fuse the two legs together, but that too mitigates our swiftness. To run well and long, both mercy and truth must be embraced without canceling each other out for a sum zero effect. Mercy is not truth, and truth is not mercy. They complement, not obliterate, each other. Mercy without truth corrupts, and truth without mercy kills. When mercy and truth kiss, we have wisdom. For short sprints we can focus on one or the other, even as we may hop a short distance on one foot, but for long steady runs, both legs must stride out in full strength. One definition of balance is to be "equally passionate in opposite directions." This would certainly be true of mercy and truth. We best preserve the power of each when we passionately embrace both without dilution. To bind mercy and truth around our neck, to write them on the tablet of our heart is to ever keep them before us in their full, married strength.

3.4

When we begin to understand the indivisible union and synergy of mercy and truth, we begin to understand God and we take great leaps in understanding our fellow men. Understanding God gains favor with Him. When God sees that we advance in the understanding of His equal passion for mercy and truth, He can trust us more liberally to represent Him in thought, word, and deed. God favors the dispenser of His mercy and truth with His power and equips them to convey the reality of His character to others. When we represent God well, we likewise better understand our fellow men and women (both the marred image of God *and* their potential for the glory of God to be revealed), and when they feel understood, we gain their favor and open hearts. Folly teaches that you have to please men and women in order to gain their favor, that you have to promise them potential. Wisdom states that favor comes from understanding God's mercy and truth, applying it to yourself, and espousing it to others. We win no long-term favor if we only mercy ourselves and others. That "mercy" is actually destructive and hateful. We heal no long-carried wounds if we only apply searing truth. Men and women cry out for the help that comes from the surgery of truth united with the salve of mercy. Wisdom receives and distributes both.

3.5

Trust originates in our hearts, not our heads. Our own understanding has a bad habit of betraying us. Facts indeed are stubborn things, but rarely do facts march un-interpreted through our minds. We view them through our hurts, biases, and brokenness, and none of us always perfectly understand. When it comes to wisdom, discernment, and understanding, we must start with the assurance, the emotional rest, and the inexplicable sense that Jehovah is good, even apart from the apparent contradiction of facts. When we lean on our own understanding (a limited and flawed head analysis) of facts, we will inevitably be mistaken. When we lean on the Lord (the decision with our heads to trust Him with our hearts), we maintain the right path, even if we walk in the dark. Faith doesn't deny facts; it bases all analysis of facts on the fact that our hearts are going to trust that God is intrinsically good and wise.

3.6

When we consistently acknowledge the Lord in small daily decisions, the grand choices of life become self-evident. In reality, there are no grand choices; there is just an amalgamation of small ones. We tend to crave God's explicit direction for the momentous choices of life—marriage, study, career, transition, promotion, change—but sail through a thousand daily choices independent of consultation with Him. Functionally, we act as if we only need God's help for big things because we can handle the small things without Him. The error in this dichotomy of dependence (thinking we only need God's help for big decisions) is twofold. First, big decisions are not divorced from small decisions; they are simply the crowning act, the summary of a legion of choices. Second, big decisions are not more important than small decisions. It is the small, simple, silent, serial choices of daily living that make one wise. When we acknowledge the Lord in all the minutia, our course is chosen and our path is set, and we do not stand bewildered at the critical crossroads of life.

3.7

Self-congratulation is stationary; it's stopping to admire our past. It is as if we cease running a fiercely contested marathon after cresting a challenging hill in order to admire how well we have run thus far. Wisdom is an active and constant moving away from evil, which in this life is always an unfinished task. We cannot simultaneously be wise in our own eyes (stopping to award ourselves accolades) *and* reverence the Lord (by constantly moving away from evil). It is not pleasant, but it is true that evil in our world is an ever-rising tide. There is never a time that we can stop climbing; we must ever press upward to higher ground. On that great day when Jesus comes, Jehovah will eradicate evil in and around us. He will swallow the ever-stalking flood. Until then we must press on, "still praying as [we] onward bound, Lord [move our] feet [to] higher ground."[2]

3.8

Humility is health to both body and soul. The more obvious result of humility is a right spirit, a right perspective about ourselves that we gain with a true understanding of the majesty of God. When we really see and understand God as the King of glory, there is no challenge in realizing what we are and what we are not. The less obvious but just as real result of humility is physical strength and wholeness. Humility sees both the strengths and weaknesses of self without prejudice and attends to them. Thus, strengths are developed, and weaknesses addressed. Pride keeps us from growing our strengths and addressing our weaknesses and keeps us sick, lame, and blind. Humility keeps our spirits right, our emotions balanced, and our bodies from the equal and opposite excesses of vanity and sloth.

3.9

We give because God is a giver, and He wants His children to look like Him. We don't give in order to receive (though receiving happens), and we don't give in order to plant seeds that we benefit from down the road (though that also happens). We give so that we look and act like God. There is not a more generous being in history than the God of heaven and earth, and He does not just give out of His largesse. He gave His only Son. God exhausted His familial resources when He sent Jesus to live and die on earth. Jesus gave all; He had nothing left when He finally gave up His spirit. Wisdom is quick to honor the Lord with material possessions, quick to give sacrificially of whatever is gained. Wisdom gives not primarily to receive (though that happens) but to look like the Giver, for in that similitude there is greater joy than any degree of material harvest.

3.10

Godly generosity has others in mind both in the beginning and end. Generosity chooses to bless others rather than to store up savings. What inevitably happens is that God recognizes a kindred spirit and opens the floodgates of heaven to replace and surpass what was donated. This extravagant replenishment is likewise not to be stored but distributed. Entry level wisdom understands that when we give, God blesses us, but then thinks the return on the investment is to be hoarded. Maturing wisdom understands that nothing is to be hoarded, and any increasing replenishment of God is intended to be distributed. God wants us to build wider distribution networks for His channeled beneficence, not bigger barns.

3.11

Wisdom looks forward to spiritual spankings. In the blessed hope when Jesus comes and restores all things (including the fallen heart of man), chastening and correction will be what we look back on with chuckles. In the now, when we are still foolish and fallen, we should look forward to chastening and correction with thanks. Why? Because they improve, refine, mature, heal, correct, direct, and protect us. The Lord's correction and chastening of us is a clear communique that He still cares, still loves, still dotes, still believes, and still trusts. It is the apathetic parent who never tells his child "no," and it is the loving parent who corrects and chastens, improves and strengthens. Correction often implies an unintended error, and chastening a willful one, and our heavenly Father addresses both types. We are wise to rejoice when He does so because we are simply being loved well. Correction and chastening communicate that God has not given up on us despite our faults and folly.

3.12

God's scrupulous attention is an indication of delight. Just as we linger over what we love, so does our attentive heavenly Father. The more we mature, the closer His inspection, for He, being the original perfectionist (who uniquely has the capacity to perfect all He gives attention to), is too perfect to let a work of His hands entertain a blemish. A foolish response to being under the magnifying glass of God is to squirm and lash out. A wise response welcomes the loving inspection, for it only leads to beautification. When God's diligent eye examines us, let us see beyond the stare to the loving and masterful Artist. Let us enter into that examination from the Artist's perspective and see that He is completing, fulfilling, and beautifying something that He is tremendously proud. God's corrections are His finishing touches on art that He intends to put on public display. He's too good of an artist to display an incomplete masterpiece.

3.13

Wisdom spreads happiness. The first beneficiary of wisdom is the bearer of that wisdom. When we understand God, God's purposes in the earth, ourselves, and our purpose in life, the immediate effect is soul happiness. It is so incredibly joyous to understand the meta-narrative of history, to see how marvelously good God is in His sovereignty, and to realize we have an active, vital, and local part to play in the unfolding drama. The second beneficiaries of wisdom are those that surround the joyous wise. When we are wise, we are happy. When we are happy, we make others happy. Happiness is infectious. Who can restrain a smile when a baby smiles and giggles? How much more when a mature adult smiles and giggles with joyful wisdom. The proximate can't hold back their smiles either.

3.14

Wisdom is an investment. Monetary investment, such as the profits of silver or the gain of gold, require patience. Likewise, we cannot expect immediate or even quick results to our wisdom. Wisdom's yield is sometimes deferred for years or decades. Wisdom is justified by her children, and it takes time for children to grow and manifest their character. What is wise may initially appear foolish, and what is foolish may initially appear wise. True wisdom is revealed and justified over time. The truly wise are prepared to appear foolish (and be criticized) in the short term and are willing to wait to be proved right over time (for the benefit of others). Wisdom's results can't be rushed, but neither can they be stopped.

3.15

Wisdom is earth's priceless treasure. Man's folly is that we don't treasure wisdom as our highest desire. If we are honest, our highest desires tend to be wealth, pleasure, and power. We all certainly want to be wise, but we'll take that as our fourth choice after we have secured for ourselves money, ease, and ability. Those that make wisdom their first desire are so rare that they delight God. This was true of Solomon and it can be true of us—if we are smart enough to want wisdom above other pressing needs. Solomon certainly needed wealth and power (ability and capacity) to rule well, but he was astute enough to realize that his greatest need was wisdom. Folly is so consumed by the lack of physical resources and strength that it fails to recognize the greater need and greater gift: wisdom. Wisdom quells the internal urge and panic for physical help or activity and petitions and seeks first to understand.

3.16

Wisdom fuels longevity. Factors like grit, positivism, resources, companionship, and fulfillment all certainly help you remain, but none contribute to staying power like wisdom does. The first fruit of wisdom (her right hand) is length of days and her subsequent fruit (her left hand) is riches and honor. Fools undercut and shorten their tenure by poor decisions, while the wise extend their service and leadership through wise choices. You can be determined, enthusiastic, rich, and popular and fail to last due to folly. But if you are wise, friendships and resources follow, which empower you to endure. Ultimately, the raw material for endurance is not external, but internal wisdom, a commodity prayed for earnestly and sought for diligently.

3.17

Peace and pleasantness result from doing the right things. As thrilling as the wrong things are in the moment, they are agonizing almost immediately after. Wrong things can have immediate appeal, but they have no long-term peace. Right things can have immediate pain, but always result in long-term health and gladness. The test of worth for any choice or activity is not immediate sensation, but long-term peace. If the long-term result is good, the choice was wise. If the medium and long-term results are harmful and peace-void, the choice was wrong.

3.18

At one time my wife and I had a Staffordshire Bull Terrier named Gracie, a marvelous dog. Our dog would latch on to a rope and I would swing her in the air around and around five feet off the ground. Holding to the rope as she sailed through the air was one thing, but as this remarkable dog swung in circles, she would still try to tug the rope from my hand, relying on her stomach muscles alone as she had zero ground for her legs to brace against. Wisdom must be latched on to, not held loosely. If there is not a bulldog determination to be wise, it won't happen. Wisdom is not gained accidentally or incidentally, but only purposefully. We must set our hearts on being wise, and once determined, latch on fiercely to whatever wisdom we have gained, lest it slip away from us. Doubly sad is the man or woman who was once wise, then acted foolishly.

3.19

Wisdom builds subterranean foundations and establishes the unseen future. In an age and culture fixated on quick growth, we must have the patience to work hard without immediately noticeable results. Quick growth is not always a friend, yet it is the altar at which pastors and missionaries often worship. Let us have the wisdom to be disciplined and to do the difficult work in the now that will reap the biggest benefit down the road. Let's be the ones planting shady oaks on sun-beaten country lanes that our grandchildren—should Jesus tarry—enjoy. Let's be the ones who take our time in discipleship, that the leaders we groom have the deep roots to weather the trials and temptations of life. Let's rejoice in smaller teams and churches if they are stronger in spirit and last past times of tribulation. Wisdom digs deep, sees far, and often has to weather the short-term scorn of being thought unfruitful.

3.20

Wisdom knows when and how to break things. Wisdom understands breaking and blessing are cyclical. Jesus blessed the bread and then He broke it (Matt. 14:19), and *then* it became a blessing again. Clouds are broken up for rain to fall; blessing precedes and follows breakings. There is not a breaking that will be wasted. God can use each one to make a blessing. There is not a blessing in this life that is intended only for self-gratification. There is always an eventual breaking that the blessing might be shared. When we are being broken, let us have the wisdom to anticipate the blessing. Even good things need to be broken. An unbroken blessing tends to become an idol. Wisdom trusts the Creator to bring blessings from breakings.

3.21

Wisdom, unfortunately, is a slippery friend. It's not like the lines we carry on our palms. It's more like a scratch on the skin that fades as it heals. Because the folly of man makes wisdom impermanent, we have to decidedly keep looking for it, preserving it. In this sense wisdom is like language learning—use it or lose it. In learning language, we retain the vocabulary we speak over and over. In wisdom learning, we retain the principles we practice over and over. We cannot be wise in theory or in stored up knowledge. Wisdom has to be kept by being spent, by being acted out over and over again. Who is the wise person? The one who acts wisely, not the one who smugly knows what should have been done.

3.22

Wisdom principally helps the dispenser. It's marvelous when the wisdom we steward helps others, but the reality is that this result is hit or miss. We can offer wisdom to others, but we can't enforce or ensure its adoption. Sometimes our wisdom is accepted; sometimes it is spurned. Whether or not others accept our wisdom (and there is grief when others disregard wisdom to their own hurt), we can swallow our own medicine and have our souls receive life by it. Wisdom helps us hold our head up, even when we are mocked or shamed. We know internally we have stood for, done, or said the godly thing; thus, we stand straight in adversity, an invisible but undeniable garland of grace around our neck.

3.23

Wisdom keeps our soul safe, but not necessarily our body. To walk safely and stumble-free does not mean you escape valleys of the shadow of death, dens of lions, prisons, or sickness. To be blunt, it is foolish to think that wisdom will shield you from physical pain, for the wise thing is often the difficult thing to do in the short term. When we are wise. we embrace (do not avoid) short-term pain, for we know it will yield long-term benefit. Wisdom has sent the wise to the stake, the cell, the chopping block, and the cross. Jesus wisely embraced His cross, scorning its shame for the joy set before Him. He never stumbled, and no evil touched His soul. Thus, it shall be with us—safe souls, stumble-free, long-term—even if there is pain and tragedy in the short- or mid-term.

3.24

When we have done what is right, when we have acted wisely, we can better compartmentalize problems in our mind. Our world is, and will increasingly be, problematic. It is impossible to avoid stress, conflict, and opposition. If all speak well of us, we are doing something wrong (Luke 6:26). God's prophetic people make enemies—through no fault of their own, but just by being faithful messengers. We will have haters, doubters, and those that resent us. It's part of our obedience. But when we lie down at night, if we have acted and spoken wisely, we are better equipped to lock those people and problems in a recessed closet of our mind and to sleep the deep sleep of the righteous. Sweet, fearless repose (asleep or awake) is the fair reward of all who know they are undeserving of punishment. We may still be dragged to the court of public opinion. We may still be condemned, even punished. But we stand strong and at rest, for we know that God knows we have been wise.

3.25

Sudden terror and trouble from the wicked will come. Jesus guaranteed that in this world we will have trouble (John 16:33). It's a given, but so is fearlessness. Fearlessness is given. It's a gift based on knowing we have been wise, knowing *the* wise One has been with us. In Matthew 14:27, when Jesus calmed the storm, He literally said, "Take courage. I AM. Do not fear." Fearlessness is the gift of those who are more aware of the I AM than they are of the danger. The fearless see terrors dimly as their gaze is consumed with the near and ever-present Lord of angel armies. It's hard to be afraid of terror when you see how small it is compared to our fearsome God.

3.26

Fortune does tend to favor the bold. In active and physical sports, the tentative tend to get hurt while the aggressive tend to emerge with the upper hand. For the most part, those who surge, commit to the tackle, confidently reach for the higher hold, or aggressively put a body on the opponent are the ones who emerge unscathed. Those who flinch, pull back, duck, hesitate, or give a half-hearted effort are injured. What is true in sports is truer in spirituality. There is an appropriate God-centered confidence. God does not want us to be spiritually tentative. He does not want us praying wimpy prayers. He does not want us preaching neutralized sermons. He does not want us singing hesitant praise. He does not appreciate timid prophecies. God wants us to be spiritually brave, spiritually bold, and spiritually confident in *Him*, which is the antithesis of pride. Being sure of *Him* is worlds apart from being sure of ourselves. Sure of Him, we are confident of not being sin-caught. Sure of ourselves we are already sin-snared.

3.27

God never sins, but He does tend to err on the side of generosity. The Bible record continually reveals a God who is slow to anger, who delights to mercy, who would rather bear pain than cause it. The God of the Bible is continually good to the righteous and the unrighteous, to the thankful and unthankful. One of the great ironies of man is that it is the very generosity of God (His patience and forbearance) that gives men and women the breath and time to insult their benevolent Creator and Sustainer. We would be wise then to emulate our generous God. If we are to err, let it be on the side of generosity and mercy even if that goodness is mocked and abused. In both our judgments and our actions, let's be generous. Generosity is a multi-directional blessing. It rewards (internally) the giver as much as it does (externally) the receiver. When good is in our power, let's give it.

3.28

God did not wait for us to be deserving before He lavished grace on us. Yet, like unjust stewards, we hold others to standards from which we were forgiven. Afraid of others abusing our generosity, we set requirements (or timeframes) for them that God waived for us. It is an irony of our craven nature that we do not naturally treat others as we want to be treated. The golden rule is more like a discipline. We must remind ourselves, discipline ourselves, to give out the same mercy we have received. Christ died for us while we were still sinners. We must be willing to grant mercy to the pre-reformed. If we can help, let's help. Let's not require the needy to jump through hoops that we in our past distress were excused from. There will come a time in the future when we do not qualify for needed mercy or assistance. What a shame if that help is denied because our heart was small when our pocket was large.

3.29

Folly is the expertise of the shortsighted. Anger (usually a secondary emotion, a response to hurt, disappointment, fear, loss, or injustice, etc.) insists on a prompt action. Foolish anger surges up within us, urging us to some mean, harsh, or rash act against the one who has offended or threatened us. Often, we lash out at those closest to us—our spouse, our family, our team members, or our colleagues. This is folly because those near to us are designed by God to be our long-term safety. If I have neighbors, even though they are not best friends, the plight, evil, danger, or enemy has to get through them before it gets to me. If I remove all my neighbors, then I remove my walls, and I have no buffer against the elements or the enemies. It is better to endure the inevitable frustration of having quirky neighbors than to shortsightedly remove them and leave yourself exposed and vulnerable. Those who are near with all their shortcomings over the long term protect you on all sides.

3.30

An essential lesson of wisdom is knowing when to fight and when to absorb conflict. It's not a matter of striving; it's a matter of timing. Both the wise and the foolish strive (fight), but fools fight at the wrong times, in the wrong ways, against the wrong people, and for the wrong reasons. Essentially, when we are always looking for a quarrel, if we always have to object, if we always have to dissent, if we always have to point out the flaw or limitation, if we start as a critic and work our way to a compliment, there is something foolish about us. The wise are much more prudent about striving. They are not weak, and woe to you if you pick a fight with the wise (for when they go to battle, they are formidable foes). The wise refuse to strive without cause. The wise strive not to strive; they fight against fighting, not as a rule but as a principle. Making and keeping peace is harder than making war, thus the wise are slow to war and quick to peace.

3.31

It is disconcerting to note how often righteousness is removed from popular. The popular kids in school do not tend to be the holy ones. The popular athletes do not tend to be the humble ones. The popular celebrities do not tend to be the moral ones. The popular politicians do not tend to be the trustworthy ones. Because competencies seem to have more noticeable shine than they do character, we sometimes pine for the acknowledgement and attention the unrighteous popular enjoy. If we are not careful, we slide toward emulating the behavior of the sinful because we are envious of their acclaim. Fools envy and copy (dress alike, talk alike, act alike, think alike, joke alike, react alike) unrighteous oppressors in hopes of replicating their success. This is double jeopardy, for on the one hand you lose your soul in the vain hope of temporal popularity and on the other you gain the popularity and lose your soul. The wise don't envy the fame of the unrighteous (who always ultimately oppress in order to maintain their status), for they know the cost of that fame and power is internal hollowness and decay.

3.32

Crass humor is easy humor. It's easy to be funny about crude things. Higher humor is the purview of those willing to work hard enough to eschew perversity. Social humorists delight in the crude, crass, mean, vulgar, and perverse because it is the easy laugh. Few are willing to dig out the laughs that result from joy, goodness, grace, and health. God is not impressed with the comedy that devalues the image of God in other men and women. In fact, the next time we are tempted to laugh at something off color, we should have a check in our spirit and remind ourselves that God thinks perversity is an abomination. Further, if we are part and parcel of things that are abominable, we restrict ourselves from God's wisdom and guidance. There's a direct link between perversity and stupidity. Man thinks it's clever to be perverse. It's actually foolish, and indeed perversity takes you further and further from wisdom as God removes His advice and counsel from you. Do not confuse witty with wise. You can be incredibly intelligent about that which is wicked—and if you are, you deafen your own ears to God's truth.

3.33

The best legacies are not tangible ones. The kindest inheritance we can leave for our children is to raise them in a home that is godly, peaceful, just, and joyous. Just homes are blessed homes. Godly homes may be poor mud huts in the African plains, or they may be crowded, dusty apartments in an Arab city, but godly homes are blessed homes. Wisdom spends less money and more time. Wisdom lavishes love more than presents. Wisdom turns off the electronics and plays on the floor or frolics outside. Homes that have wealth but are wicked are cursed of the Lord. Homes that are simple but just, right, true, peaceful, gracious, and relational are blessed. Indeed, they are the truly rich homes. If we can raise our children in homes that are God-centered (for God is just and right in all He is and does), God will bless us by our progeny rising up and calling us blessed, no matter how modest our standard of living. Conversely, if we provide our children every tangible benefit bereft of godliness, justice, integrity, love, and truth, God will curse us through our children.

3.34

Scorn is essentially a putting down of others from an assumed position of superiority. As such, God is good at scorning, for His superiority is not assumed, but real, and eternally so. God who sits in the heavens shall laugh and scorn the scornful (Psalm 2). From His unrivaled and unquestioned superiority, God will flick a finger and humble all who are arrogant. In contrast He will elevate the humble and grace them with His favor. God will pluck new Davids from their sheepfolds, elevate new Josephs from their prisons, and select new working-class fishermen to apostolically lead the Church. Because God deals with the scornful, we don't have to. We don't have to defend ourselves. We can stay silent and lowly, and patiently wait for the only One with the right to scorn to intervene on our behalf. When scorned, never feel sorry for yourself. Have pity on the one abusing you, for He who sits in the heavens is about to have a good laugh.

3.35

Wisdom's dividend is gravitas. When you live wisely, you become a person whose opinion and presence carry weight. The result of a lifetime of wise living will be an aura about you ("glory" in

Hebrew is connected to the concept of weight), an authority others can detect before you speak. They will know to pay heed to what you say and think. Strangers will sense it; children will feel it; opponents will respect it; and powers and principalities will recognize it. This gravitas will not be earned quickly, but once earned it will be forceful. Influence is the inheritance you build for yourself at the end of a long road of living wisely. But if you live foolishly, that, too, will be apparent on your visage at the end of your life. The marks and ravages of selfish living are just as physically apparent as the marks of wisdom. Be warned and be encouraged—whatever is hidden now will be revealed at the end of your days.

PROVERBS

Chapter 4

4.1

The first commandment is always to listen. Of course, listening implies obedience, not just attention. If we are to listen to Father God, the expectation is that we will do what He says. When Jesus was asked about the injunction of prime importance, He quoted the Old Testament and said: "Hear…you shall love the Lord your God" (Mark 12:29–30). In other words, "Obey this: Love God and each other." Wise people obey. Wisdom is not found in listening alone; wisdom is found in obeying what we hear. When we obey, we come to understand. The rebellious nature in us demands to understand before we obey. God tells us firmly, "Obey, and you will understand." We are not that different from Mark Twain who famously said: "It ain't those parts of the Bible that I can't understand that bother me, it is the parts that I do understand." Let's start by obeying what we understand. Let's continue by obeying what we don't understand. And let's trust that God is good and that understanding will follow our obedience.

4.2

One indicator of the onset of folly in our thinking and our spirits is when we begin to look at law and doctrine as negative and binding. To put it bluntly, when teaching and boundaries and restrictions and principles and consequences are twisted to become the "oppressive instruments of the authorities" or the "outdated wisdom of the past," then we have started to lose our way. There is right and wrong, and there is false and true. There are universal principles. Folly subtly and steadily wants to undermine absolutes. Wisdom does not swallow that poison and stands against the winds of ridicule saying: "There is right and wrong. Law is good. Teaching is a blessing. Tradition and heritage offer protection and guidance." Not all tradition is bad and not all things new are good. The wise rejoice in the doctrine of their forbearers and in the ancient laws, and do not forsake them for the passing whims of the day. It is indeed folly to remove the ancient boundary stones.

4.3

There is something strong and resilient about being tender. It is the supple trees that survive the hurricanes. It is the yielding buildings that endure earthquakes. It is the flexible Christian who is not overcome by disappointment, delay, and disaster. Wisdom's greater part is knowing which battles to fight and which ones to bypass. At times wisdom requires a rigid resoluteness. At other times wisdom demands a tender accommodation. A colleague states that a teenager could make 95 percent of his decisions, but 5 percent of his decisions require the insight of Solomon, for they are intricate problems (usually between good people) that need tenderness if there will be resolution. The wise get more tender toward people as they age and more rigid against evil. Tenderness is learned young and improved upon with maturity. Ironically, the strongest warriors tend to have the softest hearts; they have learned to be stringent in the fight against evil and supple in the delicate work of reconciliation. The wise fight for people and against wickedness.

4.4

Father figures are interested in life. In the natural family, fathers bring us into the world and teach us to thrive in it. There is incredible security in the commands of a good father. Good fathers do not enable evil. Good fathers do not shy away from orders. Good fathers do not damage their children by allowing selfish wills to become used to getting their way. Nothing is as depressing as a tyrant toddler. The tragedy of children ruling parents is that it sets up that child for misery. Misguided parents think they will damage their children by being authoritative. Children, both physical and spiritual, need commands in order to thrive. An abusive or absent father is indeed damaging, but so is a present father who does not give their child the security of "no," the safety of boundaries, the comfort of discipline, and the joy of direct instruction. Wise is the child or disciple who learns early how healthy and life-giving it is to bow.

4.5

Understanding can be lost. It can be forgotten. We need to not only pursue wisdom actively; we also need to actively retain it. There is a wonderful passage in C. S. Lewis' book *Prince Caspian* that is worth quoting at length: "But, first, remember, remember, remember the signs. Say them to yourself when you wake in the morning and when you lie down at night, and when you wake in the middle of the night. And whatever strange things may happen to you, let nothing turn your mind from following the signs. And secondly, I give you a warning. Here on the mountain I have spoken to you clearly: I will not often do so down in Narnia. Here on the mountain, the air is clear and your mind is clear; as you drop down into Narnia, the air will thicken. Take great care that it does not confuse your mind. And the signs which you have learned here will not look at all as you expect them to look, when you meet them there. That is why it is so important to know them by heart and pay no attention to appearances. Remember the signs and believe the signs. Nothing else matters." God speaks to us clearly, but the air thickens, and confusion invades. Let us not forget or turn away from the wisdom once received. As I heard Pastor M. Wayne Benson once say, "Do not doubt in the darkness what God has revealed to you in the light."

4.6

Wisdom is a romance—a recipient of love and a returner of affection. When we pursue wisdom, she loves to be found. She loves to be loved, and she loves back. Wisdom is the most faithful partner in history as far as romance goes. Wisdom never betrays us. Wisdom never seeks another lover. Wisdom never initiates a divorce. Wisdom never strays. When we pursue wisdom, as one lover to another, she preserves and keeps us. If ever you see a man or woman separated from wisdom, you can know with surety who was at fault. Wisdom never abandons us; we only abandon her. The folly in abandoning wisdom is the benefits we lose. When you see men and women who self-destructed, you know they were unfaithful to their faithful bride, wisdom. When you see the aged crowned with peace and beauty, you know they have been faithful to their preserving love.

4.7

If the main thing is to keep the main thing the main thing, then wisdom is keeping wisdom at the center of our efforts to accumulate. One of the ironies of our upstream life, a life that must always struggle against an unfriendly current, is that what is useless we accumulate easily and what is precious is so hard to both find and retain. Several times in our lives, usually when we left one country to serve in another, my wife and I gave almost everything away. When we left Sudan for Egypt, I, my wife, and our two sons each had a small backpack. A year later, we had more junk than we knew what to do with. If only we were magnets for wisdom over stuff. There are good things to accumulate—friends, experiences, culture, language, skills—but even there, in all our getting, let's prioritize accumulating wisdom. For if I walk with kings, travel the world, understand Arabic language and culture, and lead an army to war, but have not wisdom, I have nothing.

4.8

Kingdom promotion does not come primarily from being popular or even from being competent. Kingdom promotion comes from being wise. In my own heart and in my own spheres of relationship, I often detect a thirst for promotion. Occasionally, this is altruistic—it's a desire to serve. But more often it's about recognition. The young approach me and in so many words ask what their path to promotion is. They want to know what they must do in order to march up the ever ascending (in their minds) path of position and title. I recognize this because I tried to walk that path so foolishly for so long. We so easily forget that the highway to honor descends. It descends to humility and is not accessed by what we do as much as by who we are. Promotion comes from being wise, not from being competent. Promotion does not mean position as much as it means honor. God is not constrained by the titles or categories of man. He honors and advances whoever He will, either outside our processes or within them depending on whether or not the person has been wise. If there is a genuine desire in our hearts to lead (and there can be), we prepare for that by exalting and embracing wisdom.

4.9

The wise have a gracious gravitas about them. Wisdom keeps us from being frauds, for it keeps us from pretending. You can't fake grace and glory. We should live in a little bit of healthy fear—the fear of exposure as frauds. If we are wise, that fear will kick in whenever we are pretentious or duplicitous, whenever we pretend to be something we are not. We cannot pretend to be beautiful, and we cannot pretend to be wise. Those that rightly wear the crown feel no need to pretend to have authority and are not slighted when they encounter someone who doesn't know they reign (rather they are usually delighted when this happens). Let us not fixate on ruling or self-beautifying, for those efforts result in rebellion and disfigurement. Let us focus on being wise, for wisdom will grace and glorify the worthy in due time.

4.10

Obedience leads to longevity, and longevity leads to fruitfulness. There are some things that can only be accomplished through time. Some victories cannot be won by charisma, competency, or even character. They can only be won by those attributes aided by chronology. If we will hear and receive (obey and put into action) the wisdom that God offers, we will have the capacity to last. Obedience enables us to endure difficult circumstances, and in the endurance we will win victories that short-term effort cannot produce.

4.11

Obedience leads to surety, and surety leads to effectiveness. Learning the lessons wisdom longs to teach us leads us to confidence in who we are and what we should do. Confident that we are walking in the right direction, there is no need to stop for directions, to backtrack, or to take detours. Surety that we are on the right path results in efficient living. The means of surety is obedience (i.e., learn; don't just listen, but also apply what God says), and that obedience leads to internal confirmation and peace. Having gained that surety, you can turn the walk of life into an exuberant run.

4.12

Obedience clears obstacles and lets you run. There is an unnatural fear of obedience. We believe the lie that obedience constrains us, but in reality, when we obey, it liberates us. This is inviolably true of obeying God, but it's also true of obeying God-appointed authorities. When we obey (listen to and apply wisdom), our authorities notice our compliance and create a wide swath of territory for us in which we can run. When we obey, we build trust with the ones who can open and close doors for us. Our boundaries grow the more we obey. When we feel the walls closing in on us, when we feel constrained, the way to enlarge our borders is by accepting authority not by resisting it.

4.13

It's not only the pleasant things that "life" us; painful discipline also makes us healthy. A well-fed, well-educated, well-supplied child who is never disciplined will never be healthy. In truth that child will be nasty and wicked, selfish and ugly in spirit. Because we are broken, fallen, sinful humans, we will need discipline until Jesus comes. Our health depends on both encouragement and exhortation. We are but children, prone to return to the vomit of our sin. Our heavenly Father offers us both comfort and correction, and we need both in order to live well. To be beautiful in spirit in this life (before Jesus comes), we need to both encouragement and instruction. Hold on to the rebukes the Lord sends your way, for they give you life.

4.14

Evil is always a possibility for us. We cannot sit back and shake our head in wonder at the heinous crimes or sins of others without acknowledging that we have the capacity to do the same or worse. The wise man knows he is a wicked man. If it were not possible for us to do evil and wicked things, then we wouldn't be warned against walking that path. We must view every horrific revelation of another's acts through the lens. "There, but for the grace of God, go I." We must determine not to start down wicked paths, nor walk in evil habits, for they start as harmless folly and end in devastating pain.

4.15

There must be daily resistance to evil, and the only way to resist evil is to "out stubborn" it. I overcome temptation by resisting it one more time than I am tempted by it. The devil tempted Jesus in waves, waiting to return at opportune times. We have to daily turn away from wickedness. We swim against the tide. We both turn away and pass on, meaning we intentionally resist evil and then just as intentionally put distance between ourselves and temptation. The folly in us thinks we can stand near a cliff of wickedness and peer over into the chasm below, curious but not indulgent. But wisdom knows that to stand near evil's cliff is to inevitably become seduced and then to dizzily topple over, falling to our destruction.

4.16

In our natural (fallen) self we want to hurt others. How many times do we rewind a conversation in our head and think of the appropriate rebuttal or stinging rebuke (only it's too late). Because we're broken, we lash out, sometimes even appearing as smiling assassins. Some of the sweetest acting people become devastating murderers with their words, and some of the most murderous (or life-taking) actions are words of praise, forgiveness, or grace withheld. When we devise ways to make others hurt, lack, fall, or even "get a taste their own medicine," it's foolish evil, even when wrapped in wise-sounding words. If our motivation is to hurt, not heal, we will act wickedly.

4.17

Without Jesus' saving power, death is what "lifes" us. I recently noticed how enjoyable it was to shoot my friends with paintballs.

It alarmed me. We played an elimination game, and the adrenaline that surged in me as I hunted down the last few young lads startled me. I fed off the fear in them as they scrambled to escape. It was the same adrenaline that energizes a hunter or a taker of life. So easily we slip into "hunting" mode with the people that hurt, disappoint, or insult us. There is a real energy and sustenance as well as a perverse pleasure in hunting something or someone to diminish or take its life. It is, incidentally, the true and evil spirit behind abortion and euthanasia—the evil energy derived from taking life. Wise energy preserves and gives life and refuses to feed on that which hurts others.

4.18

God's life glows and grows. There is such health in living in the light. Most of evil's power is broken when the evil thing or thought is brought into the light. When people live in the presence (light) of Jesus, you can tell. There is a beam that emanates from their faces and spirits. To be around them is to sense joy and peace. It is the shining face of Moses, a radiance that is neither bought nor manufactured, a shining that only comes from being in the presence of the God of light and from keeping all our actions and motives open before Him and others. Fools hide things, but the wise have no secrets. A life lived in transparent openness to the light of God is a life that blossoms in influence and fruitfulness. Living in the light grows you; living with secrets shrinks you.

4.19

Evil and self-deception go hand in hand. Self-lies are the most binding. When we are not transparent and accountable with others, we eventually lose the capacity to be honest with ourselves. What starts simply enough with managing how others perceive us becomes incredibly complicated as we try to manage how we perceive ourselves. The twists and turns in our own head blind us to our true selves and we don't even know that we stumble, much less what we stumble over. The way to preserve a realistic view of ourselves is with honesty, vulnerability, and accountability with others about who we are—warts and all. The way to lose accurate self-perception, or the road to blindness, is to walk without accountability and honesty. Any form of dishonesty (internal or external) is essentially to poke your own eyes with a stick.

4.20

Don't take wise friends for granted, and if they only ever agree with you, they are not wise. Pay attention to diverse sources of wisdom, including the sources that critique you. We should have a natural wariness of those who only complement us. At the same time, no wise coach only criticizes. No good doctor believes you can survive on medicine. No wise grandmother thinks you will thrive on sugar. Our good Teacher reminds us that we are in trouble if all men speak well of us (Luke 6:26). He also affirms that the power of life and death are in the tongue (Prov. 18:21). Wisdom rebukes and encourages, exhorts and warns. Surround yourself with friends who will speak truth in love, and if you want to be a wise friend, you must speak the whole counsel of God.

4.21

Don't think that truth requires no maintenance. We need to center and re-center. It is a blessed and needed exercise to return to the truths of God's character and the gospel. God knows we need to constantly refocus on what is simple and true. That's why holy communion should be repeated with great frequency and why repeated Sabbath rest is so critical. We cannot assume that once we understand a truth, we need not revisit it. A wise storekeeper brings out both old and new from his stock. The spice of our spiritual life is in discovering new things about God and His creation. The strength of our spiritual life is in returning to old truths, being struck with fresh awe, and standing on the promises of God.

4.22

God's truth through His word brings total health. It's astounding that Jesus refers to His words as spirit and life (John 6:63). It's astounding that God used and uses words to create. Due to the fallen nature of man and our subsequent abuse of words, we have overreacted and attempted to diminish the authority and impact of words. God created us to respond to the spoken word, especially His words. The wise person then positions himself or herself to hear the word of God constantly. Read it in the mornings, sing it in the shower, pray it around the table, memorize it on the commute, share it with the neighbor, and preach it in the pulpit. The wise find ways to inundate their ears with the word of God. It's the best health food on offer. The fool fills their ears with talk radio, sports, celebrity nonsense, political acrimony, gossip, un-word of God chatter, banality, and noise. Those type of words will just make you sick.

4.23

A strong heart is a soft heart. We must be super disciplined to keep our heart soft. Experience so easily leads us to cynicism. Information too easily leads to pain. Leadership often makes us jaded because we've seen so much junk, all the effects of broken people breaking people. The current of living relentlessly tugs us to a critical spirit. Even our own sin makes us pessimists. A strong heart determines that it will stay soft, that it will absorb hurt, disappointment, and reality, and yet believe that God can redeem people and circumstances. The spirit needs as much exercise as the body. The difference being that while physical exercise makes muscles hard, spiritual exercise keeps the heart soft. A soft heart gives life.

4.24

Lying and perversity cause hard hearts. The primary way a soft heart turns hard is through incremental jokes and deceptions. It can start so benignly. A smile at someone's comment that is just a touch off color but still within the norms of social acceptability. A small exaggeration about your role in a funny story. A tiny evasion of truth where you confessed 95 percent of your sin, leaving out one small, yet critical, part. Hard hearts do not primarily result from external observations; they result by accumulated internal disobediences. Every time we run through a Holy Spirit stop sign, whether in word or deed, we add another layer of callousness to our conscience. Smiling at someone else's off-color remarks leads to us stating our own. Exaggeration leads to fabrication. Omission in the confession of sin leads to commission of it. The fool indulges small deceptions and perversities, concessions that lead incrementally to a hard heart. The wise are ruthless about their own lies and perversity, and they determine to have nothing to do with them, either from their mouths or in their ears.

4.25

The wise put blinders on themselves. The fool scoffs at any restrictions, arrogantly (or at least overconfidently) saying that we should be able to walk through the public sphere without what we see affecting us. The logic of the fool goes that we can't avoid seeing what we see, so we must be strong enough to see it and remain unaffected. But the wise person is sufficiently conversant with the weakness in her own heart to know that what goes through the gate of her eye affects the mind and heart. We can't unsee what we see, and we don't easily stop thinking about what we see. We have to take the radical step of limiting what we see. This is the real strength, the strength to avoid looking at places that would sear our eye gate with unhelpful scenes. Sometimes the wisest thing is to walk through an airport looking at the floor or the ceiling tiles, or at the very least looking at people from the chin up. The wise impose some restrictions on what they see, restrictions that seem excessive but are actually just safe. The foolish have no restrictions on their eye gate, and in their overconfidence, they assimilate more filth into their imaginations than can be filtered out.

4.26

We walk on a knife edge, especially when in leadership. When the path has cliffs on both sides, it's easy to overcorrect and overcorrection can be disastrous. As we mature in life and grow in leadership responsibilities, the path before us becomes even narrower. The only way to maintain the path is to watch it. Some appreciation of scenery must be surrendered—not all, but some. We maintain the narrow path by deliberately focusing on where we are going and by intentionally refraining from both wandering and overcorrecting. Carefully watch where you step! When you walk with your head up (enjoying your accomplishments), you tend to step on loose stones. You may see more but walk less. When you walk with your head down, you may not see all that is accomplished, but you will certainly travel farther and safer.

4.27

Plodders tend to win most long races. Missionary William Carey said he owed everything to plodding. C. S. Lewis in *The Last Battle* talked about pressing "further up and further in." The race is truly not to the swift, but to the stubborn (kind of like learning Arabic). Wisdom knows that if we just keep going, if we just keep moving, slow and sure, we will eventually arrive. Folly stops or takes detours. We take vacations from abiding in Jesus, exercising, or eating nutritious food at our own peril. Wise living never ceases plodding in the essential disciplines.

PROVERBS
Chapter 5

5.1

Wisdom bows the ear to God's voice. It makes a determined effort to see the world from God's perspective. Wisdom realizes that we may not like what God tells us to do (that He might even ask us to do unpleasant things), but if we trust Him, our obedience leads to pleasant postures. Wisdom does not approach the Bible as a book about man, but as a book about God. We approach the Bible with awe, for God sanctifies it to speak to us about Himself. Bible warnings then are not negative restrictions but positive invitations to be like God, which in the end is pleasant to us and to all around us.

5.2

We keep wisdom by passing it on through the generations. Public knowledge collectively preserves truth; this is the power of transparency and accountability. What is in the light has the best chance at health and life. Gnosticism has ever been the enemy of the body of Christ and the overall health of the Church because the ironic claim to enlightenment is undermined by keeping secrets in the dark. When knowledge is the domain of the elite, the whole world suffers. Truth is best kept pure and gives the most life when the widest possible population has access to it. Knowledge is kept by sharing it.

5.3

What is familiar can be balanced for it is entirely known. What is foreign is alluring because it is imperfectly known. Immorality is attractive because it is foreign and mysterious, and outside the normal. The adventure of immorality blinds us to the total package, which weighed by any sane person is not worth the price. Sexual immorality foolishly or willingly overlooks (or refuses to consider) all consequences of the endeavor, delighting only in what is appealing. Immorality is one of the most shortsighted and incomplete of indulgences. Immorality is the self-deception that you can be the first in history to indulge in deviant sexual pleasure without the inevitable searing pain and devastating consequences that always follow.

5.4

A friend stated both accurately and crudely: "Sexual sin is like pooping in your pants. It feels good for about one second, and then you are in misery." Lust does indeed energize as it rushes through our bodies, but the fleeting pleasure of a season, or even a few seconds, is disgustingly defiling and devastating. No brief and illicit pleasure is worth the long, painful road back to cleanliness and health.

5.5

Sexual sin kills. Hunters of wolves have been known to freeze blood around sharp razor blades. A wolf will, in his taste for blood, literally lick himself to death as unwittingly feeds on his own blood. Sexual sin, unrepentant and continued, is slow suicide. We incrementally indulge ourselves to death. Make no mistake about it, sexual sin is hell. We cannot underestimate its burning, tormenting power. The wise will not take even one step on that descending staircase. Sexual sin does not scare the fool, to his own unfortunate demise.

5.6

Sexual sin attacks your personal foundations. Sexual sin destroys your personhood, the base of who you are. Sexual sin destines you to a life of unsteadiness at the moral, emotional, and spiritual level. God in His grace can forgive any repentant heart, but the consequences of sexual sin are so severe that the immoral will always walk with not just a limp, but some unsteadiness of gait. We cannot, for risk of discouraging those who have fallen into immorality, soften the warning. To sin sexually is to commit your course of life to a degree of unneeded unsteadiness. There is a surety, an innocence, and even an empowerment that will never be regained in its original purity if you sin sexually.

5.7

Purity is an elongated decision, continually remade. Because we swim against a current of sensuality, we can never stop kicking our spiritual legs and stroking with our spiritual arms. Increasingly, sexual images and invitations seek us out, and it's impossible in this current, evil age to avoid exposure to perversity of all kinds. Decisions I made yesterday must be reinforced by decisions I make today. I must decide today to turn my eyes away from alluring images. I must decide today to force errant thoughts from my mind by quoting Scripture. I must decide today to be accountable and to confess all temptations *before* they lead to sin. Yesterday's purity cannot guard me from today's evil. I must decide to be pure today, so help me God.

5.8

Some enemies need to be avoided. It is hubris to think we can fight all opponents at any given time. The wise warrior chooses the ground and timing of battle, while the arrogant warrior fights from disadvantaged ground and at foolish times. When it comes to sexual temptation, we must have the humility of Joseph, which is the wisdom to run away. Sexual sin is so alluring that none of us can withstand constant exposure to its siren song. None of us, young or old, male or female. We must run away, avoid being near it. Wisdom makes the practical decision to avoid places, people, times, events, and stimulants that are sensual. Wisdom is lowly enough to know that it must flee some enemies, and that sexual temptation is one of those giants.

5.9

Sexual sin ultimately undermines vigor. To sin sexually is in effect to throw your strength away. Honor is not the only casualty of immorality, so is energy. Even post-repentance and forgiveness, there is a cruel piper that must be paid. The road back from sexual sin is emotionally and spiritually exhausting for all involved, not just the immoral. The Bible does us the kindness of stating bluntly that sexual sin has unimaginable consequences. If we are not scared and sobered by the effects of immorality, then we are not listening. And not listening to this warning is the height of folly. May we listen to the weeping testimony of those who have found this to be true.

5.10

Sexual sin is financial suicide. One of the reasons the Bible warns us so stringently about sexual sin is because the consequences are so widespread. One such consequence is fiscal. Pastors, ministers, and missionaries who sin sexually are dismissed from the congregations and fellowships that support them. There is the short-term practical pain of losing a job and the long-term practical pain of losing credibility, which then has a direct effect on trust, opportunities, and invitations. Laity who sin sexually speed toward divorce, alimony, fractured families, and a litany of complications that affect practical living. Serial immorality leads to increasing financial difficulty. You may scoff at the connection between sexual sin and financial strain, but it's the warning of the Bible and of the unfortunate reality of men and women through the ages. Invest in your family's future emotional and financial stability by staying faithful and pure.

5.11

Sexual sin leads to physical deformity. Like it or not, politically correct or not, sexual sin has always led to flesh and body being consumed. God has attached terrible physical consequences to sexual sin. We must ask ourselves why. There is something so powerful and precious about purity that God without apology says that its violation will be punished. God's deterrents and punishments seem to increase in proportion to how He values what is violated. The more beautiful the creation of God, the more heinous the crime when that creation is marred, the greater the punishment for that crime. Physical afflictions that result from sexual sin are intended to lead to mourning, for the mourning helps us remember and guard the pristine beauty of God's intentions. In this way harsh consequences are a mercy to all who follow and observe, for they graphically remind us of the great value of that which must not be lost or sullied.

5.12

Our sinful state hates what would help and save us. The father of lies is very aware of that which would "life" us, and so in attempted preemptive action, he always tries to make what is good look bad. The devil knows that correction is good for the soul, so he frames it as oppression. The devil knows that discipline leads to delight, so he frames it as legalism. The devil knows that structure leads to freedom, so he frames it as restriction. The devil knows that order leads to creativity, so he frames it as imposition. Wisdom loves instruction and correction. Folly listens to the lie whisperer and despises the very things that deliver and empower.

5.13

The fool is self-made, for foolishness is chosen. Folly is not about intelligence, for some of the brightest men and women are fools. Those that refuse to listen, refuse counsel, and refuse instruction choose to be fools. It is in fact easier for the educated and intelligent to be fools, for they are more prone to disdain advice. Natural intelligence tends to groom an aversion to thinking others can speak into our lives. Wise is the intelligent person who rejoices to learn from the simple, the surprising, and the small, and foolish is the one who reacts in anger or defensiveness when friends oppose their will or way.

5.14

Sexual sin leads to public ruin. Part of the allure of sexual sin is the adrenaline rush of secrecy. There is an added excitement to what is illicit because it is unknown by others. There is a strange drug attached to hidden disobedience. Let us not deceive ourselves, what is sinfully done in secret will be broadcast in the public sphere. Sexual sin always manifests in time, always garners public attention and scorn, and always destroys publicly those who sinned privately. Whenever the filthy suggestion of impropriety barges into our minds, we should bash it with the truth that ultimately every evil thought acted on will be displayed for everyone to see and criticize. Wisdom only does what can be revealed publicly without shame. Folly self-deceives and says that there can ever be a private, sinful act.

5.15

Purity is a byproduct of contentment. When we compare our spouse to another, whether that comparison involves physical, emotional, or spiritual attributes, we lust. In effect, we are not satisfied with what we have but desire that which belongs to another. When we compare our status as singles with envious eyes toward the married, we lust. For in that comparison, we lust for what we do not have, for what our Sovereign Lord has not assigned (perhaps not yet, perhaps never will). A significant step towards purity involves being content with what we have, with who we have, with who we don't have, and with what who we have doesn't have.

5.16

Some things are not to be shared. We violate our intimate friends both when we jealously clench them to ourselves *and* when we share too much of them with others. For example, some anecdotes should only be shared by pure lovers. Some words should only be said to close friends. We must both protect and promote those we love the fiercest. Some looks, touches, and all sexual intimacies should only be experienced inside the marriage covenant. Sexual encounters outside marriage are wasted; they only end one way, a devastating loss to all involved. There is never a long-term gain or blessing from sexual sin. Never.

5.17

Giving must extend in concentric circles. We must first give to God. We must next give to immediate family. We then give to the body of Christ (the family of God) and then give to the family of man. In one sense all giving is family oriented but properly radiates out from the heavenly Father to spouse to father/mother/children to spiritual siblings, and to God's children everywhere. There is something indecent if the prescribed order is revoked or ignored. Giving (of ourselves, our wealth, or our bodies) contrary to the divine priority is indecent and inappropriate; it is death making. Giving according to the divine order is pure and life-giving.

5.18

Faithful longevity is an irreplaceable joy. The longer we are faithful in our intimate relationships, the greater our joy in that union. There is something heavenly about a couple that has been married for sixty years when they have spent those decades in absolute fidelity to one another. In the spiritual dimensions, such intimacy over time is like a glue that holds society together and pushes back the tides of evil. This understated and under-celebrated beauty is of such dignity and spiritual import that heaven rejoices in it though man ignores. Eternity will reveal how such long-standing faithfulness served in the grand scheme of things as a pulsating reminder of the character of God. Holy marriages like these contribute to the ten good persons in Sodom that withheld the wrath of God.

5.19

Do not despise yourself or others for aging. Sexuality is more spiritual and emotional than physical; it is so much more than a sexual act. Singles, created in the image of God, are sexual beings, and chastity is sexuality consecrated to God. As couples age and their bodies decline, sexuality is heightened, not lessened. We learn to revel in the intimacy of true union, a union that sex illustrates but does not define. Singles also mature in their sexuality, not defined or lessened by an abstinence from sexual acts. Satisfaction breeds purity. Purity breeds satisfaction.

5.20

Counterfeits ultimately deeply disappoint. There is something supremely beautiful and precious about relational intimacy, whether emotional or physical. When that intimacy is chaste, it is life-giving; when that intimacy is selfish or inappropriate, it is life-taking. Intimacy is not to be judged in quality by a short-term appraisal, for the pleasure of the short term can blind us to the torment of the long. Counterfeits bring short-term pleasure and long-term pain. The only sexual unions that bring long-term pleasure are those between a husband and wife. All other short-term sexual pleasures are counterfeit, for they rip out our souls, they destroy others around us, and they ultimately bring pain and sorrow. Why go there? Why not embrace sex within the friendly confines of one man married to one woman and reap the harvest of unbroken joy, long after the physical pleasures have past?

5.21

Because God sees everything, we should act as if He is standing right there. Because He is. We don't pick our nose when we know others are present or watching. Yet, look what we do beneath the gaze of a disappointed God. We must become increasingly comfortable and aware that there is no privacy with God. God is present and sees into our dreams, into our solitude, into our thoughts, into our motives. God is in our secret places. If we really believed in the omnipresence and omniscience of God, it would radically affect our behavior. Most of the sins we commit are done in a foolish if unarticulated hope that God is not aware. We are the child who covers our own eyes in the delusion that if we cannot see, others cannot see us. When tempted, we must remind ourselves that God is not only there, but He stares at us lovingly.

5.22

Sin is a self-locking chain. Habitual sin is a steady digging of our own grave. Others do not entrap us, no matter how enticing they are. We are self-assassins. We lock ourselves in prison. We slowly stab ourselves to death. It is convenient to blame the power of vices or predators, but we have no one to blame but ourselves. In our folly we self-trap by the willful, disobedient, and self-centered choices we constantly make. Unfortunately, the converse is not true—we cannot self-deliver. Arrogant as we are, we deny both realities: that we self-imprison and that we are helpless to self-release. We excel at making prisons, but we are clueless at making keys. We can but plead for a Savior who will rescue us from our own folly.

5.23

Disobedience is undefeated. It always wins, and it always completely dominates, even to the death. When we refuse to listen to biblical correction (which is always linked to obeying), the end is always macabre disfigurement of life. Health dies, marriages die, friendships die, unity dies, dreams die, usefulness dies, integrity dies, peace dies, joy dies. All these deaths are the inevitable result of accommodating disobedience. The Spirit of God through the Bible and His gentle voice is kind enough to be sober. We are warned explicitly that little disobediences have one end—death. Small disobediences lead us astray, and accumulated disobediences kill us.

PROVERBS
Chapter 6

6.1

We are not God. To try and meet the needs of the world is both presumptuous and exhausting. Sometimes the most damaging thing we can do to a friend is to help them, and damaging others always damages ourselves. The help that damages others is the help that inserts a human helper in place of the divine. The Scripture refers to the Holy Spirit as our Helper, and yet so often we do not allow Him that function or space. Rushing in to save, we cut in front of the Holy Spirit and often confuse or truncate what He is trying to do. Some of the most priceless lessons of faith can only be learned by duress and endurance. Our shortsighted concern often propels us to rescue, when the best thing we can do is stand back and pray. Wisdom learns not to overextend help. Wisdom understands there is only One limitless in His ability, and He is not me.

6.2

Our biggest liability is our mouth. Our mouth makes promises and boasts that we cannot sustain, and thus it snares us. As the spokesperson of our soul, our mouth continually betrays how foolish and vain we are. As the Bible condemns all of us as fools in our own wisdom, the wisest of the foolish is the one who stays silent. The safest of fools is the one who stays silent, makes few promises and fewer boasts. Eventually our mouth will reveal what is in our heart, and again the Bible does not mince words or truths—no one has a good heart. All of us are self-deceived to some degree; all of us are broken and wicked to complete depravity. There is *no* one who does good, not even one (Rom. 3:10). Let us open our mouth cautiously, reminded that it quickly reveals our arrogant heart and often commits the body to impractical, unhealthy promises. Shutting up is wising up.

6.3

Humility always precedes deliverance. The way up out of bondage and calamity is always to first fall down on our knees in genuine repentance. Deliverance does not negate consequences and surgeries leave scars. Too often we remain undelivered because we are not willing to meet the bill of our deliverance. We want to be saved without humiliation, rescued without consequences, spared without discipline. Lasting deliverance demands we acknowledge our folly and turn from it, admitting that we chose it and refusing to blame anyone else for our predicament. Too often we plea to be saved from the consequences of our sin without being separated from it. We like our sin but not its consequences, so we try and negotiate a way to have one without the other. This is foolishness. Wisdom understands that we must declare: "I am the idiot that got myself into this mess, and I am the idiot who cannot get out of the mess without help." It is certainly painful to be honest about being a fool, but it is a necessary step to freedom.

6.4

Right things don't become easier to do with delay. When in bondage, the first step out is humbling ourselves, so we might as well gather up our courage and take the plunge. We cannot escape predicaments established by easy, pleasurable, and foolish actions without painful, antidotal, and right actions. The wise hasten to their punishment, discipline, correction, and even their humiliation, for they recognize the incontrovertible law of sin: The medicine of humility must be taken and pride swallowed for sickness to be overcome and health returned. The one in the greatest pain for the longest time (and the greatest fool) is the one who refuses or delays humility. The wise one knows there is no escaping humility, so he hastens to it, not sleeping or napping until it is done.

6.5

Arrogance is a slow killer. To be arrogant is akin to being caught in a snare. Typically the snare doesn't kill you immediately; it just holds you until the hunter comes to finish you off. Arrogance is a long, slow death, agonizing for others to watch because the snared one is largely oblivious. The irony of arrogance is that to yourself, you appear magnificent but to others you appear pitiful, starving, weak, and vulnerable. Bound by your self-deception, you don't see that your soul is shrinking daily, and you don't hear the steady steps of the approaching hunter.

6.6

Laziness is foolish unpreparedness. Wisdom is industrious preparation. The wise believer gathers in regular community prepared for the moving of the Spirit. Our corporate worship is beautified by the personal abiding in Jesus that preceded the gatherings.

To go to church unprepared is foolish. To go to church after a week of personal abiding, rich reflection in the Scriptures, faithful and regular passionate prayer, and quick daily obedience is to go ready both to receive and to give. It is wisdom. To exit a week of indolent and lazy spirituality and to go to church expecting to receive or be renewed is foolish. Renewal belongs to the prepared, and decay to the slothful. Grace should never be a covering for laziness. Those who are most diligent benefit from the most grace.

6.7

Sound follower-ship does not wait for orders. It takes initiative and does what needs to be done. The best followers are those who lead by example and are industrious enough to take ownership of the people, projects, or programs they steward. Knowing what needs to be done by being told is certainly helpful and clarifying, but leaders rejoice in followers who are wise enough to recognize what needs to be done without being told—and then do something about it whether singularly or by coordinating a response. Foolish followers merely respond to direction. Wise followers take initiative and in their surrendered enthusiasm help guide both movement and movements.

6.8

Wisdom lives with one eye and one foot in the future. The future is consequence, preserved by wise acts in the present. When we live partially in the future, we have the wherewithal to deny ourselves pleasures in the present that we might guarantee them down the road. Disbursed and delayed gratification is lasting and growing gratification. Folly panics about the future and tries to gorge on pleasure now, wasting both present and future joy. Wisdom is relaxed and measured and, consequently, has peace today and provision tomorrow.

6.9

Rest must be rationed. A falling world requires a rising man. In this life we'll probably never get all the sleep that we want, though we should wisely take what we need. The wise learn to manage their fatigue, measure their rest, and make ground for God's purposes. There is something sinister about the prospect of reaching the end of our life un-tired and rested. A life without fatigue is a life wasted. We are not to glory in being tired, but neither are we to shun it. Weariness is an indicator of labor and labor an indicator of obedient faithfulness. We work hard, take our little slumber, and rise earlier than our bodies desires, for the King is coming, and the night, too, when no man can or will work.

6.10

We are slowly destroyed through countless little actions and inactions. Sudden calamity of character is a misnomer—it does not exist. No one decays overnight. No one gets up in the morning and decides to commit adultery. Devastating sins are those that were mulled over and accommodated for days, weeks, months, and years. If we daily indulge the small siren whispers of the flesh and daily ignore the sweet wooing of the Spirit, we will indeed one day commit the most heinous acts. Yet because the converse is also true, we can be at peace. If we daily listen to the Spirit, feed on the Word of God, and obey what Jesus tells us, in the hour of temptation we will not fall. Our security or demise is never in the moment. It is in the countless little actions or inactions prior.

The wise are preserved in the same way that the foolish are condemned little by little.

6.11

You cannot overcome the consequences of a life of laziness or selfish decisions with one heroic act or last testament declaration. The inevitable laws of sowing overrule all panicked conversions. Forgiveness can always be granted—it was given and received with a last breath on the cross—but consequences can never be annulled. What I did yesterday affects today, and what I do today will affect tomorrow, and what I do in the next thousand tomorrows will shape my destiny and the destiny of those around me. Tragically, the painful consequences of repeated small acts of folly and selfishness are always born in community, but beautifully, so are the life-giving consequences of a multitude of unseen kindnesses.

6.12

Wickedness as expressed in perversity has no value. Because perversity disguises itself with a cloak of humor, we are sometimes seduced into accepting what is vile. We countenance junk because its wrapping makes us smile. Television, movies, and late-night talk shows all excel at promoting what is disgusting by presenting it with wit. Foolishly we allow that perversity into our ears, and it's not long before it begins to penetrate our thoughts and hearts. Wisdom does not smile at what is evil, even when that evil is dressed up by clever words and phrases.

6.13

Cool, suave innuendo—smart enough to cut down others and subtly be sensuous—is not wisdom. It's merely a twisted intelligence smart enough to become stupid. There is a definite intentional cleverness to posture and words that lead us beyond the borders of propriety. These jokes and nuances start simple, probing for a listening ear, for a small opening. Without being prudes we need to guard our ears, hearts, spirits, eyes, and faces from any accommodation of clever crudeness. Men and women need to be appropriately guarded (even in the household of faith, especially in the household of faith) against speaking or listening in any ways that flirt with flirting.

6.14

Perversity always divides. Purity unites. Perversity starts by exiling the truth from pleasure and ends in divorce, breakage, brokenness, and isolation. Do not let the trap of enjoying an inside, off-color joke, a crafty but crude comment, or a sneaky, sexual pun beguile you. Alliances based on deception, criticism, jealousies, or lust never last; they only destroy. Pure words, pure jokes, pure actions, and pure thoughts bring homes and hearts together. Do not be of the gang that divides through small, repeated perversities. Be of the tribe that builds and unites through small and public encouragements, truths, and affirmations.

6.15

Rapid rise through perversity is sure to end in a sudden, startling collapse. Our fallen cultures frantically search for the next comic, entertainer, or thespian. We discover these public figures and elevate them because they are charming, beautiful, witty, or strong. We overlook their flaws; in fact, we find their muted flaws part of their charm. Despising character, we worship what is broken until the day scandal reveals a covered brokenness that even our hypocrisy cannot countenance. We should be slow to elevate anyone to the pedestal of praise, and we should never do so by overlooking their feet of clay. At the end of the day, we will all be exposed and fall, and pedestal praise only accelerates the day of our demise. There is only One who will never disappoint. There is only One worthy of unending praise.

6.16

The Lord hates certain things. In fact, the Lord has degrees of animosity. There are things He hates with a passion. Because humans have so distorted hate, we struggle to attribute any positive connotation to hate. Yet hate, like zeal, drive, and ambition, when correctly applied is a good thing. Hate is the desire to destroy something. God hates divorce; He wants to destroy it. God hates wickedness; He wants to eliminate it. God hates death; He will destroy it. It is a reverse perversity to tolerate, accept, and like something that should be destroyed. To want to destroy what is wicked is a God-shaped emotion—it is appropriate hate and justified hate. Let us love the things that God loves, and let us hate what He hates.

6.17

Pride, deceit, and violence are triplets. They are inseparably linked, and one cannot exist without its siblings lurking nearby. Pride is such an imposter that it can only be sustained by deceit. Deceit is so self-defeating that it eventually exposes itself and only remains in command by coercion. We cannot be proud without eventually deceiving and forcing our will, opinions, or preferences on others. Folly thinks we can indulge in a little pride while staying in the truth. We can't. Pride leads inescapably to deceit.

We may further think that a little pride and little white lies are relatively harmless. They are not. Indubitably they lead to the forceful defense of our fallenness. Wisdom shudders at violence and deceit and recognizes that escape from those two terrors begins by evading every form of pride.

6.18

To be quick and constant with words or actions that hurt others is to be anti-God. God's nature is so inescapably linked to tender mercies that any anti-mercy, anti-loving, anti-kindness efforts are actually anti-God rebellions. When we critique, slander, abuse, or insult others, we in effect raise our defiant tongues against the God of heaven, the God who is slow to anger, abounding in love, faithful to a thousand generations. This principle not only applies to the innocent and to our friends. It's just as true for the ones that we don't like, for the ones that hurt us. God expects us to have His perspective towards our enemies. We are not authorized to act or speak counter to God's character to anyone—friend or foe. We are to view and communicate the large heart of heaven to all, no matter our feelings or frustrations about them.

6.19

Of all the things God detests, one of the highest is dis-unity. In fact, Scripture refers to the one who brings disunity as an abomination, someone hated by God. This reality should make us quake in our boots, bridle our tongues, and walk circumspectly in times of tension. If we are the instrument of unnecessary and self-centered division, God not only hates that rupture, but He hates us for bringing it—meaning He will actively seek to destroy us. Is that strong? Indeed, it is, but that is how passionately God is against the one who divides. Wisdom sits up sobered and takes note, determining never to incur the hate of God by being the foolish false witness and sower of discord.

6.20

A confusion of gender leads to a loss of wisdom. Fathers (men) and mothers (women) have complementary insight into the character of God, which is the fount of all wisdom. Women were made as helpers comparable to men (Gen. 2:18), equal in their ability to represent qualities of the divine image in humanity. Man without woman is incomplete, and vice versa. We cannot be fully wise without the insight and perspective of both genders. The way to preserve wisdom is, therefore, not to blend the genders and thereby diminish both. Women need men to be masculine and men need women to be feminine. Society depends on a celebration of these differences, and in the blurring of gender distinctive we lose our common sight. We best help one another and most beautifully represent God when we are true to our birth gender, a choice the all-wise One has made for us.

6.21

We need physical reminders of internal truth. Men are internally and intrinsically male and should therefore dress and act like it. There should be a strength, confidence, and rigor, a warrior aspect to how men comport and compose themselves. Women are internally and intrinsically female and should therefore dress and act like it. There should be a regal beauty, dignity, and a modest and appealing aspect to how women carry and communicate their personality. Men should speak with the reserve, balance, wisdom, wit, judgment, and force of a king. Women should speak with the gentleness, charm, discernment, joy, and welcome of a queen. Let the simple clarity and winsomeness of our external behavior and speech represent the great dignity of our gender within.

6.22

Wisdom is potable. It cannot be stolen from us or misplaced. It cannot be diminished by use or fatigued by application. We transfer wisdom with us wherever we travel—it is our constant companion. Wisdom can only be squandered or ignored. With just a modicum of attention, wisdom grows, ever latent within us. Whenever we stray into folly by word or deed, it's not because we lacked the resource to avoid the trap. We have only ourselves to blame.

6.23

That which hurts you also illuminates. Critics and skeptics are gifts to us, for in their aspersions they often bring to light a brokenness or a liability early on in its development in us. If we are secure enough to ferret out the truth through the condemnation of others, we remain healthy in the long term as our malady is exposed and dealt with before it becomes too serious. Rebuke comes just as beneficially from antagonists as it does from admirers, and usually with more frequency. The wise person turns an intentional (if filtering) ear to the voices that object, for they are often the most kind in the long term, no matter their sting in the present.

6.24

Evil is a flatterer. Evil uses flattery to create short-term excitement and makes you feel good about yourself in the immediate and horrible in the long term. Evil distorts your self-image and deceives you into thinking you are above the rules, immune to consequences, deserving of privilege, worthy of exceptions. Evil whispers that what you do publicly is too important to be sabotaged by what you do privately and suggests that there is an allowable dissonance between what you teach and proclaim and what you practice. Folly is seduced by these flattering lies, while wisdom turns a deaf ear to them and opts for long-term stability over short-term excitement.

6.25

Even the blind lust, for lust begins in the heart, races up to the imagination, and then looks for application through the eyes. While blinders, filters, accountability, and averted eyes in the public sphere are helpful and necessary, the battle is not in the eyes, but in the heart. Alluring images now stare at us more brazenly than ever before in history. The digital age has empowered the sirens to come into our homes, phones, and other electronic devices. Now more than ever, it is crucial that the heart is defended from such unyielding assault. Yet in this unfair battle we have hope, for victory is not won or maintained by the eyes but by the heart. The heart is a space of which we still have control, for no billboard is erected there without our signature of assent.

6.26

Sexual sin cheapens the indulger. Sexual sin is self-mutilation, self-robbery. We undermine our own stock when we accommodate any form of sexual impropriety—whether that be with the heart, mind, imagination, eyes, hands, or body. Every time we accommodate sexual indiscretion, we undermine our own spiritual stock. Crassly, we are worth less spiritual stock (less empowered, less anointed, less spiritually powerful, less trustworthy) every time we indulge the flesh. Spiritual vitality is lost irretrievably with immoral sexual concessions. Sexual sin seems to be of the gravest, death-inducing rebellions in Scripture. Forgiveness? Thankfully, yes. Return to former effectiveness and usefulness? Sadly no.

6.27

Sexual sin has a 100-percent disaster rate. Some disasters are immediate and public; others quietly eat the sinner up from the inside out. Some who sin sexually are like a tree struck by lightning, immediately felled to the ground. Others are like a tree eaten by worms from the inside out; to all appearances the tree is strong and mighty until the day of its collapse. Whether by lighting or worm, the result is sure. There is no escaping the ugly consequences of sexual sin. Folly thinks that we can be the first (and only) in history to have our sin undetected and unpunished. Wisdom knows this is impossible.

6.28

Sexual sin sears both body and character. It is a fire that burns and scars. Sexual sin is a betrayal of the highest order, treacherous not only to the people dishonored but to the very fabric of the sinner. God places such a high value on holy intimacy, marriage, and trusting and yielded union that when those are violated, He decrees sharp, unrelenting consequences to the perpetrator. This drastic effect is because God knows how painful and damaging sexual sin is to anyone it touches, and He wants to warn us dramatically away from it. Those who have sinned sexually are the first to hope that their pain would serve as a merciful warning to others. There is a temptation to soften what the Bible says about the consequences of sexual sin so as not to heap hurt on those who have succumbed, but that is not fair to our young. Let the warning go out. The kindest message we send to the future is in our pain.

6.29

Sexual sin, particularly adultery, is so serious because it is a violation of multiple sacred covenants and has a wide ripple of insecurity and instability. Adultery breaks two marriage covenants and three spiritual covenants—the covenant with God of each of the actors and the covenant of propriety with each other. Adultery breaks two family covenants as both actors betray their individual families. The emotional and spiritual damage done to children, parents, siblings, and relatives in the horror of adultery is unquantifiable. Adultery breaks two social covenants as both actors betray friends, leaders, disciples, and acquaintances. Adultery breaks two public covenants; both actors prove to society at large that they are untrustworthy, selfish, unstable, and unworthy of public trust. The range of covenantal havoc triggered by adultery is staggering, atomic in its devastation. Let us not be the idiots who do anything to get anywhere near the possibility. No precaution is too extreme when the damage costs are tallied.

6.30

Wisdom judges without condemning. The foolish condemn without empathy, while the wise endeavor to judge (and punish) with mercy. A fallen world continually propels broken people to do unlawful acts. The foolish regard the act and the world in isolation from one another and either unfairly blames one or exonerates both. The wise ever regards both the person and the context and judges mercifully (deals with the issue including punitive, corrective, and appropriate measures), neither exonerating both or unjustly blaming only one.

6.31

Consequences cannot be waived when difficulty prompts misguided, if desperate, action. Mercy does not remove consequences—that is perversion. Mercy is only true to itself when it addresses injustice comprehensively. Restitution and forgiveness are not mutually exclusive; they are the two legs on which mercy walks.

6.32

Sexual sin is a two-edged sword maiming both the user and the other. Sexual sin not only steals from the other (even by their consent), it also self-inflicts injury. The tragic irony of sexual sin is that self-pain is artfully and convincingly disguised as self-pleasure. What seems to be gratifying is actually destroying. The wise are not fooled by the appearance of pleasure. The wise constantly bear in mind that sexual sin is pain, pain, pain, no matter how loudly it pretends to be pleasure. The tragedy of most sexual sin is that those who fall know this (that sexual sin is but pain), but they foolishly indulge in the appearance of pleasure knowing deep within that they only hurt themselves.

6.33

You never fully recover from sexual sin—there is irretrievable loss. After David sinned, he remained king, but his family and kingdom disintegrated around him and his last days contained more sorrow than joy. Sexual sin cannot be forgotten, neither by the sinner nor those around him or her. Whenever you appear, whenever you speak, whenever you are before the public, the memory of your shame will lurk in your mind or in theirs. God forgives as does man. God restores ministry opportunities as does man. But history is not removed nor forgotten. Those who once ran without hindrance will still be able to run, but with a limp.

6.34

Some breaches of trust have no other resolution than a harsh response, and sexual betrayal is one of them. God seems to endorse a furious reaction to sexual twistedness, and He does so because He strongly hates it. Sexual sin cannot be dealt with partially or reservedly. It must be dealt with firmly, quickly, and finally. Sexual sin will always result in emotional lashing out privately and publicly. This is because sexuality is so beautiful, and the more beautiful a gift of God, the more anguish when that gift is abused. God is angered when His beauty is disfigured as should we be.

6.35

Wisdom recognizes there is no escape from the extreme consequences of some sins, so our only good recourse is to avoid them altogether. The painful cost continually and internally borne by those who have fallen into sexual sin is a painful necessity for the good of the community. There is no appeasement for the pain or consequences of sexual sin. It cannot be undone. It cannot be forgotten. Its consequences can only be lived with. So don't be the fool who commits sexual sin. Just don't do it. The penalty is public as a mercy. The consequences are so harsh that all must be warned, even if in warning we cause pain to those who have fallen.

PROVERBS
Chapter 7

7.1

Truth starts external to humans (God is the treasury) and slowly penetrates our inward parts. We are meant to store up truth as treasure. Think of it in the childlike way. Think of a little girl in an Easter dress hunting for Easter eggs. Even as she finds one and delightedly and excitedly places it in her basket, so too should we hunt down nuggets of truth and treasure them within. Think of the hard-working farmer storing up grain for winter, or the blue-collar worker faithfully saving up to buy a necessity for his struggling family. Treasure is kept in order to be spent, spent in the day of need. So, too, is truth stored to be spent. In the day of need, those who have delightedly stored up wisdom will both survive peril and prevail over it.

7.2

God's laws are the lens through which we should view the world. When faced with choices, grand or small, we peer at the choice knowing that if we choose God's way, it leads to life. When God's law is our lens, the appearance of what we study changes. What seemed alluring (if it is wicked) is exposed as repugnant. What seemed odious (if it is for His great and merciful will) is revealed as attractive. When God's law is our lens and our delight, we see past form to substance, we reach for no disguised poison, and we press toward eternal good though the path requires temporal pain.

7.3

God's truth must be the basis of both our actions and our emotions. Truth performed with dour reluctances loses its luster. Truth acted on passionately delights both actor and observer. We need to be emotional about truth. Truth is not only adorned by sobriety, it also glows with joy. Truth should make us weep and make us dance. Truth should both stun us to silent wonder and lift us to our feet in shouts of praise. Let's be emotional about truth.

7.4

Treat truth as family. Be intimate, familiar, and comfortable with wisdom. Healthy family relationships emerge over time through both tactile and spiritual interaction. We spend so much time with one another, we intuitively know when something is amiss with sibling or parent. They don't have to make a lot of fuss, we see the minor twitch of nostril, the tiny lift of eyebrow, the little flush of color in the ears, and we know what it means. So should it be with wisdom and understanding. We should be so conversant with it that any little deviation from the norm is immediately discerned. We don't have to study evil to recognize it. Rather, let's study good. Intimate knowledge of what is right immediately alerts us to what is wrong.

7.5

Familiarity with what is pure, true, and wise is a safeguard against unguarded moments. Our habits discipline us and our daily walk with wisdom protects us from a moment of folly. If our habit has been to wisely avert our eyes from what is scandalous, when the scandalous ambushes us, we will reflexively run, caring not what we drop in our haste. No one is immune from a moment of weakness, but in those sudden snares of temptation it is as unlikely that the habitually pure will succumb as it is probable that the undisciplined will fall. My security or failing tomorrow is determined by my discipline or laxity today.

7.6

The painful observation of others self-destructing can have one redeeming result—it can warn us. Whatever misery the foolish choices of others causes them, let there be a small mercy in their agony, a mercy that keeps us and others from making a similar foolish choice. Don't waste the pain of another by not viscerally reacting to their plight, by putting distance between you and your temptation. It's too late for the blunderer to evade tragic consequences, but it's not too late for the observer. Whenever you hear or see someone fall morally, it is a double waste if your resolve to purity is not strengthened, if your heart does not fly to repent, and if your actions do not immediately lead you to climb higher up the solid rock.

7.7

Simple doesn't have to be stupid. Childlike doesn't have to be childish. Innocence doesn't have to be naïve. We don't have to experience sin's burning to know it hurts us. We can learn of the power of fire through a cautious proximity; we don't have to plunge our hand into the flame. The foolish are stupid, childish, and naïve. The wise are simple, childlike, and innocent. We must know enough of the damage of immorality to avoid it, without knowing too much that we are sullied (by information even if not by experience).

7.8

Patterns matter and paths have an addicting power—for good or for evil. In the East African revival of the 1950s, extended prayer became common, and Christians would walk the same path to their place of prayer day after day, beating worn paths bare by their frequent visits. If a Christian ceased to pray, their friends would note, "Friend, there is grass growing on your path." If our repeated path is to prayer, that discipline contributes to our protection. Frequent is the sad verification of the immoral that their first step to disaster was when they stopped walking the path of prayer. We lead ourselves into temptation when we stop leading ourselves to pray.

7.9

Secrecy is always detrimental to purity. Bringing temptation into the light breaks most of its power. The wisest thing we can do is to early and often share our vulnerabilities with safe others. The shame of expressing temptation to a friend is infinitesimal compared to the shame of private acts becoming publicly known, broadcast one day from the rooftops. Those who escape big sin and broad shame are those who constantly and voluntarily bring their little sin and shame into the light. They are wise enough to know that their hope is in being known, not in being hidden.

7.10

Craftiness is a precursor to sexual sin. There is demonic wisdom. There is cunning that is opposite to wisdom, a kind of cleverness (joking, false intimacy) that leads to immorality. We should not rejoice in twisted cleverness in others or in ourselves, for it is the sign of a predator. Sexual wolves are charming in both genders. Crafty hearts wear attractive clothes, speak slick words, act and dress suavely, but have leprous bodies. If you notice in yourself a tendency to be crafty, you should be very alarmed, you should be scared not proud.

7.11

Rebellion makes you susceptible to sexual sin. When you chafe under the boundaries that others (fairly or unfairly) set for you, you open yourself up to disdain other boundaries. There is a fine line between a free spirit and a rebellious one. Coloring outside the lines does not take ingenuity; it just needs impudence. Real creativity is to color within the lines in unique patterns and vibrancy. Wisdom does not make a habit of leaping over boundaries. That is actually folly disguised as bravado. Wisdom marries creativity and finds life within the boundaries that God (and others who learned the hard way) have prescribed. This is why Paul calls the marriage bed undefiled. Real sexual joy comes from creativity discovered within the bonds of marriage.

7.12

Sexual temptation is a lurker. E. Stanley Jones advises that the middle aged need a re-regeneration as morals tend to be discarded after long adoption. When it comes to our battle for purity, we are in a championship bout, and we must keep our guard up for all twelve rounds. Immorality has a cruel left hook and jabs away steadily, patiently waiting for us to drop our guard, waiting for those moments when we don't protect our vulnerabilities. A wise boxer is not discouraged that he must defend for the length of the bout. He reconciles himself to that reality and trains accordingly. A foolish boxer yields to fatigue and quickly regrets it. On that great day of the Lord, the final bell will ring, and we can drop our guard. What a day that will be! Until then, we can never drop our guard.

7.13

Shame serves as a protection against impropriety. In that sense shame as compared with shamelessness is a good thing. Wisdom gets embarrassed about some things. Shamelessness has no embarrassment and thus is the folly of no protection. Sinful cultures relentlessly attack shame, framing it as prudishness. Folly says we should never be ashamed. Wisdom rebukes that lie and welcomes shame as a gift, a safety, a help, and a friend. Folly mocks all shame while wisdom unimpressed rejoins with benevolent intent: "Have you no shame? For you could surely use some for your own and the common good."

7.14

Super spirituality can lead to improper sensuality. Sex is at its core a spiritual act, a spiritual union. Chaste, unmarried couples growing in intimacy are often surprised by the strength of the sexual impulse. As they share life, they become more and more intimate spiritually. Eventually their spiritual union lacks only one intimacy—physical consummation. I often warn young couples that praying together can easily lead to sleeping together, strange as that may sound. Those who therefore overplay (through subtle arrogance) their spiritual relationships, vocabulary, or behavior often set themselves up for improper liaisons. When we bond spiritually, there can be a desire to also bond sexually. The wise are aware, not afraid.

7.15

Perversity is persistent, and thus must be fought accordingly. We can't fight perversion idly. It must be total war. In our media (print, video, audio), public discourse, and social media, there is a relentless assault on decency. As in all major wars we must have the wisdom to know when to stand and fight, and when to swiftly withdraw as the forces amassed against us are too mighty. Folly fights battles you are either unprepared for or overmatched in. For me it's not wise to have access to social media. For me it's wise to severely limit my online presence. For me it's folly not to have accountability software and foolish not to severely restrict what is at my fingertips. For me it's folly to go to certain places and have certain things in my ears and eyes. Part of my persistent war against perversity is to constantly starve it.

7.16

Most temptations are not crass. We must be on guard against the beautiful, elegant, and refined traps of the devil. Sexual sin woos us more than wows us. There is a subtlety to illicit sensuality. It is a slowly rising tide, not a sudden and crashing tsunami. These elegant temptations are deceptions that often originate within us. We tell ourselves enough small subtle lies that we become susceptible to big foolish ones. The foolish want to be fooled and so they dig the ground out from under their own feet through a series of sophisticated half-truths.

7.17

In our battle for purity, if we are wise, we will guard against the intangibles, the illogical attractions. Context can confuse and distract us. The foolish linger in relational ambiances that have seductive sounds, smells, and textures. The physical yielding that is central to sexual sin is but the fruit. The root is when we foolishly place ourselves in an emotional environment where our needs and wants are met inappropriately—by persons or things or self. Wisdom is willing to have some needs and wants unmet rather than met by the wrong person or in the wrong way.

7.18

Wisdom does not confuse lust with love. Folly (even in marriage) conflates the two. Lust at its core does injury to another through stealing, deceiving, withholding, or misappropriating. Love always promotes and guards the interest of each other. Love defends, protects, serves, and always respects person, privacy, and property. Sexual sin has invisible arms (that reach out much further than the confines of a local embrace) and invisible legs (which take a long run of many steps to arrive at the present sin). Lust is blindly in love with self, while love lusts to bless others, seeing far beyond what is near or visible.

7.19

Wisdom is wary of inappropriate adventure. Sexual sin includes the thrill of the chase and the attraction of danger. It's fueled by the feeling of exhilaration about doing what is wrong. Folly wrongly assumes that the greatest kick is in doing what is forbidden. Wisdom knows there is no better adrenaline and no higher reward than doing what is right and pure. Purity is the best and safest drug. Purity needs not descend into the mud of lesser sexual narcotics. Nothings soars as high or is more sexually fulfilling and rewarding as a married man and woman who are year after year, decade after decade, all lifelong completely faithful and given to one another.

7.20

Beware the descent into a false reliance on a "grace period" for sexual sin. The single thinks that pre-marriage immorality is of less consequence than post-marriage failure, little realizing that immorality's effects linger in mind and spirit, spoiling all that follows. The married one supposes that a little pornography here and there is not debilitating, little realizing that something beautiful dies with every wayward perusal. One of immorality's frequent lies is that you will get away with it, that you are the exception, that you will not be discovered. This deception redirects the sinner away from considering the sin as the discoverer. The Bible tells us our sin will find us out, not our friend, spouse, or neighbor. Sin keeps no secrets and rejoices in the public humiliation of its victims. Your sin will not stay hidden, for the sin itself will manifest in perverse delight at its destructive power. The foolish align with the very thing that will expose them.

7.21

Sexual sin appeals to our ego. Sensuality is a flatterer and enticer, and immorality draws us in by pride. Hence, the first line of defense is humility. Purity and pride are like oil and water, humility and holiness like magnets. We cannot sustain purity when our hearts are proud, and we cannot sustain holiness without humility. Those who desire to escape sexual sin must be diligent to stay lowly, as arrogance is the first step to adultery.

7.22

Sexual sin will absolutely humiliate the offender. It will slaughter his or her dignity, confidence, moral authority, reputation, and emotional health. Sexual sin reveals the real fool no matter the elaborate pretensions of intelligence. The effects of sexual sin are so obvious and so well recorded that the one who falls has no excuse for his or her idiocy. Sexual sin is doubly shaming for it not only reveals our craven, animal sensuality, it also reveals our stupidity. Sophistication is no protection from sexual sin; neither is cleverness, charisma, wit, or confidence. Sexual sin is so potent an enemy that we should be soberly scared into a caution devoid of any pretension.

7.23

Sexual sin will cost your life vibrancy. The thrill of the chase, the drug of illicit adventure, and the adrenaline rush of lust all drown out the voice that warns, "To sin sexually is to suffer and die an agonizing death." Sexual sin reveals how often the intelligent can be idiots, forsaking long-term joy for momentary pleasure. The real wisdom is the determined, unwavering choice for long-term health, a choice which recognizes short-term snares. The way to avoid the arrows of lust is not to dodge them as they land all around us, it is to remove ourselves from their reach. Lust arrows can only fly so far, but they fly fast and furious. The wise remain out of their range.

7.24

We need a healthy fear of sexual sin. We should tremble now rather than shake later. If we are wise, we will take a long look at all the pain sexual sin caused in the Bible, in history, and in society around us (including family and friends). Every time we hear of someone failing sexually, let us go into a private place, fall on our knees, tremble in prayer, and confess, "There *but* for the grace of God, go I." Let us offer a prayer for the fallen to the ever merciful One, and let us commit once more that we will not walk that path—not one step, not one glance, not one click, not one act.

7.25

The avoidance of sexual sin hinges on pre-determined clinical decisions, not in-the-moment emotional or physical reactions. While in our right minds, while outside the raging zone of temptation, while in the clear light of day, while in the simple light of communion with Jesus, we must rule out the possibility of any small steps that lead to significant stumbling. Yes, we depend on mercy and divine aid, but we are responsible for disciplined pre-determinations. Let us practically put (and keep) sexual sin on the list of things we will never consider. We all make internal determinations. Some are moral, and some are neutral morally but personal convictions. These determinations may be to never drink alcohol, get a tattoo, become a Communist, eat feces, murder children, strangle puppies, or a range of other choices. The point is that we all have lists of no-fly zones, things we won't internally debate or consider. They are completely off the table and unthinkable to us, and we would never even approach them as a possible. They are anathema. The wise have sexual sin at the top of that list.

7.26

The strong are not invulnerable to sexual sin. Shockingly they are more susceptible. Public figures, preachers, teachers, mentors, leaders, and those in the public eye are more prone to sexual sin for two reasons. The obvious is that when a leader falls, especially one who has called for purity, the shame to the name of Christ is greater, the damage to the body of Christ deeper, and Satan cackles in demonic glee. The less obvious reason is that when we praise our public figures and leaders, we participate in creating a delusion in their minds—a delusion based on the lie that their contribution is so valuable that their errors will be overlooked. When we praise the public figure, we may be well intentioned, but often the effect is to cause them to lower their shield of humility and lift their head of pride up into the enemies line of fire. What the strong need is more prayer, not more praise.

7.27

Sexual sin leads to torment—unrelenting, spiraling torment. All sin is forgiven, but memories are hardly ever erased, and consequences are never removed. Sexual sin destroys families, ministries, churches, and communities. The ripple effects of sexual sin start in the heart and psyche of the sinner and extend out to every circle of influence and cause anguish all along the way. The book of Proverbs may seem excessive in the amount of text used to warn about sexual sin, but the inspired author does so because he has experienced the bitter fruit of his sexually deviant root. Solomon from painful experience pleads with us over the centuries not to walk the unrelenting path of pain and death that he trod. He or she who has ears to hear *and fear*, let them hear and fear.

PROVERBS
Chapter 8

8.1

Fools keep their status by determination. It is rigid stubbornness that keeps you from wisdom. There are unlimited opportunities to learn. Every day teaches us where we are wrong, if we will but listen to wisdom's cry. If we are not wiser today than we were yesterday, if we are not wiser this year than last, it is not the fault of wisdom. We retain our foolishness by sheer grit. Life is the repeated opportunity to learn. Wisdom never tires. Thus, the old fool is the stubborn fool.

8.2

The marketplace is full of wisdom. The God of truth generously sprinkles His nuggets of wisdom in every stratum and vocation of society. Truth is so ubiquitous and necessary to basic human function that even lies need a little (or a lot) of truth sprinkled in them in order to be credible. Those who rise early and faithfully and launch out into the marketplace are privileged in that they are assigned to a treasure hunt every day. Work is made joyful when discovery replaces drudgery, as the discovery of God's truth nuggets are hidden liberally for us to uncover all day long.

8.3

Wisdom is not privileged, hidden, or secret information. Wisdom is an equal opportunity offering. Wisdom is offered on the front end of life to all. We can choose to listen to wisdom's call before we experience sin's fall. On the early approach to the city of daily life, there are voices that warn, instruct, and advise. We can either take that wisdom at its word and avoid pain, or we can ignore that broadcast help and learn the hard way. It is one of life's wonders that we don't have to learn through our own pain or joy. The pain of others can (if we are wise) exempt us from our own sorrow, and the joy of others can (if we are humble) speed us to our own delights. Foolish are the persons who refuse to learn from others' pain and joy. Proud are the persons who demand their learning be only by their own experience.

8.4

Wisdom actively and repeatedly pursues us. At the end of the day, we have no excuse for our foolish choices. The defensive person is the one whose spirit knows he has erred even if his mind and emotions refuse to admit it. Over and over again the book of Proverbs reminds us that wisdom is making a public, general call. No one is without excuse. When we fall, we fall because we would not listen. The positive application of this truth is that those hungry to be taught will always be helped. We never have to worry about being left ignorant. Wisdom is constantly available free to those that will receive it.

8.5

Naïveté is not harmless. It may be a gentle folly, but it is a folly all the same. We cannot be content to be naïve, nor proud of that lesser status. To be naïve is not to be innocent; to be naïve is to be uninformed to your own detriment and the detriment of others. Wisdom insists that we grow from naïveté to understanding. Naïveté insisted upon is foolishness embraced because it leads us to imprudent decisions. Imprudent decisions lead to the damage of self and others. Foolishness always ends up wounding, while wisdom ends in healing.

8.6

Wisdom's first volley is verbal. The benefit of wisdom is seen over time as a consequence of actions, but the first shot in the war to be wise is spoken. Wisdom is justified by her heritage but introduced by her heralds. Wisdom can be gained by listening to the wise and obeying their advice. Wisdom can also be gained by ignoring the wise, disobeying their advice, and experiencing the lesson painfully. Fools repeatedly choose painful lessons. The wise repeatedly choose to learn from the painful experiences of others.

8.7

Wells only give one type of water, and wicked speech perverts our well. When our mouths speak what is wicked, we pervert what emerged from our mouths prior and pollutes what will emerge from our mouths in the future. The wise realize that they cannot speak wickedly on the margins without that speech destroying all they say from the center. A few wicked words undo all the wisdom that has come before and all that will follow. The wise determine that no wickedness will escape their mouth so that no damage might be done to their truth.

8.8

Speech needs to be consistent if it is to stay wise. The wise diligently trace wickedness backwards from their mouth to its origin in the creases of their heart, ruthlessly digging out what is crooked or perverse. Both wisdom and folly are comprehensive; neither allow for dual citizenship. To belong to one camp is to be excluded from the other. While foolishness may appear wise and wisdom may appear foolish, in essence they are antithetical and can never be joined. The wise determinedly swallow what is crooked or perverse, hunt it down within, destroy it, and limit themselves to say, think, and feel what is right.

8.9

Understanding is sequential; it builds on prior wisdom. As wisdom builds, it increasingly makes more sense. Wisdom in essence is simple and so different from sophistry (i.e., the art of making what is stupid look smart). Wisdom is simple and plain, unadorned by flattery or exaggeration. Folly is complicated, exaggerated, hyperbolic, and clouded. When in an internal debate as to what is wise and what is foolish, the often-wise thing to do is the simple, plain, uncomplicated path. Simple is not to be confused with easy; the wise thing is often the hard thing. The right thing to do is usually not complicated; it's just hard.

8.10

Wisdom is the wage of the diligent. We don't just luckily stumble our way to wisdom; we must work to be wise. Wisdom is mined from deep in the ground, not discovered as we amble down the beach. Wisdom is much more valuable than money because it's much harder to earn. Money is not easily gained; it demands hard labor. So how much more wisdom! There is a greater degree of difficulty in procuring it. Those who desire wisdom must determine to labor long and hard for it. Those who desire wisdom must strategically plan and long persevere if they will attain their goal. Wisdom is always attained intentionally. It is not acquired randomly.

8.11

Wisdom is beautiful in the short term and security in the long term. Ministry tends to make a way for itself. The cynical report is that those who rise to prominence in ministry were favored, while the reality more oftentimes is that they were faithful. When we are wise, it beautifies us in the now and it opens doors for us in the future. It is shortsighted to want position, power, wealth, recognition, longevity, and influence. It is wise to want wisdom. For as Solomon learned (and then unlearned), if one gains wisdom, all the other desirables are accrued. Wisdom sources position, power, wealth, recognition, longevity, and influence; it is not derived from them.

8.12

Knowledge and discretion are byproducts of *prudent* wisdom. Knowledge and wisdom are different things. Some of the smartest people in the world are fools. The accumulation of knowledge does not increase the likelihood of being wise. In fact, sometimes it retards one's chances. The less one applies what one knows is right, the less one is wise. Thus, if one grows in both knowledge and deferred obedience, one grows in folly. Wisdom requires correct application of what is continually learned. The wise have twenty years of experience, while the fools have one year of experience repeated twenty times.

8.13

Love and hate are not opposites. If you fear the Lord, you will love Him, and if you love Him, you will hate some things. Loving God includes hating what He hates. We typically understand hate to be negative, but functionally it means to be passionately against some things, passionate enough to have the energy and motivation to destroy them. We should hate divorce. We should hate gossip. We should hate deception. We should hate betrayal. We should hate injustice. All these hates are signs that we love God, that we respect Him so much that we join Him in His passions. The fool loves what he should hate. The wise hate evil, pride, arrogance, and the evil way.

8.14

God owns wisdom and counsel so completely that He *is* counsel, wisdom, and understanding. Jesus is *the* truth. Truth is so much more complete than a principle—it is a Person. The strength of God derives from the fact that He not only possesses wisdom and understanding in infinite amounts, but He *is* wisdom and understanding infinitely. Therefore, He can give away wisdom and understanding without ever being depleted and diminished. No transaction can add to or subtract from God's wisdom. The wise therefore never cease asking counsel, even on repeated experiences. The fools presume they know how to do something the second time, and in their hubris they fail.

8.15

Leadership rises and falls according to the measure of counsel, wisdom, and understanding in its fabric. Counsel inherently means a plurality of voices that speak to a situation. A wise leader understands that she has blind spots and is only protected from bad decisions through listening to the perspective of others. Wisdom does not make decisions in the confinement of isolated ideas. The first opinion seems correct until it is tested by other voices. Do not be hasty in deciding—even after listening to good people—and do not listen to only one good counselor. To lead well you must listen to a plurality of voices and then decide as you can best discern the right way within.

8.16

Judgment is noble; it is not easy. Justice does not please everyone. In fact, justice tends to upset more widely than injustice. Noble justice is that which makes the right decision no matter the consequences. At the end of the day, order and leadership are maintained and strengthened by making the right decisions, not the popular ones. This strength is not apparent in the short term. It may seem that the right choices initially undermine security, but in the long term the right choices (despite the initial collateral damage) are always the most stabilizing and the most noble.

8.17

We initiate the release of wisdom by seeking it. When we seek wisdom, it finds and cares for us. Wisdom is the winsome woman who waits to be pursued. It is not fitting for the woman of decorum to chase her man, nor is it fitting or likely that wisdom will pursue us. We pursue wisdom, and she, enthused and honored by the pursuit, gives herself to us and cares for us loyally. We cannot be shy or reserved in our pursuit of wisdom. We will wait vainly for her to ask us to dance. We must bravely cross the dance hall floor and ask for her companionship. And no one who asks to dance with wisdom in good faith is disappointed.

8.18

Honor is so much more valuable than money. The truly rich are those who maintain their integrity all lifelong. That enduring righteousness (the honor derived from right standing with God, others, and yourself as much as depends on you) is attained by the daily acting out of what is right, of what is wise. Wisdom is not to be confused with intelligence. Some of the brightest humans are fools, for they do not act with honor or do the right thing on a daily basis. All their learning drives them mad. To seek wisdom is not an intellectual or theoretical pursuit. Seeking wisdom is a daily application of lessons learned. Seeking wisdom is doing the right things over and over and over again, unnoticed initially and with no fanfare, but recognized unmistakably with honor at the end of a wise life.

8.19

Wisdom's yield (the interest on her investment) is better than the power or capacity that money engenders. To be rich in wisdom is to have the real power on earth. Millions have been deceived into thinking that external coercion or force give influence and control. The real influencers of the future are those who are rich in wisdom. If you want to shape tomorrow, invest in becoming wise today.

8.20

True wisdom is only found and maintained through steadily making the right choices and consistently living prudently. The path of wisdom is well-worn and simple. It is a narrow road. Wisdom does not walk off the path, nor does it remove ancient boundary stones. Wisdom does not consider doubt a virtue, nor become bored with common truths. Wisdom shares the simple joy of God in repeated goodness, as C. S. Lewis expounds God's childlike delight with another sunrise by saying daily: "Do it again!" Wisdom sees the simple beauty in what is good and daily cries: "Do it again!"

8.21

When we delight in wisdom, God delights in storing up treasure for us: emotional, relational, spiritual, and physical. God's treasures, of course, are never meant to be hoarded. If God gives us greater emotional capacity, it is so we can steady others. If God gives us greater relational influence, it is so we can share His joy. If God gives us greater spiritual depth, it is so we can feed His flock. If God gives us greater physical strength, it is to serve and carry the weak. Wisdom then both earns God's treasures and realizes they are received only to be passed on. Wisdom never hoards.

8.22

Being God-possessed is a wonderful thing. In *Voyage to Venus* by C. S. Lewis, the protagonist is on a new earth competing with a devil-empowered colleague for the mind and heart of a new Eve. The devil-aided man tries to make the new Eve sin while the protagonist tries to counsel her to stay pure and true. The protagonist sees all the demonic wisdom in his adversary and feels hopeless in his own strength to contend. He realizes the only hope is if he is filled with the Holy Spirit and wisdom of God to the extent (and more) that his competitor is filled with the devil. So it must be with us. To compete against the twisted wisdom of this fallen world, we must be possessed with God and all His wisdom. One of the wisest things we can do is to seek to be filled and possessed by the Holy Spirit of God, "the Spirit of wisdom and understanding, the Spirit of counsel and might, the Spirit of knowledge and the fear of the Lord" (Isa. 11:2).

8.23

Wisdom predates us all and will outlast us all. We don't discover wisdom; we submit to it. One tragedy of being human is that we rarely learn from the mistakes of our forbearers. We insist on making our own errors and learning the same lessons they learned over and over again. In the big scheme of things, this is a colossal waste of time and energy, and a needless experience of great pain. The wisest of earth don't insist on gaining wisdom the hard or long way. They take their fathers and mothers in faith and wisdom at their word and run with it. When we are humble enough to learn from the experiences of others, we have more energy and time to advance in wisdom. Collectively and sadly, humans have too much hubris to so advance. Generationally, we insist on starting over. Wisdom invites us to avoid this waste.

8.24

Wisdom, concrete as it is, predates the material. The eternal laws of wisdom predate time; they were established from everlasting. Wisdom argues for devolution, not the ever-ascending intelligence of mana pressing forward towards an enlightenment that lies ahead of us. Light and truth, wisdom and knowledge were before us and are now thus behind us as we have fallen from their heights. Whatever progress man makes in wisdom is merely a scrambling back to our starting place. We are reaching to regain the heights from which we fell—and often vainly as we are so committed to our own foolish mistakes. Humans should blush at our actual folly, not flush with our illusory fame.

8.25

The present is secured by a blend of past truth and future consequences. Because wisdom is "older than the hills," it knows inevitable consequences of human choices. Wisdom precedes time, and time has seen countless humans make choices and has seen enough iterations of those choices and their results to predict the future unerringly. We cannot have the arrogance to think that we of all the humans in history will achieve different results from our choices. Because there is order to choice and consequence, we know that what has unfailingly happened before us morally will unfailingly happen after us. Our present then can be secured by wisely choosing what inevitably brings life and wisely avoiding what inevitably yields death.

8.26

We see the future by looking back. The clear repository of wisdom is behind us. The Bible narrative does us a tender mercy when it refuses to veil the frailty and fallen nature of its subjects. The whole tale told allows us to cheer the victories and wince at the failures. One of the most tender mercies we can thus render to children and disciples is to be likewise transparent with our lives. To hide our follies and foibles from those we lead or teach is to restrict them from the full-orbed wisdom deposited in the repository of our past experience. Let us be kind by being transparent, even when that revelation shows where we were unwise.

8.27

Wisdom prepares and does not ad lib. Preparation is the best foundation for spontaneity. When we thoroughly know (heart and head, experience and theory) our subject, we are best placed to set our notes down and harmonize the melody for a stanza or two. But those unfamiliar with the melody are foolish, not brave when they are extemporaneous. Preparation (teaching, sermons, lectures, parenting, public and private presentations) is the best posturing for the outpouring and anointing of the Holy Spirit. Critics of the prepared (manuscript, well-studied) preacher claim that he leaves no room for the inspiring Holy Spirit. The reality is that the Holy Spirit is not barred from inspiring during the hours of preparation, and neither is He (or the preacher) bound to the manuscript at hand. As the old hymn states: "Through days of preparation, Thy grace has made us strong, and now O King eternal, we lift our battle song."[3]

8.28

Wisdom is not always visible. Like foundations beneath a building or sun behind clouds, wisdom is evidentially there even when we can't see it. God sometimes acts in a way where His wisdom is veiled to us. We scratch our head and comfort our bereaved and can't quite understand why the Omnipotent allowed such pain. We join Sarah Edwards in spirit as she writes to her daughter Esther after the loss of their husband and father Jonathan in 1758:

My very dear Child, what shall I say? A holy and good God has covered us with a dark cloud. O that we may kiss the rod and lay our hands upon our mouths! The Lord has done it. He has made me adore His goodness, that we had him so long. But my God lives; and He has my heart. O what a legacy my husband and your father has left us! We are given to God; and there I am and love to be. Your ever affectionate mother....[4]

8.29

Wisdom sets limits. The "do nots!" of Scripture and life are some of the wisest injunctions. We often display our wisdom not by our indulgences but by our restraints. Observe what a person says "no" to, and you will have great insight into her character. A person, a parent, a collective, a church, a state, and a world without boundaries is foolish. A child who was only told "yes" or redirected to other activities always grows into an incorrigible adult. The soul never denied is never supplied with wisdom. Wisdom's "no" is just as loving and important as her "yes." To be told "no" is to be loved.

8.30

Wisdom is a master craftsman, a craftsman that brings joy. Master craftsman are not satisfied with good. They labor for great. When you are the marble, the medium, the clay, or the canvas in question, you do not usually have the patience of the artist. You would gladly settle for good, or even for the chisel to cease. But wisdom seeks beauty and joy and works long hours, enduring the process, for the joy set before—the joy of both artist and art.

8.31

Wisdom delights in finding a hospitable host. We have all been the bestower and the bestowed of begrudging hospitality. When hospitality is a duty, neither guest nor host nor anyone under the roof is at peace. So it is with the guest of wisdom, personalized in the Spirit of God. When His presence and insight (nudging, whispering, gentle advising) is appreciated, there is a common joy that host and holy share. When the presence and advice of the wise One is spurned, no one is happy. God is happy when we heed Him. When God gets happy, it is impossible for the divine host to stay sad.

8.32

Listening is obeying. We have not heard until we have done. Biblically, to hear is to act. Therefore, the wise are men and women of action. What they hear daily (from their reading of the Bible and communion with the Spirit), they act on it that very day. To be wise is to put into practice that day that which you read in the Bible that morning. Christianity is not complex; it's just hard. We object to what the Bible says, not because it's confusing, but because it's difficult. The wise listen to the daily difficulties consistently and over time build the muscle of obedience to the strength in which there is no delay between their hearing and their doing.

8.33

Don't disdain the wisdom that comes from unexpected people and places. We all have our favorite sage. We all have our favorite preacher. We all have our favorite mystic, philosopher, mentor, or even book of the Bible. Without lessening their influence, wisdom is open to the insight of an enemy, a critic, a pagan, a rebel, a child, and even a fool. Even as no human is completely wise and foolproof, no fool is completely foolish or "wiseproof." The wise have ears that accept wisdom, no matter how unlikely or unlikable the source.

8.34

It's not totally inappropriate to eavesdrop on wisdom. Truth intended for others can always serve the spectator. Wise fields harvested by others can always be gleaned again as there are nuggets inevitably left behind. Growth in wisdom is an active endeavor. Getting wiser is not necessarily like getting richer in which accumulated wealth bears its own interest. Getting wiser is like swimming upstream; if you're not active, you lose ground. We cannot be passive in gaining wisdom. We must seek, strive, ask, knock, and not be too proud to eat the crumbs that fall from the tables of the sons.

8.35

Wisdom gives life and leads to favor. Wisdom makes eyes sparkle and mouths spread into irrepressible grins. To be dour is no sign of wisdom; it's just a sign of selfishness. Wisdom gives life and favor and always breaks containment. Wisdom biblically is not hidden in a monastery or perched on some ascetic mountain. Biblical wisdom is found in the kitchen, on the tractor, at the lunch table, and in the vegetable aisle. Wisdom beams out in relational circles, neither owned nor contained by the source you hear it from but rippling out through you to others. At the center of it all is a joyous Lord whose wisdom makes Him glad, whose joy makes Him dispense favor, whose nature as a giver demands all joy, and whose favor received be passed on.

8.36

Wisdom not only keeps you in joy; it also keeps you in health. To sin against wisdom (to scorn it) is to hate what will invigorate you and to love what will kill you. The shame of folly is that it's so self-defeating. Folly advertises itself as adventure and masquerades as freedom, but it's merely disguised chains. Wisdom does not boast so loud, nor does it parade itself, but once acquired, wisdom's restraint yields a harvest of joy and freedom. Folly chooses the boundaries of freedom. Wisdom choses the freedom of boundaries.

PROVERBS
Chapter 9

9.1

Wisdom is a shelter laboriously carved from immovable rock. To become wise takes time and hard work. Wisdom has to be worked for, it has to be earned, for wisdom is derived more from labor than from listening. We can listen to wise words, and we can observe caves hewn from rock, but until we take up hammer and chisel and blister our hands for a while, we will not attain wisdom. Wisdom, in this sense, is practical and experiential, not memorized and recited.

9.2

In the same way that wisdom is slowly earned, it is slowly shared. It takes time to impart wisdom to others and it must be dispensed in doses. We are all children with limited capacity to apprehend until we have done so. We do a disservice to our disciples if we fill their heads with theory and don't allow them time to stumble forward experientially. Wisdom gives a few words about swimming and then takes its child into the water. It utters a few more words and grants a little more liquid liberty with saving arms ever nearby. Helping others live in wisdom is a long process. Wisdom and patience are bedfellows.

9.3

Folly is chosen and without excuse. Wisdom continually makes a public appeal. Those who are unwise are so because they shut their eyes and stuff their fingers in their ears. They hum childish nonsense to drown out wisdom's song. Thus, whatever ditch they fall in or wall they crash into is by their own choice. Wisdom is not stationary. It seeks, it hounds, it sends out messengers to trail after the fool, it repeatedly offers help. The first step of wisdom for the fool is the acknowledgment that whatever trouble ensnares him is there by choice. The fool always chooses the ditch of his dismay.

9.4

To be wise requires we leave our favored path and make practical changes. Growth from folly to wisdom requires turning, it requires repentance. Accumulated knowledge does not make us wiser, but practical changes do. The fool is the one who does not allow experiential pain to cause lifestyle changes. Everyone in life encounters pain. The wise not only make changes when pained, but they make the right changes. Low-level folly makes no changes when hurt, while sophisticated folly draws the wrong conclusions from pain and receives more pain as a consequence.

9.5

Enduring wisdom is more commonly gained by a consistent diet, not a drastic one. Even as the best way to lose weight is to eat nutritiously and exercise regularly, the best way to gain wisdom is a slow, steady intake of truth mixed with a daily application of that very truth. Crises and trauma have their place, but their success rate in wisdom retention is mixed at best. Persecution, for example, has made some better and others bitter. Those who consistently discover a small truth, incorporate that truth into their active behavior (obey it by living it), and then model that truth with others (share it) have a far superior result. One gains wisdom through discovery, obedience, and sharing.

9.6

The soul of the human is one-handed. Despite our delusion that we're complicated beings, we're actually quite simple and have the capacity to focus on one thing well. If we are to retain wisdom, we will have to release folly. The story of the monkey grabbing an apple through an iron-barred fence is apropos. When the monkey's fist clenched the apple, he could not draw his hand back through the bar of the fence. A gardener approached, and the monkey had to either release the apple or forgo freedom. Folly is an apple, sweet to our desire, that must be released for us to gain wisdom. We have one hand to grab one thing, and if we cling to folly, we forgo wisdom.

9.7

Sometimes the wisest thing we can do is shut up. Discretion can indeed be the better part of valor, especially if our interaction is with fools. It is the fool, after all, who gives the pig something valuable that the pig cannot recognize nor eat. There are certain types of people (scoffers and wicked) who are adept at taking intended good and turning it to harm. Even if your intention is to help or to bless, you can actually hurt them (scoffers and wicked), yourself, or other participants in your attempt to correct. The wise realize that sometimes only the spankings of time can drive out scoffing and evil.

9.8

When we don't accept correction, we verify our status as fools. Critics are God-ordained, and if we will recognize them as such, agents of mercy. There is almost always a nugget of truth in the rebuke of both friends and enemies whether or not their comments originate in a merciful heart. We know that the blows of a friend are kind, but the wise see kindness in the harshness of enemies as well. Sometimes it takes a low blow to knock the pretension and self-delusion out of us. The wise neither seek criticism nor ignore it.

9.9

Wisdom is not static. The proof that you're wise is that you're wiser today than you were yesterday, that you've grown and increased in capacity. Wisdom is not a diploma to hang on the wall, a credential conferred by ceremony, or a medal brought out for parade day. Wisdom is like fresh bread; it's real if when broken, hot steam lifts and soft morsels soothe. Wisdom is a bit like manna, ever new, yesterday's portion already useless. The wise are so today, ever new, actively and increasingly.

9.10

The path to wisdom begins with submission and respect, not with doubt. To know God is to know. Wisdom starts with a Person, not with a precept. The wisest thing we can do is to begin with the simple presuppositions that (1) there is a God and (2) I am not Him. Wisdom then does not put God on trial but assumes God is good and God has reasons for what He ordains. I have a friend who felt he could not ask a Muslim to doubt Islam if he (my friend) did not first likewise doubt Christianity, the Bible, and Christ. Thinking himself wise, he acted the fool and lost his faith. How much wiser my friend would have been to seek the reasons for accepted precepts, not to doubt the Person and Source of the decree.

9.11

Time is sweeter when we are wiser. To the fool eternity is a horror. To the wise the long seems short. Good choices in the practical lead to health and perseverance, stability in trouble, and provision in distress. But even more eternally, good choices in the now make the present sweet and the future sweeter. There is no angst over time for those who have been wise. The present and the future are equally anticipated, and there is no fear that folly from the past will overtake. Wisdom increases our appreciation of both time and timelessness.

9.12

We cannot live on the wisdom of others. We must have our own supply. No manual we read by the sages, no observation of parent or mentor, no familiarity with philosophy, and no external source of wisdom will override our will when we are under duress. When under pressure, all external sources and records disappear, and we must confront our dragons and demons with only what we have fostered within. Mercifully, the best Counselor resides within, so we are never abandoned. But that is the point. To the measure we've accumulated our own store of wisdom and to the degree we are united with the Spirit of wisdom, there will be the measure and degree of right choices in times of trouble or confusion.

9.13

Truth is loud but not dissonant. Wisdom is publicly available but in a non-abrasive way. Folly, however, is invasive, clamorous, rude, bullying, and domineering. Wisdom is genteel; folly is coarse. Wisdom respects you; folly will seek to domineer you. When you feel pressured, manipulated, or coerced, that is folly pursuing you. When you feel drawn, wooed, and invited, wisdom's call is honoring and valuing you. When we seek to help others, let us not present wisdom's gift through folly's means.

9.14

Folly is a self-promoter and tends to use crass speech and coarse joking. Folly is adept at making her way into commercials, public broadcasts, the arts, and entertainment, and also unfortunately, into sermons, lectures, and Bible studies. The market of life does not cordon off a section of the central square for fools. Fools are granted equal access into every general discourse and often given a prominent place in the movies, universities, novels, or news. Fools are not required to wear a jester's hat. More often, they are given a golden voice and a charming smile. The highest places of society roll out the red carpet for folly, while wisdom takes a humbler path.

9.15

Wisdom doesn't deviate. It has purpose and a fixed eye on the preferred future. Clarity, simplicity, and unity tend to characterize wise choices. Like a farmer aiming his plow at a fixed point at the end of the field, wisdom looks neither right or left once that fixed point is determined. Wisdom plods straight on. Folly, however, ambles from side to side, easily distracted by the calls of a variety of vendors. When making choices, especially those in communal decisions, we should make sure the choice is simple, clear, and unifying. Once we determine what it is, we fix our eyes on the destination and don't detour or self-doubt.

9.16

Foolishness preys on the naïve. Naivety is not neutral, and it is not harmless. Naivety does not keep us safe and is an illusory shelter for the timid. In a world at spiritual war, we must choose sides. Wisdom does not bury her head in the sand, and she does not remain unaligned. Wisdom determines what is right and just, and wholeheartedly launches all her resources towards the aim of good. We are not to be naïve about the devil's devices. We are able to recognize them, so that we can disarm them. We cannot ignore the devil's devices or not engage the fight hoping it will pass us by. This is total war. We must choose a side.

9.17

Folly has a certain deceptive adrenaline rush. It is deceptive not because the adventure is false, but because it is fatal. Foolishness tells you to throw yourself from a height because there is the excitement of flying for a few moments. But the end is death. Foolishness beckons you to sexual sin for the genuine excitement and pleasure of the moment. But the end is death. Foolishness calls you to drunkenness, gluttony, overindulgence, and a thousand other vices by promoting a legitimate short-term joy. But the end is death. Wisdom looks past adrenaline to joy, lasting joy.

9.18

The false and temporary joys of foolishness end up killing you. Not only that, but folly connects you to a tribe of the foolish. One horror of hell surely must be the accumulated arrogance, rebellion, disobedience, criticalness, snobbery, and selfishness of the masses. How horrible to be surrounded by others just as foolish as you are, for nothing so offends the fool as the sight of folly in another. Fools excel at pointing out what is wrong with others. Imagine the millions in torment, adding to the flames by criticizing each other. Imagine by contrast the beauty of heaven where the congregation of the humble, submitted, obedient, affirming, inclusive, and selfless get together. That is the tribe to which I long to belong.

PROVERBS
Chapter 10

10.1

Wisdom and folly have generational implications. No blanket brings as much warmth to the aged as children who live rightly, act wisely, and think biblically. No riches or retirement package can assuage the grief of the elderly when their offspring live selfishly and carnally, in disobedience to the God of the Bible. The joy of wisdom is that it moves reciprocally through the generations: the wisdom of the child brings joy to parents, joy to the child for bringing joy to the parents, and joy to the grandchildren when they discern how their ancestors have loved one another. Likewise, grief and folly move multi-directionally through the generations, causing great harm and pain wherever they are planted.

10.2

There are many ways to die. A moral death can be as painful as a physical death. In fact, loved ones may be more pained watching their relatives wither morally than they would be observing physical decline. Moral decay can be hidden for a season, even from those closest to us, but when our physical faculties give way, our spirits are revealed. We should soberly anticipate the revelation of our morality as our physicality declines. Whatever is deep within us will be revealed. The only protection is to ensure that what is in us now is pure, true, wise, submitted, honorific, gracious, tender, and kind. When we lose our minds, our morals emerge unguarded. Let us secretly treasure up that which brings honor, not shame, when it is revealed.

10.3

Doing the right things is its own satisfaction. There is a part of our fallen nature that longs to be satisfied by recognition and praise. The wise are satisfied by doing what is right, not in being recognized for doing what is right. By the same token, doing the wrong things is enduringly unsatisfying, even if pleasurable in the moment. Fools are satisfied with being noticed, even if they do rude, crass, or depraved things. That satisfaction proves unsatisfying and leads the fool to worse acts for even more fleeting fame and more satisfaction. The only way out of that degenerating cycle of futility is to start doing the right things when nobody is watching.

10.4

Laziness empties both mind and coffers. Hard work fills up both your soul and your bank. It's revealing that the first act of God recorded in Genesis is that He worked and took pleasure in good work. Neither retirement nor heaven are designed for non-workers. Labor is heavenly. Work is satisfying. Good work is God-glorifying. Rest is complementary to labor. We were created to do both, not to fixate on one. Rest without labor is gluttony, and labor without rest is both pride and folly. Both are self-destructive.

God's character is a beautiful harmony of work and rest as should ours be, even in repose.

10.5

All humans must endure winter or dry season or famine. Wisdom recognizes the seasons of life and prepares for lean times by storing up for them. An African fable tells of the king who asked for a ring that would make him happy in sad times and sad in happy times. He was presented a ring inscribed with the Swahili expression *hilo nalo itapita*, which means "this too shall pass." Famine came, enemies invaded, and the kingdom tottered on the verge of economic and civil collapse, but the king looked at his ring and was at peace. "This too shall pass." Prosperity and peace dawned, stability and increase flowed. The king looked at his ring and knowing that harvest doesn't last forever, stewarded the growth wisely, storing it up for the good of all in the next season of trial. Wisdom neither soars to giddy heights of unrealism, nor plummets to the despair of pessimism. Wisdom holds steady and digs into stored-up treasure to bridge the gaps.

10.6

Violence in word or deed is ultimately self-harm. Violence cuts us off from provision, for it narrows the field of potential help when we are in distress. We never know when we'll need a neighbor to help us in our duress. When we've hurt others, we seal their ears, eyes, and hearts to our needs. Blessing is the opposite of injury. When we serve and bless others, we invest acts of kindness that yield blessing and help in our time of need. The wise bless (and avoid unnecessary injury of others), both for the joy of being like

Jesus and for the insurance of open ears, caring eyes, and compassionate hearts available in times of crisis down the road.

10.7

Those who do evil stink and decay, while those who do right shine and waft beauty long after they're gone. Memory is sensory, positive or negative, according to the one being remembered. The righteous bring joy long after they're dead as friends remember their grace. The evil cause a shudder long after they're buried when their name is invoked. Wisdom realizes that physical death is not the end of our influence. Wisdom determines to bring posthumous joy through present day graciousness. May our wise living in the moment bring smiles and cheer long after we leave our school, job, church, field, post, neighborhood, or the earth.

10.8

You have to shut up to listen and you have to listen to be wise. Ruin never comes from listening. It's "loose lips" that sink ships, not big ears. Listening in order to be wise requires application. The person who listens but does not apply, turn, repent, adjust, learn, adapt, or change is just as foolish as the prattler who doesn't listen at all. We can be proud of taking counsel and considering others' perspective, but at the end of the day wisdom is active.

10.9

Safety lies in treating others well, not in scheming or maneuvering for power and enforced protection. Ultimately, safety is in people, not in police or programs. We have a small cottage in rural Kenya, far from any town, stores, or law enforcement. The cottage nestles into the African bush at the end of a dirt road. Our long-term protection is linked to how graciously and generously we interact with the local population. If we are kind to the community, the community will be kind to us. Our protection against rascals in the community comes from within the community. It is linked in potency to the favor and good with which they view us, which in turn is determined by how loving, compassionate, and neighborly we've been to them.

10.10

The clever and charismatic who make friends and gain advantage by force of personality not backed by strength of character will fall. Wisdom does not allow charisma to outstrip character. The fool relies on his charisma and ascends to impressive heights to only eventually commit very public, devastating sins. The wise do not throttle charisma but regulate it and endeavor to build on character, with charisma as the garnish, not the building block.

10.11

The right thing to do with our mouths is to speak life. We should prophecy with a view to life. We should preach with a view to life. We should speak publicly and privately with a view to life. Life speech is honest and does not shy away from painful truths, but it also offers remedy, not punishment. The righteous craft and deliver speech in such a way that aims for life. Our listeners will rise to the level of faith we have for their future. Foolish talk either aims for or results in death, discouragement, doom, depression, or deceit. We can judge the wisdom of words based on whether or not they lead to life.

10.12

Love covers sin. Love swallows anger. The wise pour water on inflammatory or painful information; fools pour gasoline. The wise understand that they can be the terminus for pain if they are willing to absorb it (by grace) and not pass it on. So much brokenness in the world results from hurting people hurting people. Wisdom determines to break that chain by deservedly (or un-deservedly) refusing to pass on gossip, malice, slander, accusation, or ill will. Love is discreet and gracious, even when provoked. Hatred does not swallow pain but regurgitates it and adds to its rancor the bitter contents of one's own stomach. Love dissolves tension, while hate inflames it.

10.13

God speaks first, then strikes. Both are acts of love, but the severity is determined by where we are on the continuum of wisdom. Those who are wise hear and obey the first time, and they pass the wisdom on in order to help others. Those who are fools listen to neither God, nor man. The delinquent choose sovereign spankings, for they are never the first choice of the heavenly Father. At the same time, no good parent refrains from spanking their child. Today, laws in the foolish West increasingly take away corporal punishment, and the wisdom of that over-reaction is dubious at best. But striking does not have to be physical to be effective. Good parents discipline early and consistently and love enough to incur appropriate pain in order to avoid long-term problems. Pain is in the arsenal of the loving, the good, and the wise (parents, doctors, therapists, coaches, trainers, leaders, teachers), not just the hateful, the wicked, and the fools.

10.14

Every piece of wisdom stored is a step away from the cliff of insanity and danger. Folly skips blithely towards the edge and prances foolishly on slippery and treacherous ground. If life is lived on an elevated plateau, ringed with fearsome cliffs, it is not wise to dwell or dance near the edge. The wise live far from any moral, physical, emotional, and relational cliffs. The fools cavalierly camp near the edge, and ultimately *always* fall into shame and death.

10.15

Money is a force for good when it is wisely used to bless others. The common, greater good is our good. Individual savings or storehouses do not ensure security in life. We live connected to a community, and if the community falls, isolated wealth will not be sufficient, it will not save the hoarder. Individual wealth saves only for a short time; communal wealth holds disaster at bay. Shared resources may be less comfortable and indulgent, but they do last longer. Wisdom understands that we can only ultimately protect ourselves by providing for others. Folly selfishly seeks the illusion of self-preservation. Long-term survival and health for individuals and nations is linked to their commitment to the well-being of others.

10.16

Do right things and eventually right things happen to you. Do wrong things and they too will ultimately come around to bite you. This is not karma; this is God's law of sowing and reaping. It is an inviable law that God has put in motion, as sure as gravity. The wise treat others as they want to be treated. Fools treat others disrespectfully and then are shocked and offended when they receive similar treatment. You are kind to your future self when you are gracious to your current neighbors. When you are cruel to those around you, you are cruel to your future self.

10.17

Every one of us needs course correction from time to time because to some degree we are all self-deceived. To refuse correction (because we are not humble enough to admit we are wrong) is to not only lose our way, but to lead others astray. The real tragedy of the unteachable is not the damage they do to themselves, but the damage they do to others. If only those we respect or those in direct authority gave instruction, it would be easier to receive, but often critics and enemies give life-saving instruction. The wise receive instruction, even when laced with scorn or offered in a mean-spirited way. The wise receive this painful correction for they realize it will ultimately "life" many. God's grace can turn mean-spirited, individual critique into wisdom that blesses the community—if we are but wise enough to receive it.

10.18

Hatred has to be exposed in order to be eradicated. Hatred is not automatically negative, as to be so passionately against something as to want to destroy it (and some things are so wicked and vile they should be destroyed), the Bible is clear that God hates and will destroy some things. But when hatred is merely concealed bigotry, it is most dangerous because it lurks, waiting to pounce on the unaware. The wise have an obligation to expose demonic hatred—the self-serving hatred in ourselves and in others. Exposing hatred is not a justification for slander. Fools spread slander; the wise expose hatred. Knowing what slander is and what hatred is requires discernment and prudence, and when hatred is identified, the kindest good we can do is to expose it. Whenever evil is brought to light, it immediately loses much of its venom.

10.19

The more you talk, the more likely you'll not only err, but sin. In fact, the Bible is shockingly frank in categorically stating that if you talk much, you will sin. By contrast wisdom talks less than you could, less than you want to. Restraint of words (as wisdom) implies there is opportunity and desire to retort, lash out, or be cute, flippant, mean, critical, or coarse, and you chose not to. It's a wise idea to fast words, to discipline ourselves against the folly of verbal gluttony.

10.20

Hearts eventually expose themselves through their junior (and less sneaky) partner, the tongue. What is in the heart will eventually manifest through the mouth. When we are tired, angry, stressed, bitter, hurt, or disappointed, that which is really in us leaps out into public view. We excuse the unguarded reaction or word as exceptional: "Oh, that was not me. I was just upset." Actually, that was the real me. That was the sneaky heart being exposed by the less artful mouth. Righteous tongues reveal righteous hearts when righteous hearts are under pressure. The wise know that whatever is within will one day be shouted without, from rooftops, even, so the only safety is to make sure that what's within is silver, not dross.

10.21

Words matter, and words break more hearts than sticks and stones may break bones. Life and death are indeed in the power of the tongue, and the wise remember this constantly. Wise tongues continually give life, speak life, offer life, and extend life. Foolish words steal life, erode life, demean life, discourage life, and denounce life. When tongues call for life, we know they are wise. When they call for death—especially when they call for the death of the innocent, the frail, the aged, the unborn, and the defenseless—then we know they are most foolish, despite their angry arrogance.

10.22

God's presence brings joy to wealth, experiences, friends, and wisdom. When we have riches, opportunity, followers, family, and intelligence without God's presence, we find that they only end in sorrow. God's presence allows us to encounter neutral things, good things, even painful things, with joy. Thus, the wise prioritize the presence of God over His blessings. The foolish confuse God's blessings with His presence, and missing His presence, they stunningly find that good things can bring sorrow.

10.23

There is an initial thrill in what is wicked, but the fool can't see beyond the adrenaline rush of the present to the mutual pain and collateral damage of the future. The wise have better eyes, or at least longer sight; they see the inevitable consequences of short-term pleasure and reject the pleasures that lead to pain. Wisdom looks over the near horizons of quick and selfish sport to embrace the lasting pleasures that lead to mutual joy.

10.24

What consumes you becomes your destiny. In the end you get what you crave: either to your destruction or to your deliverance. For example, if you crave attention, you will do whatever you need to get it, and in getting it, you will lose your soul. When your desires are evil or even self-serving, they attract the attention of demonic powers, and those desires open you up to the desires of those evil powers. Finding an open gate, they surge in. They betray you, having only one thought: your destruction. They use your own desires against you. Conversely, if you long for what is good and pure, you open yourself to the desires of a holy God. God, finding the open gate of your desire, surges in and, rather than betraying you, completes you. He guides, refines, and blesses your desires, fulfilling them in ways better than you ever imagined.

10.25

Righteousness is earthquake-, cyclone-, disaster-proof building material. Righteousness, as far as a building material, is not flashy, but firm. Foolish lives are built on what is externally appealing. Wise lives are built on what is internally unshakable. The winds of life strike the wise and the foolish. What is wise remains standing after the storm. We have the advantage of looking back through history, of watching others pass through storms, and of seeing what stood after the storms. We would be wise to build our lives with those same materials, and we would be wise to learn from others' pain and from their enduring joy.

10.26

Human laziness is a constant displeasure to God. The people of God have been sent forth into His earth to labor. We were created to exert effort for the King's glory. When God's people do not reflect God's work ethic, it not only disappoints Him, but it also aggravates Him. The Bible opens with God at work. He sets the example early on. And He has been constant ever since. Hard work that is wise takes sabbaths in order to rise early and labor on. Foolish work either never takes sabbaths or never sweats.

10.27

We reverence the Lord in how we eat, exercise, and sleep. Respect of the Lord is not restricted to houses of worship or moments of prayer and reflection. We do not fully respect the Lord if we do not fully respect Him with our bodies. To neglect the body or to indulge a lifestyle harmful to it (i.e., to God's temple) is wickedness. If we respect God in how we care for the body, we will physically live longer in a healthier state. If we consistently act wickedly by disrespecting our body, we disrespect the Creator of our body resulting in early death.

10.28

Wisdom takes the long view of life. It is not beguiled by quick results and has the patience to do the simple things over and over to get lasting results. Wisdom understands that life is a marathon, not a sprint, and thus sets out with a long-distance pace. Marathon pace does not mean a lifetime of grimace for a quick grin at the finish line. Marathon pace inserts gladness all along the way. Dour wisdom is not godly wisdom. A measured and disciplined but joyless life is not godly life. Wise, godly living is both joyful and disciplined. It runs on the legs of current gladness and future hope.

10.29

God's way is the strong way and the long way. There is neither relenting nor hurrying with God. As the old hymn "Immortal, Invisible, God Only Wise" says, He is "unresting, unhasting, and silent as light." God steadily and constantly presses on without fanfare, and He gives us wisdom to do likewise. This doesn't mean we never linger in His presence (abide), rest, sleep, or sabbath. It actually means the opposite. Wisdom realizes that rest is a step of flowing forward, not a step aside. Wisdom coordinates rhythms of life so that the total effect is a strong and ceaseless advance. Those who do not pause, who rush, who do not learn to wait on the Lord will wilt and fade. Such a life, even when motivated by good, is foolish and doomed to burn out.

10.30

"Do you not know that the saints will judge the world" (1 Cor. 6:2). Right living leads to long ruling. Ultimately those who obey what God tells them to do will lead and remain in leadership. It is not the charismatic but the obedient that God entrusts with authority. Those who don't obey (righteousness is obeying what God says to do; wickedness is disobeying what God says to do) just don't last long, not in God years. Glimpses of this truth will be seen in this age, but in the age to come this truth will be seen without exception.

10.31

Perversity ultimately gets wearisome, even to the perverse, for it has no creative, value-adding, or life-giving power. When words only deplete, there will come a despair of words, and the tongues that drip poison will eventually be cut off, even by the wicked.

However, we never tire of hearing pure speech as it adds life, gives hope, and brings value. If your words reduce value, you know they (and you) are foolish. When your words add value, you walk in wisdom.

10.32

We are creatures of habit. We need to train our mouths so that when our filters are gone (because the hour is late, or we're old, tired, or stressed), good flows from them. Should we live a long life, it's probable that our bodies will outlast our mental faculties. How glorious in that day if what emerges from our mouths is joy, grace, peace, purity, praise, and prayer. How revealing if what comes from us when we have lost all restraint is foolish. Of course, mouths only represent hearts. The only guarantee that the mouth speaks honorably when all restraint is gone is if what's in our heart is pure. We've all been given a season of grace, and we would be wise to prepare now for that filter-free day.

PROVERBS

Chapter 11

11.1

Truth and accuracy pave the path to humility and wisdom. Exaggeration (either making too much or making too little of ourselves) is pride. When we make too little of ourselves, we deceive. It's our pride calling out for someone to object and praise us. Inaccuracy is deception, and every time we are inaccurate, we lay a paving stone in the opposite direction of humility. Humility tells the truth. Wisdom is accurate. Dishonesty and deception are arrogant, and they are an abomination to the Lord, even when sweetly said by seemingly sweet people.

11.2

Ironically pride always leads to shame because it's inherently foolish, and ironically the intelligent are most prone to pride, for they've confused their good intellect with good character. Intelligence and integrity are not synonymous. In fact, intelligence usually goes to war with integrity; they are more often enemies than friends. Humility, on the other hand, always leads to wisdom, for it's the wise who are the first to admit they do not know and they cannot achieve in their own strength or knowledge. The opposite of wisdom is pride.

11.3

The right way is an internal posture, not an external path. The right way finds the right path over continually changing terrain. Life is not mapped out for us. We stand before a wilderness of choices with no roads. No life has a precedent—we all stand before frontier territory. We must have internal integrity if we are to safely navigate our uniquely uncharted territory. If we carry within us perversity, we have lost the way before we take one step. The best guarantee for knowing our "life way" then is to be a person of integrity and to ruthlessly expunge all perversity from within.

11.4

There is a day of wrath, and your fate on that day is not determined by your wealth, gifts, or intelligence, but by your relationships. A day is coming when King Jesus will return to this earth to judge the living and the dead. There will be a general resurrection, and the living and the dead will be judged. We will be judged and rewarded by our works according to the Bible (Matt. 16:27; 1 Cor. 3:8; Rev. 20:12–13). If you treated King Jesus rightly (through repentance, obedience, faith, and submission), you will be granted eternal life through grace. If you treated King Jesus's people and creation rightly, you will be rewarded accordingly. If you treated King Jesus or His kingdom un-rightly, you will die. You will suffer eternal death—and that is the height of foolishness.

11.5

Do the right thing no matter how high the initial cost. For no matter how high that cost, it's far cheaper in the long run. When we do the wrong thing initially (in order to avoid or reduce pain), we always pay a premium. It is wise to suffer in the short term in order to rejoice in the long. Short-term joy is always inferior to long-term joy. Short-term pain is always better than long-term pain. Pain deferred is pain magnified. Pain encountered bravely reduces sadness and induces joy. Be kind to your future self; do the right thing today.

11.6

Righteous living is pre-escape. When we do the right things on a daily, simple, continual, and diligent basis, we guarantee ourselves that no sin will entrap us. No one commits grievous sins on a whim. Great sins are just the announcement of a litany of smaller ones. When we faithfully live rightly (which means, we live as God decrees in the Bible), we inoculate ourselves from moral failings. We escape treacherous and dramatic snares by daily, un-dramatic righteousness.

11.7

In 258 A.D., Lawrence of Rome, while being roasted alive on a gridiron, turned to his executioners with a smile and said: "You may turn me over now. I am done on this side." Then used his last breath to pray for the people of Rome. When we make the decision daily to die to self, then in the critical moments we chose well. The martyrs who died well did not summon up unusual character on their final day. Martyrs who endured unimaginable deaths with dignity did so because that day was merely their final deposit on a life of dying daily. They knew their dying was about to be over and their living was truly about to begin. Wicked people cannot die well, for they have not lived well and have no hope.

11.8

Time alone vindicates some righteous acts. Evil acts (no matter how well they're disguised as good) always end in dishonor. God always delivers the righteous. Sometimes by escape (miraculous extraction from danger), sometimes by endurance (unusual grace to glorify Him through difficulty), and sometimes by eternity (taking one home, free from all danger forever). Eventually, honor stands and is recognized; eventually, dishonor is exposed and falls. The wise, then, live with honor. It is their legacy, even if they're considered foolish while they live.

11.9

Words both hurt and heal. We must use them wisely. A kind tongue delivers. A harsh tongue destroys. Unfortunately, kind people can lapse to harsh tongues, and the harshness is magnified because it is unusual. We cannot assume that we will automatically sustain kindness. Kindness is a choice; for among all of us who are fallen, it is not our natural state. The wise work at being kind, and kindness is maintained and disseminated. The fools take their own kindness for granted and the cost to others is prohibitive.

11.10

Both success and failure bring joy to the public. We love to assassinate the ones we have enthroned. The perversity of men enjoys destroying a man as much as they enjoy exalting him, which is why Jesus cautioned: "Woe to you when all men speak well of you" (Luke 6:26). However, there is appropriate celebration when the wicked fall. But this celebration should not be personal lest it be vindictive, just as celebration of the righteous should not be personal lest it be idolatrous. When we celebrate who and what is righteous, we are celebrating the God who is right to bless them. When we celebrate the removal of who and what is wicked, we are celebrating the God who is right to destroy them.

11.11

Wisdom and folly both have communal implications. Life is communal. Societies sink when the preponderance of their citizens are un-Christlike and they rise when the preponderance of their citizens are Christlike. No country can be converted, and Christian countries are misnomers. Society and civilizations are, in fact, doomed to fail, and the timing of that fall determined by how much salt preserves and how much light repulses darkness. So then in civic society we should not put our primary energies into Christian law or public Christian trappings and truisms, but into living Christlike lives. It has not helped anyone to have "in God we trust" stamped on our money, but oh, the impact if that was stamped on many of our hearts!

11.12

Don't speak all you see and don't despise what you don't understand. We are always commanded to tell the truth, but we are not always commanded to tell all the truth. Prudence can indeed be the better part of valor, and the one devoid of wisdom is too liberal with his criticisms. Wisdom waits for the right time and dispenses criticism carefully, kindly, and constructively, and in small, separate doses.

11.13

Faithfulness is a gossip-swallower. The faithful person is where slander, gossip, libel, and cruel truths go to die. The wise person doesn't listen to mean speech and certainly never passes it on. Wisdom keeps secrets so well it even forgets them, for the wise never wields what he or she alone knows against any other. The foolish have good memories and can quickly dredge up and loudly relay the shame of others.

11.14

We are not safe when we have only one human voice (living or dead) in our ears. Because all humans are limited, none of us has all the truth. In all our character, experience, and gifts, we all carry a piece of God's wisdom. The wise are not enamored with one sage. Rather, the wise realize that all God's people have a nugget of His truth. The wise realize that even godless people have wisdom. The wise realize that critics can be wisdom's mouth and that dissenters often hurl truth with their opposition. Fools give a disproportionate amount of weight to one favorite human to their own hurt. Fools make enemies of the truth by refusing to hear truth from their enemies.

11.15

Don't mistake generosity for wisdom. Unwise giving can cause great damage to both the receiver and the giver. Wise giving does not create dependency. Wise giving does not put the human giver at the center of the gift. Wise giving does not demand control. It is wise to be generous and it is generous to be wise, but they are not identical, nor do they automatically coincide. If your generosity has placed you in the center as the solution or the receiver in the center as a dependent, you have given unwisely. Wise giving points to both deity and dignity.

11.16

It is better to have honor than to have wealth, and the way to the true wealth of honor is through grace, not force. Some women's beauty is forcefully presented, and in so doing they lose honor, for they maintain outward beauty without inward grace. The woman who is gracious from the inside out retains an honor that beautifies with age. The woman who concentrates her forces on the preservation of external beauty only loses both beauty and honor as time unfolds. To be ruthless with our resources is ultimately to squander them; we ultimately only keep what we freely give away.

11.17

Mercy is a seed the sower harvests, even if the sower remains or becomes financially poor. Both mercy and cruelty are multi-generational harvests. Successive descendants benefit from the mercy sown by merciful ancestors. God has perfect long-term memory, and if you "mercy" the poor and unfortunate, God will "mercy" those who follow you. If you are cruel to the unrelated near to you, you will sow cruelty to be reaped by those related far to you.

11.18

Hidden things tend to be evil things. Right does light, and light makes right. There is no honor, nor any long-term good, in deception. Deception always wounds, even when the lie is "honorable" or well-intentioned. The wise find a way not to lie. The wise choose short-term awkwardness over long-term agony. The right thing to do is to bring all things into the light. The wise thing to do is to live in the light. The godly thing to do is to work hard and have no falsehood in your behavior or speech.

11.19

Right things give life. Thus, the test of whether an action is right is if it gives life in the long term. Right is not determined by the lack of initial pain. A surgeon's knife (and the short-term cutting pain it brings) is the right thing because it is the life thing. Wrong things bring long-term decay and death, primarily to the protagonist. It is always the wrong doer (not the victim) who suffers the most long-term pain. This is the law of God. His warning is that life-giving actions are always a reward to the life-giver and that life-taking actions are always a punishment to the life-taker.

11.20

God delights in pure humor, pure speech, and pure minds. Crass humor is always near at hand, always easy to produce, and ultimately always angry. Crude humor is just a clever disguise for murder. Pure humor takes more effort and gives more life. The Lord hates the ones who use perverse humor to wound, and He loves those who use life-giving humor to heal. If your humor does not heal, it is likely wicked. We are to be blameless in our humor, a delight to the God of pure joy.

11.21

Wise strength is not found in numbers or in popular opinion but in alignment with truth. Right makes might; might does not make right. To be right is always to be in the majority, even if you are the only one standing for that truth, for as Mary Slessor said, "God plus one is always the majority." Since God is truth and is always right, to side with truth is to side with God, which is to side with right, which is to side with might. Strength then comes from understanding where God stands on an issue, then standing next to Him.

11.22

To lack modesty is to "uglify." Folly says that the more of your body you reveal (through either tight or revealing clothes), the more beautiful you are. Wisdom knows that taste and discretion are beauty's most attractive accessories. This principle is true both for the bodies of men and women, and for their personhoods. We can be transparent without being vulgar, we can be open without being crude, and we can be honest without telling all the facts. We are beautiful when we are modest on both the inside and out.

11.23

Pure hearts want good for others, even for the others that don't like them. When you wish ill on others, even enemies, you chose wrath and destruction for yourself. Wisdom recognizes that the Spirit of Jesus leads us to call down love and mercy from heaven, not fire. The terrible decrees of judgment are for God alone to determine. We are to throw ourselves and all others at the feet of the One who is good, merciful, abounding in love—and slow to anger. One of the chief identifying attributes of the righteous is that they ask God to mercy all and allow Him to assign wrath in His inscrutable sovereign wisdom.

11.24

In human relationships, you save the most by being inexplicably generous. Generosity of wealth and resources so delights God that He out-blesses the giver. Miserly action is so contrary to the nature of God that He distances Himself from it by afflicting the miser. There is no "Scrooge" in our Sovereign. God is a giver, and He wants His children to look like Him. Our motivation for giving is obedience and the result is we look like our heavenly Father. When God sees His children acting like He acts (outlandishly generous), He gives them more so they can give that away, too, and in the process, look even more like Him.

11.25

God can't resist blessing the generous in Spirit. God goes out of the way to bless the "blessers." When God sees someone patiently serving others, He rushes to serve them. When God sees someone denying self by helping others move from hurt to healing, God moves heaven and earth to heal the healer. When God sees someone returning good for evil, He hastens to lavish His good. God is quick to bless those who bless because He knows He can trust them with His power and resources. God knows the generous will disperse, not hoard, the goodness of God. When we feel unblessed and under-resourced, our recourse is to demonstrate to God we can be trusted with more by giving what we have away.

11.26

The goodwill of your neighbors is a better reserve than money in the bank. Relational equity lasts through all disasters and is renewable. We are wise if we spend more time investing in people than we do in stocks, bonds, business, and cash. All the treasures in the world can be consumed in sudden disaster or global shifts, but no tragedy can touch the treasures of true friendship. Tragedy, disaster, and blight magnify the resources of relationship even while they devour the resources of mammon.

11.27

One of God's laws is that humans will always be allowed to find what they seek. Those who seek good are seeking the God who is good. They will find both Him and His favor. Those who seek evil will find the devil and all his trouble. Seeking evil is seeking harm, self-harm. Evil seeking is fueled by false adrenaline, false in that the evil seeker attempts to hurt another and succeeds to primarily hurt himself.

11.28

At the end of the day, it is depth of character, not piles of cash, that helps individuals, communities, churches, and nations flourish. Those that depend on money for their advancement build edifices, programs, or projects that quickly go up and suddenly fall or fail. Those that depend on doing the right things to and with people build relationships that endure long after external props and programs have waxed and waned. The wise build people before they build buildings. The wise trust their people, not their programs.

11.29

God promotes by merit, not by bloodline. All honor begins in the home. When we respect our parents and all God-placed authority, we show ourselves worthy of handling authority wisely. When we dishonor our parents or any layer of God-placed authority, we demonstrate that we are neither ready, nor worthy, to be in authority ourselves. We prepare for positions of authority not by ruling small fiefdoms well, but by obeying small leaders with a pure heart. At the end of the day, those who submit well will be given authority and authoritative fools will bow at their feet.

11.30

The wisest thing you can do in life is to win souls and grow your own spiritual tree. The true riches of this world and beyond are disciples. The universal and timeless mandate is for us to make disciples. The wise compete for souls—not with each other, but with the powers of darkness. Fools do not fight for souls. If you are not fighting for souls or fighting to make disciples, you have lost the plot, you have lost the path of wisdom. Our legacy will be judged on our spiritual tree in the courts of heaven, on whether we made disciples that made disciples that made disciples.

11.31

The spirit world has no secrets and no privacy. All hidden motives and secret actions are publicly known, recorded, and broadcast in the spirit realm. In the practical realm, we live in our little delusions that we can hide what is really within us. But this is folly. The wise realize that all righteousness will be known and rewarded and that all folly will be known and judged. Reward and judgment are not only a reality of our lives after death; they are certain even here on this earth. No righteous person will go unrewarded, and no evil person will go unjudged. To think otherwise is deluded idiocy.

PROVERBS

Chapter 12

12.1

Stupidity is avoided by embracing the sting that is integral to instruction. The wise understand that knowledge comes through teaching and that teaching must include corrective rebuke. The wise become wise through painless success; wisdom is attained by painful failure. The wise are those who have recognized, admitted, and learned from their mistakes. The fool is the one who is not courageous enough to embrace the pain that learning requires. My most encouraging mentor in my doctoral studies reminded me often: "PhDs are not earned by the smart, but by those who can organize information and endure pain."

12.2

God alone rewards good intentions as He is the only one who can truly know internal motives. We often do the right things for the wrong reasons. We can fool others, but we cannot fool God. If we do good things for selfish motives, there will be no long-term blessing. On the flip side, we have no right to judge the motives of others. We can question a person's decisions, but no human can see clearly into the heart of another. Wisdom judges decisions but leaves evaluation of motive to God alone.

12.3

The right thing is the lasting thing. Wisdom has the courage to make the decision that is healthy for the long term, even if it is unpopular in the short term. Parents, pastors, and politicians so often make the cowardly choice—they yield to the immediate demand at the expense of the future. Foolishness sacrifices the future. Wisdom makes sacrifices today for the establishment of tomorrow.

12.4

In marriage, complete equality does not mean either absorption or uniformity. It does not mean democracy (which can have its own tyrannies). And it does not mean the husband abdicates his role as the spiritual authority in the home. A wife of excellence adds a regal glow to the marriage. My wife is my moral and spiritual equal. She is of equal value before God. She has equal wisdom and equal input into daily life and decisions for our home, our finances, our future, and our children. What she does not have is equal spiritual authority. The biblical marriage is led by the man and crowned by the woman.

12.5

There can be no agreement or union between right words/deeds and deceit/duplicity. Right living never, ever deceives. Right speaking always tells the truth, even to the hurt of the speaker. Biblically, if truth cannot be spoken (in full or in part), our only recourse is silence, even if that silence is misunderstood. The defense of the misunderstood silent is time. Time reveals all. It is better to be quiet and thought a fool, then to panic and prove it. If you are wise, events over time will justify your silence.

12.6

Wickedness waits for others to become vulnerable in order to hurt them, prove a point, or take advantage of a situation. Righteousness covers the vulnerabilities of others, even if those others are enemies. It is the fool who exposes or attacks the vulnerable—simply because we all have vulnerabilities, and the eternal laws dictate that we will receive in the same measure that we give. The wise know that one day they will need their own vulnerabilities covered, so protecting others is a down payment on receiving in kind down the road. We best protect ourselves by defending others, even the other who has done us harm.

12.7

In the short-term battle, it often looks like evil is winning. But evil can never win the war. Even when evil wins battles, its doom is sure, for evil always self-destructs. The nature of evil is to destroy; it cannot help but destroy itself. One of the defining factors of the demonic hoards is how they hate and envy one another. Contrast that to the angelic hosts who love and rejoice over one another. Both armies take their styles from their generals. On a daily basis then, do the right thing, the righteous thing, the long-term thing, and you will stand long after quick-sprinting rascals fall.

12.8

There is no long-term honor in perversity. There is certainly a measure of short-term pleasure and fleeting fame for the wicked, but the laughs and cheers turn to scorn and jeers as the nature of this world is to tear down our celebrities with as much relish as we use to establish them. For the wise it is the opposite: Short-term jeers turn to cheers, and scorn to praise. The wise have the patience to wait for the final verdict, the wise have the prudence to want eternal, higher commendation, and the wise do not fixate on what the lower, vulgar courts have to say.

12.9

Wisdom is secure in what it thinks about itself. The wise do not measure themselves with a false yardstick. They do not think too much or too little of themselves. In fact, they turn away from fixating on self-measurement. Fools compare themselves to others. The wise avoid comparisons to people and are content to compare themselves to God and to their former selves. Foolishness asks, "Am I better or worse than others?" Wisdom asks, "Am I more like Jesus today than I was yesterday?"

12.10

Strength is kind, and restrained strength is winsome and attractive. When a strong man is gentle, there is a masculine beauty about him. When a beautiful woman is modest, there is a feminine strength about her. Neither strength nor beauty is magnified when it is flaunted. In fact, when we draw attention to our good qualities, we invariably tarnish them. Strength and beauty are designed to care for others, not to draw attention or to promote ourselves. Real beauty cares for the disadvantaged, the poor, the creation, including animals. Self-centered strength and beauty (even when used to help others) is corrupt and ultimately cruel.

12.11

Beware the allure of shortcuts. Quick money, fast fame, and early promotion all have a downside. There is a deep satisfaction and maturity that emerges from the process, and time spent sharpening our tools is never wasted. Vain and frivolous things have no heart and ultimately disappoint. What is true lasts forever and satisfies completely.

12.12

Real, lasting growth can't be rushed. Honor must be earned or conferred; it cannot be borrowed or stolen. We can only grow as high as we dig deep, and the real strength of character is subterranean. Who we are when no one sees us is our true self. Strength of character rests on a thousand little lessons and a million little obediences that no one has witnessed.

12.13

Much trouble is avoided through disciplined silence. Often the righteous come through trouble because they did not speak. The righteous do not inflame already tense situations through angry words. The righteous absorb criticism and swallow gossip to defuse it through their silence. The foolish use words to make things worse, while the righteous use restraint to help things heal.

12.14

Words are boomerangs; they always return to smite or bless you. Works are homing pigeons; they always come back to roost. A central teaching of the Bible is that we always reap what we sow. Sow kind words and you will receive them. Water others and you will be watered. Forgive and you will be forgiven. Give and it will be given to you. The great eternal Farmer guarantees the central law of harvest. For good and for bad, we always reap what we sow.

12.15

To not listen to others is foolish, no matter how wise, seasoned, mature, intelligent, and experienced you are. In fact, the wise listen and consult more than the inexperienced, for real wisdom is in recognizing how much you do not know. The height of folly is to think you are too advanced for advice, too rational for rebuke, or too capable for correction. Some of the most competent and charismatic leaders are the most foolish. Their giftings have betrayed them into believing the lie that they know better than all. A great trap of the enemy is to deceive us into thinking that because we are wise or gifted in one area that we are gifted in all.

12.16

Shame can make you angry, and anger (as a secondary emotion) reveals your heart. It is not always wise or helpful for the depravity of our heart to be publicly revealed. God publicly reveals shameful postures and actions as a last resort. He is kind enough to give us opportunity for private repentance first. When we lose our composure, we forfeit the offer of private discipline, and our depravity is then displayed to all. Both are mercies, but private shame is easier to swallow and process than public humility is.

12.17

Little truths are cosmic in implication. There are no little truths in that each truth is magnificent, and there are no big truths in that big truths are merely collections of little ones. Lies have to be built on truth and are, in fact, truths seasoned with little lies.

Lies are twisted truths, and truths are the absence of any deceit, dishonesty, and pride. To be persons of truth we must have no lie about us; we must be all light with nothing twisted.

12.18

The wise are slow to speak and are fine word surgeons. Precision in our words is godly. False witness is not restricted to blatant deception. False witness includes exaggeration, the withholding of critical life-giving information, and the bludgeoning of others verbally. True witness is intended to heal, not harm, even if the truth hurts.

12.19

Lies have short-term attraction. Truth is not rushed, and time verifies it. By nature what is false cannot endure. If a foundation is faulty, the house will eventually fall, no matter the apparent beauty. When surrounded by lies, one of our chief weapons is time. Truth is wise enough to wait, for wisdom knows that lies always self-destruct eventually. Truth is wise enough to discern the ugliness lurking behind attractive lies.

12.20

All deceit is evil, and flattery and exaggeration are deceit in infant form. Wise counselors broker no deceit, neither in themselves nor in those they counsel. To empower deceit by leaving it unchallenged is neither wise nor loving. It is unloving because deceit always ends in sadness and truth always ends in joy. Deceit and truth are on opposite trajectories. Deceit usually begins in mirth and promises a joy that it cannot deliver, while truth often starts soberly and penetrates painfully before terminating in life and joy.

12.21

Doing the right thing is the best long-term life insurance. There is a difference between hurt and harm. No grave harm (disabling, crippling, despairing, debilitating, joy-conquering evil) will come to those who act rightly. They may quite certainly be hurt in the process (slandered, betrayed, rebuked, corrected, disciplined, misunderstood, and accused), but evil will not penetrate their souls even while good soaks through the wounds. Doing the wrong thing, however, always ends in harm to both perpetrator and victim.

12.22

God loves the truth. Being truth, God loves truth brokers. He loves men and women who are wise, gentle, bold, courageous, and winsome in the verbal communication of His character and will. In the wisdom of God, the critical communication of His gospel has been committed to the foolishness of preaching. The risk of unfaithful messaging is high, and the scandal of hypocritical messengers is constant. Still, God commits His word to lips of clay. Perhaps because the damage is so consistent and the cost of error so high, God takes special joy in mouths that He can trust.

12.23

Wisdom does not broadcast what can hurt others; neither does it promote what can help at the wrong time (too early or too late) or in the wrong tenor (arrogantly or condescendingly). Foolishness not only broadcasts what hurts others (and self); it also proclaims the right things at the wrong time and in the wrong spirit. How sad it is when the right message does harm because it was foolishly delivered.

12.24

It is the hard, faithful workers who determine policy, principle, and vision in the end. God has balanced the influences that go into His institutions by ordaining both positional and moral inputs. Positional authority is of God and is to be respected. Practitioner authority is also ordained of God, and He expects positional leaders to "obey" it. Strategy is, therefore, most wise when it is a harmony of voices from those in leadership positions and those in the field. Those who work hard and faithfully in each sphere will be the long-term shapers of the body.

12.25

Praise overcomes depression. When we have anxious hearts, we tend to descend into negative self-talk or even distracted navel-gazing. Our own selves are indeed a fairly depressing view, especially when we are in trial and temptation, for there is not much good to look at there. Depression is often the result of chronically taking our eyes off Jesus and fixating on ourselves, our unfortunate circumstances, or our antagonistic associates. Good words (praise) about a good God lift us from our despair. Our circumstances don't necessarily change quickly, but because we are looking at Someone beautifully radiant, we don't flinch at the darkness.

12.26

No one is influence proof. We need to surround ourselves with the godly. We also need to surround ourselves with those who are better than us, smarter than us, holier than us, more gifted than us, and wiser than us. I have played squash for forty years, and whenever I play my equal or my lesser (skill-wise), my skill deteriorates. I only improve at the sport when I play someone who is better than me and who beats me. This is true with friendship and peers. In order to grow, we must love being the lesser and intentionally pursue our betters. How small and limited the leader who insecurely surrounds himself only with those he can teach, lead, and conquer. To be bettered is to be better.

12.27

Delay is not always wisdom. When you know the right thing to do, act quickly and decisively. If one error is "ready, fire, aim," it's equal and opposite errors are "ready, ready, aim," or "ready, aim, aim," or "ready, ready, ready." The goal is to fire, to act, to be bold. Readiness and aiming simply protect the efficacy of our action, but they are no substitute for it.

12.28

Wisdom and life are synonymous. Wisdom always leads to life even if the path goes by way of the cross. Right things always result in an explosion of life. Wrong things always eventually kill, even if they initially allure. Right things foster the environment for life to expand. Wrong things create a climate that chokes creativity, personality, and conditions to thrive. We confuse right things with easy things and wrong things with hard things. The right thing is often initially the hard thing and ultimately the life thing. The wrong thing is usually the easy thing but ultimately the death thing. Choose the hard thing. Choose life.

PROVERBS
Chapter 13

13.1

Wisdom doesn't have to talk. Often it's a silent observer. In meetings we can gain insight by watching those who choose not to speak or who intentionally choose to speak sparingly. The wise both listen and submit, hear and obey. The wisest one who ever lived was the most obedient, the quickest to heed. Scoffing, sarcasm, and crude humor all use intelligence to prove their stupidity, a stupidity evidenced by a failure to listen to rebuke. Mocking is folly dressed up in clever clothes.

13.2

Words that help others nourish the speaker, while words that unduly wound malnourish the same. Using our words to build others up is a faithful use of this God-given verbal resource. Using our words to cause harm, to break peace, or to cause disunity is a most unfaithful application of the tongue. The Lord of speech is dishonored and angered when our mouths cause strife, and He is glorified when our words heal, give life, and bless.

13.3

The more you talk, the more you damage yourself. The wise speak less than they listen. The wise learn to fast words as often as they fast food. Too much input of food is bad for the body, too much output of words is bad for the soul. Fasting food reminds the body to bow to the soul. Fasting words reminds the mouth to bow to the heart—God's heart.

13.4

Wisdom moves past ideas to activity. A wise idea is an active idea, an idea with the diligence to move past dreams to action. It is action that differentiates wisdom from intelligence, for wisdom acts in timely fashion. The Bible refers to God as wise much more often than it refers to Him as intelligent or smart because He acts appropriately and in timely fashion. God recognizes the fullness of time and is diligent to prepare, act, and persevere. Likewise, those who are diligent will be rich in experience and eternity.

13.5

The liar ends up hating himself, for lying is a curse the speaker utters against himself. The liar ends up being hated, for lying brings harm and no one celebrates the one who destroys. The righteous hate lying, for they are wise enough to know that lying results in harm and they refuse to open that door to death. It is wise to ruthlessly eliminate falsehood from all our speech and living, for there is no other end to falsehood but shame.

13.6

The best self-defense mechanism is to make a habit of doing what the Bible and Christ tell us to do. The best long-term insurance policy is to obey what God says to do, no matter how costly and difficult that obedience is. When we do the right (biblical/Christ-like) things, the right consequences ultimately overtake us. When we do the wrong things (selfish/wicked), then evil things ultimately find and devour us.

13.7

True riches are character based. The wealthy men and women are the virtuous. Those who spend their virtue to gain money eventually lose both. Those who keep their virtue, even if it means they lose money, in the end gain both. The chase for money leaves you virtue void. The pursuit of virtue makes you wealthy, whether you have any money or not.

13.8

Those with great financial wealth have more fears and more potential for loss than those who have nothing to lose. What is true of money is also true of honor. Those who hoard honor and seek praise have much to lose if no one fawns over them. Those who do not live for the praise of men are unwavering when they go without it. When money and fame do not motivate or control us, we are more immune to the scorn of men and more alive to the pleasures of heaven.

13.9

There is an inherent joy to right things, a lasting joy. We know something is right when the joy of it lingers long after the experience. Wrong things may be exciting, pleasurable, or fun in the moment, but that "joy" never lasts. We know something is wrong when it has no enduring joy. The wise opt for activities that bring joy long after the action is over, and they avoid the joys that please in the moment but give pain in the future.

13.10

No lasting good comes from arrogance, but a multitude of good comes from walking in humility. Humility can be gained by counsel. Physically, we can't see all of ourselves. We can't see the back of our own head, and we can't really see how we walk. The same is true for character. We can't see all of ourselves. We can't see the dark side of our character, and we need others to help us discern how to walk humbly. We need the eyes of others to help us see ourselves as we really are, as we really walk.

13.11

Rush and shortcuts lead to loss and shortfall. Every good thing is built slowly, and every lasting work has an unseen foundation. When we labor for ideas, understanding, wisdom, or truth, we can grasp them and stand on them in ways impossible than if we dishonestly acquired those same concepts. The dishonest acquirement of truth is that which does not experience it, but merely memorizes or parrots it. The wise are those who work for wisdom, and the fools are those who try to steal it.

13.12

Don't make others unnecessarily ill by deferring their hope, by making them wait for the help you can provide. If you can help, help. If it's in your power to meet a need, meet the need. If God gave you the wherewithal to bless others, do so. So easily we can rationalize away our assistance because in our "wisdom" we think it will cripple others. There can be a fine line between discerning and stingy. If we are to err, let us err on the side of hope and life.

13.13

Respect is always rewarded. When we respect what the Bible says, when we take Jesus at His word, we always reap blessing. To not respect the Word, to despise what Jesus says is to be destroyed. The challenge is, we respect the easy things He and His word say, but we despise the difficult things. To respect the Word and the commands of Jesus is akin to keeping the law; we can't just respect some of it. To despise some of what Jesus says (i.e., the hard things) is to despise all of what He says, and that leads to destruction.

13.14

Higher life is the only cure for lower life. When we live wisely, it leads to ascending joy. Human life is lived on an immense island, an island ringed with cliffs of folly. This immense island scales upward to beautiful, safe ground. Wise living takes us further and further away from the cliffs of folly and higher and higher into the pleasures of right living. The more we climb into wisdom, the more joyful we become. The exertion is worth the reward, for we are further from the cliffs and gladder in the way.

13.15

Hurt and harm radiate from the unfaithful. Faithfulness sometimes hurts, but it never harms. Unfaithfulness always does long-term damage, even if it avoids short-term hurt. In the long term, faithfulness opens doors and unfaithfulness closes them. In ministry, service, and life generally, the wise are those who do the right things in the short term (which usually are the hard things) and in so doing, gain long-term favor and open doors. The foolish are those who lack the character to do what is either lowly or painful in the short term, while their long-term future becomes a series of slammed shut doors.

13.16

Prudence is not hesitancy based on fear, but discretion based on patience. Fools are cavalier with the truth, either unwisely spreading it or too casually listening to it. It's not always wise to reveal all that's in your heart and mind. Ultimately, promiscuous self-revelation is demeaning to you and to all whom you broadcast. This is the tragedy of our age and electronic media—we can now exhibit our self-centered folly to the world.

13.17

To not be a faithful messenger of the character of Jehovah as revealed in the Bible, including all its strident truths and warnings, is to be a wicked messenger that brings disease. Faithful ambassadors bring health, even if the means are surgical. God's ambassadors always speak of both wrath and mercy, and the result is health for those who heed. Pseudo-ambassadors tremble at wrath and thus corrupt mercy, which brings long-term trouble to all the ears that itched for affirmation. The great wickedness of messengers stems from reluctance to speak painful words. There can be no cure without accurate diagnosis.

13.18

To delay response to correction is to disdain help. If we do not immediately repent when we are confronted, the damage of our folly quickly multiplies. The only bad time to repent is later; quick repentance is a hallmark of the wise. Those who listen to rebuke, from those of greater, equal, or lesser status, do not lose face or honor, but gain both. The greater the soul, the more open the person to correction from anywhere, anyone, anytime. Small souls can't stand criticism or correction, while large souls seek it out.

13.19

Fools never accomplish their deepest desires because they refuse to relinquish their shallow ones. The wise forgo their immediate pleasures for delayed gratification instead. The wise sell, avoid, and ignore a litany of small charms in pursuit of the pearl of great price. When small sacrifices are made for great desires, the greater joy attained cascades down into all the smaller ones, illuminating the soul comprehensively. No great approvals are made outside one thousand little voluntary and daily denials.

13.20

The wise pursue friends morally better than themselves. The comfort of a friendship based on the lowest common denominator cripples us, while a discomfort in friendship based on proximity to character which we do not yet have compels and propels us to ascend the moral heights. When we walk with those stronger, better, fiercer, truer, gladder, kinder, and lowlier than we are, we end up like them, we end up dissatisfied with who we are, and we long for the divine image we see reflected in them. When we only gravitate to those who share our level of character or holiness, we foolishly commit ourselves to a life of moral decline.

13.21

Good stalks the righteous. It hunts them down relentlessly. When you live as God would have you live, when you treat others as Jesus would have you treat them, you cannot escape blessing. There is no investment with a higher yield than that of doing what is right. Whether proactively helping another or responsively returning mercy for hate, when we do good, we give to God, and He repays with ridiculous interest. The foolish who initiate evil, however, find that investment is likewise repaid with similar ridiculous interest.

13.22

Good has multi-generational implications. My grandfather was an incredibly generous man, and his children, grandchildren, and great grandchildren have reaped the benefit. I am convinced that one of the reasons my family is so generously provided for is because our ancestor repeatedly gave significant financial gifts to his church, the Billy Graham Association, and missionaries around the world. Contrary to Shakespeare's pessimism in the mouth of Mark Antony,[5] the good that men do does indeed live after them, it is not interred with their bones. The best thing we can do for our children is to give our money away. The best inheritance we give our children is not a lack of work ethic and a hoarding mentality, but a robust generosity that loves to pass resources on.

13.23

Injustice is poor community stewardship. It is a grave error to think that the poor and lowly cannot contribute to society, church, leadership, or innovation. The combined latent power of the poor is the most overlooked and underutilized resource in history. So dazzled are we by isolated wealth, we miss the treasures buried all around us. The wise seek out ways those without large reserves of money can contribute, lead, advise, instruct, develop, and speak. A foolish pastor or leader or Christian does not seek out the wisdom or input or participation of the financially poor.

13.24

Discipline is most helpful when it is early and often. Teaching boundaries and the immediate consequence of disobedience is the most loving thing we can impart to those we lead. To mete out loving consequences promptly is compassion in action. We are helped by the "no" as much if not more than the "yes." He who spares his rod hates also himself. He who loves himself disciplines his children promptly. If you spare the rod and do not discipline promptly, you create little tyrants that in turn create heartache for you in the long term.

13.25

Good deeds are so much more satisfying than good food. Contentment is a derivative of right choices and character. Full hearts have more nutrients than full bellies, and it is better to be physically hungry than morally starved. When we live right, the simplest lifestyle is full of peace and satisfaction. When we live in sin, the best foods are sawdust, the best homes confining, the best cars boring, and the best clothes irritating. Right souls make the physical world delightful and the most spartan fare a pleasure. Wrong souls remove the pleasure from all good things.

PROVERBS
Chapter 14

14.1

We can never blame others for destruction that we have seeded and harvested. The instinct in self-preserving humans is the foolish casting of blame on others (animate or otherwise). God sternly warns us that fools blame their parents, their friends, their government, their luck, the fates, the weather, or the devil. The wise do not blame but accept the responsibility of work. If your moral or physical house is falling down around you because you undermined yourself through laziness, deceit, greed, or hate, you can blame no one but yourself. If your character and moral house are to stand the test of time, you must labor at it brick by brick, choice by choice, day by day.

14.2

Perversity is first a despising of God. When we speak crassly, we do not believe God is present, nor that He is holy. No good person would ever talk crassly before his parents, the innocent, or the ones he respects and reveres. To speak and act perversely is to foolishly pretend that God does not see or that He does not care.

If we really respect the Lord, we will always speak and act in such a way that is conscious of His immediate presence and pleasure. Fools ignore the omniscience and purity of God. The wise ever honor both.

14.3

Pride always undermines self-preservation. The best way to survive war or peace is to keep your head down, mind your own business, be quiet and faithful in your assignment, and avoid desiring recognition. The one who sticks his head up gets shot or punched; the one who seeks recognition and calls attention to himself calls down the rod of correction. "Loose lips sink ships" goes the wartime idiom and that includes relationships, reputations, careers, and credibility. The lips of the wise tend to be tight lips which save "ships." Slow to speak and slow to anger is the way to preservation.

14.4

Growth is messy. Growth requires the liberation and accommodation of strong personalities. To be involved in growing people requires a tolerance for mistakes, stress, disappointment, and friction. Great leaders always have limitations and blind spots. Growing leaders always make mistakes. Young leaders usually let their enthusiasm overcome their prudence. Whenever there is robust growth, there is some collateral damage. Wise eldership learns to set strong personalities free with just enough freedom to spur innovative advance and just enough boundary to ensure consolidated, preserved gain. Sometimes the nobility of leadership is evidenced by quietly shoveling manure from the stall.

14.5

Faithfulness can hurt in the short term. To be faithful is to be more concerned with the common good than personal reception. Very few set out to lie for the sheer joy of it. Most of us lie to save face, to escape shame or punishment, or to have our peers and/or judges think better of us. The folly of lying is that it trades short-term comfort for long-term self-respect. To be a faithful witness is to be a broker in truth no matter what it costs you today. The wise speak truth even when it strikes them, for they know that tomorrow's respect is linked to today's honesty. Fools trade long-term honor (including self-respect) for short-term escape.

14.6

Knowledge follows understanding. We invert it and think that if we know facts, we are wise. In reality, it is only the wise who can rightly interpret the facts. Many are the brilliant fools of this world blinded by their biased and carnal interpretation of facts, incapable of rightly discerning the times or the signs. As God is Spirit and as His Spirit is truth, there is also a spirit of truth. There is a posture of humility before God that opens the lowly to the understanding of God. This spirit of understanding becomes the filter with which we sift facts. Facts sifted by understanding lead us to accurate knowledge. Scoffers reject the reality that they need God's help and God's Spirit to understand facts. They foolishly think that true knowledge can be gained outside divinely enabled understanding. They have earned their PhD in ultimate idiocy.

14.7

False guilt causes us to linger with those who add no value to life. Godly conviction tells us to move on from the persons advancing their own agendas and retarding the mission of God. Folly is enamored by power and wealth. This world gives microphones to those with big wallets and big muscles, even if they have empty heads. We fawn over the foolish if they can entertain us or throw us some bone of position or power. Wisdom is disgusted by the bold and beautiful when they have nothing of God's truth to offer. Wisdom knows that the gifts of the foolish are vaporous and wastes no time wanting them.

14.8

One of the greatest gifts you can give others is to be self-aware. Some of the greatest damage done to others is by those who are self-deceived. Leaders, friends, parents, mentors, and spouses who are self-aware are able to give life because they self-censor the damage latent within. The self-deceived damage others without knowing it. The self-deceived are toxic in relationships and devastating in leadership positions, not because they have no good to offer, but because they unwittingly mingle a little bit of unrestrained poison in their good. The wise are truthful with themselves and make every effort to disperse only from their clear fountains, ever aware that it is possible to serve others their filth.

14.9

Wisdom embraces good guilt as a friend. Maturity understands that good guilt is the conviction of the Holy Spirit and bad guilt is the condemnation of the accuser. We attain the status of a blasphemous fool when we build a callous on our conscience so thick we can no longer be dismayed or cautioned at the prick of the Holy Spirit. This is no light malady. In fact, the Bible refers to it as unpardonable. To so harden our heart to good guilt that we can no longer hear the Holy Spirit is to place ourselves in jeopardy of never being able to repent. And without repentance, there is no pardon. Fools mock guilt and deny it entrance. The wise open the door on their knees.

14.10

Some things are not to be shared, even with the most intimate humans. Some sorrows are only made sweet by taking them to Jesus and to no one else. Pain sometimes leads us to compound our sorrows by sharing it when we should have submitted it to the Man of sorrows. Ecstasy sometimes leads us to gloat or brag, and in so doing we sully the victory. Some joys are only preserved when they are taken to the Father for a private shout and cheer. Wisdom recognizes which sorrows and joys are mitigated or enhanced by public expression and which ones are borne or bathed in sharing them only with Jesus.

14.11

What seems so strong, permanent, and immovable will always come tumbling down if it's built on wickedness. What seems frail, weak, and transitory will always last if it's built on what is right. Time has over and over again shown that hollow trees fall in a night and hollow regimes crumble in a day. History has shown that little kindnesses and gentle graces far outlast armies and kings. For those who wish to build enduring legacies, wisdom dictates that the strongest dynasties are built on character and the weakest ones on charisma.

14.12

Life's wise choices aren't always obvious. Roads straight in the near distance can veer when they pass beyond our sight. Seas calm in harbor can rage over the horizon. Careers stable today may be obscure tomorrow. Man has not been burdened with omniscience but blessed with dependence. It is folly to make choices based only on the stretch we can see before us. God who, outside of time, knows the end from the beginning is the only One who sees every twist and turn of our future. Choices, then, must always be run by Him. We consult Him first and He gives us peace about a certain direction. We step out on that path and walk it as long as there is peace in our hearts, no matter what rages before our eyes.

14.13

Laughter is part and parcel of dealing with pain. It's not the only way and it's not the primary way, but it is part of the medicine. The danger in this admission is that sometimes we don't see the pain inside others because of their external mirth. It is not unusual for a comedian to be depressed and suicidal; laughter has gone beyond medicine to a numbing drug. Wisdom knows when to laugh and when to cry. Folly only laughs or only cries. Wisdom sees behind mirth to pain and in loving timeliness helps the weeping to smile.

14.14

Self-satisfaction is dangerous and leads to falling. God-satisfaction is safe and leads to joy. The reason self-satisfaction is dangerous is because there is so little of it. We are so finite, so limited, so bound, and so blinded. Our souls and beings were created with the capacity to receive so much more than we can provide for ourselves spiritually, emotionally, and relationally. When we are self-satisfied, we are doomed to emptiness and privation. God, on the other hand, in His limitless goodness, energy, wonder, beauty, power, strength, and creative newness is so much more than we can contain, and we are ever satisfied in His ever-more supply. A good man is a God-fixated man, ever-receiving, ever-overflowing.

14.15

It is not wise to believe everything the news, your books, your teachers, or your friends have to say. All men and women have biases and blinders, and all men and women speak error more frequently than they know or believe. There is only One who is *The Word*, only One full of grace and truth, only One who never exaggerates, distorts, withholds, or misleads. There is only One whose every word can be trusted. The wise, therefore, filter all human words by the Word's words. The prudent run every alleged truth by the Truth's truth. Simply put, the wise are Jesus, Bible people.

14.16

Wisdom reverences when folly rages. The wise question themselves just enough to consider the opinions of others. They may not agree, and they may not follow the opinions of others, but they always listen with a respectful ear. Opposing opinions almost always have nuggets of truth. Fools have neither the patience nor the humility to mine truth out of others. Self-confidence is an unfaithful friend and, when combined with impulsive or rash temper, leads inevitably to disaster. Both unrestrained self-doubt and self-confidence betray us. Wisdom is being confident enough to hear dissenting opinions and disciplined enough to take the time to make the choice best for all.

14.17

Anger and impulsiveness create a terrible combination. Anger when "slow-tempered" is actually a godly trait. God is described as being "slow to anger," and we are told to "be angry and do not sin." There are some things that should stir the people of God to anger. Wisdom then combines anger with process, deliberation, and counsel before action. Foolishness leaps from anger to action rashly and causes more harm than good. Unfortunately, anger quickly acted on often leads to wicked acts and an exacerbation of the problem. When anger rises in us, it is imperative that we slow down, take counsel, and do the diligence required to channel that passion towards righteous acts and righteous ends.

14.18

Decisions are like dominoes. To tip the domino of rush is to end up foolish. To tip the domino of prudence is to end up wise. Haste doesn't just waste materials; it wastes minds, souls, lives, and futures. Prudence doesn't just save the prudent; it saves all those who surround. Both our rush and our waiting always have collateral implications. They never just impact one issue, and they never just affect one person. Rush in one decision leads to multiple negative consequences for multiple different people. Patience in one decision leads to a thousand different benefits for a plethora of diverse people. Real wisdom knows and remembers that every little decision has far ranging consequences.

14.19

Wisdom is a long game, a game won long after the game ends. Many events seemingly end in tragedy, with the wicked in charge, gloating, and unpunished. The wise are unperturbed when the Napoleons of our day crown themselves, for they know that what seems like unassailable strength is just a shadow. Looming behind all self-crowned despots and demonic ideology of man is the eternal specter of the Power, the God Most High. The wise look past temporal thrones to eternal ones and know that any wicked principality is doomed to fail and destined to bow before the King. Do what is good; it is the smart thing over time, for a good God will always ultimately crush what is evil. Do not fear or cower when evil gains the throne, or the courts, or the legislature, or the kingdom, or the province, or the village, or even the family member. Why? Because evil's "rage we can endure, for lo, his doom is sure; one little word shall fell him."[6]

14.20

You identify real friends when you have nothing to give them, neither money, favor, grace, nor even time, yet they graciously mercy you. The evil in man's heart is never better revealed than in its propensity to get rather than to give. The more our heart is oriented toward giving, without expectation of return, the more we look like Jesus, the more we embody true friendship. True friendship is not egalitarian; it is condescension. "Jesus! What a friend of sinners!" "What a friend we have in Jesus." Not because He is our equal, but because we have nothing of substance to give Him, yet He wants to be with us and lavish gifts on us that we can never repay. The rich man thinks he has many friends, but all he has are vassals. You will know your friends by the unrequited grace they shower on you, not by what you shower on them. Friends are gifts received, not flatterers purchased.

14.21

The parable of the Good Samaritan reminds us that our neighbor is the one right next to us in need, the one nearby. Our neighbor is not the one we like. Our neighbor is not the one we look like. Our neighbor is not the one we enjoy being with. Our neighbor is not the one who helps us in our time of need. Our neighbor is the one we help simply because God sovereignly put them right next to us. To be a good neighbor is not to wait until the miserable have shed their dignity and asked for help. A good neighbor proactively seeks to give mercy to those who are near, those who are poor, and in doing so, finds great soul satisfaction. We forget what is so quickly the best way to overcome our sadness: Find someone near to bless, to mercy, to serve, and happy we shall be.

14.22

Evil has the sinister side effect of blinding those who practice it. It is an insidious blindness because it creates an alternate universe in which you see. It is a leprous blindness because you hurt others and yourself without feeling it, at least initially. Evildoers are blind without knowing it and self-destructing without realizing it. Evil is doubly deceitful, for most people do not realize they are acting out evil. Many have been the seeing who, blind to the damage of their actions and attitudes, have lost their sight and then lost their way. By contrast, those who labor to do good, those who make plans to help, heal, and bless, their eyesight improves. The do-gooders see both trouble and blessing from a mile away;

they then easily avoid the snares and collect the treasures of mercy and truth strewn all around them.

14.23

Sometimes the reward of work is the work itself. God created us with the capacity to exert energy with the intention of a double profit: the joy of result and the joy of the process. Undoubtedly, we celebrate when the masterpiece is finished, when the tool is refined, when the goal is gained, but God created the process itself to also make us smile. If we merely enjoy the result, we miss half the fun. The wise enjoy both the process and the prize. When there is no joy in labor, there will be no richness of result. Poverty of soul and character is the result of those who forsake the joy of work. Regardless of economic status, the truly wealthy are those who embrace the joy of hard work.

14.24

It is a tragedy that in our modern world we frantically chase the wrong treasure. Think of the effect on our world if men and women would pursue wisdom with the same veracity that they pursue education, power, fame, and money. In neglecting to make wisdom our global priority, we have all become impoverished. The folly of man is that we mistake vulgarities for virtue. That which helps the least amount of people is what we prize, and in selfishly pursuing it we actually undermine the community. The wise realize that the common good is the road to wealth, and forsaking personal gain, they dedicate their life to the aid of others. This is their crown, and it is a communal wealth, for in their wisdom all society prospers.

14.25

Truth is always on the side of life and deliverance. If a judgment comes down from a superior court that jeopardizes innocent life, we know it's a foolish pronouncement from deceitful liars. A true witness does not care about cost to self, only about cost to truth. A true witness shields the truth, flinging even its mortal body in the path of any threat. A true witness would rather die than see the death of truth. A false witness is cowardly, caring more for self-preservation than for the preservation of truth. A false witness will never give his life for another, nor for what is good. A false witness can only think of what is safe for self, while a true witness can only think of what is good for others, especially for those too weak to defend themselves. The false witness kills the weak, and the true witness saves them.

14.26

The greatest legacy we can give our children is to have room in our hearts only for the fear of the Lord. When a child, young or old, sees their parents bow with tremble-joy before the King of kings and stand fearlessly against the storms and tyrants of life, steel is imparted into their souls. A spiritual impartation of strength is given to children who see their parents stand up for Jesus in daily life. The way to secure the future for your children is not primarily through sheltering them from engaging the world, but by fearlessly engaging the world in a manner loyal to the King. Wisdom doesn't hide her children from evil; wisdom shows her children how to attack it. Wisdom doesn't hide her obedience from her children; wisdom shows her children how to daily submit to the Savior. Wisdom shows how to salute and leap into action when given orders. When we fear the Lord, we instill in our children a double confidence: They know how to bow before the King and they know how to live surrounded by enemies unbowed and unscathed.

14.27

In God's economy fear leads to life. In the fallen realm of earth fear leads to panic, seizure, immobility, and death. When we have a high view of God, we make choices that lead to health and strength. When we truly believe that God is omniscient and omnipresent, we are acutely aware that He is not only right next to us all the time, but He also knows our hearts. There is then no action and no motivation that God is not intimately aware of—and He will judge both. That fear, that healthy respect, gives us impetus to do the things that lead to life and to avoid the things that lead to death. Godly fear motivates toward life-giving action. Human and fallen fears lead to immobility. Sometimes it's the things we don't do that kill us.

14.28

Leadership, in essence, means people not only want to follow you, but they are able to follow you. This is why pioneers don't necessarily make good leaders, at least when they forge ahead in a manner or pace with which no one can keep up. Honorable leadership is far enough ahead that followers can clearly see what to do and how to do it, but not so far ahead that no meaningful lessons can be drawn from their thinking or behavior. When a leader is close enough to her followers that they can imitate her life, they can then assemble (over time) enough human resource power to do incredible things. When a leader is too far in front (or too far behind), she is never able to mobilize enough people to win wars and conquer giants.

14.29

Quick action, when impulsive, is not to be confused with wisdom. In fact, to be impulsive is almost always foolish. The Old Testament includes "slow to anger" in a definitive description of God's character: "The Lord is merciful and gracious, slow to anger and abounding in mercy" (Psalm 103:8). Wisdom, then, must include wrath (for wrath/anger is a definitive part of God's character), but only if we are slow to anger. When we are quick to anger, we slip away from God's nature and into our carnal impulsive folly. God's wisdom is very slow to get angry and is able to be angry without sinning.

14.30

Envy, like bitterness, is doubly evil because it causes double sickness. Those who are jealous poison both their own spirits and their own bodies. C. S. Lewis remarked that our souls and bodies are so closely connected they catch each other's diseases. So, when our soul is envious, our body gets sick. The same is true when the soul is the opposite of envious. When we act in ways that are generous, trusting, empowering, and liberating, we become physically healthier. The wise, therefore, proactively take care of their physical bodies by having healthy souls. The foolish allow jealousy and envy to make their souls small and their bodies weak.

14.31

It's foolish to think that we are stronger than those who cannot defend themselves. When an evil heart pursues selfish gain because the bully within thinks it can oppress with impunity, a critical error is made. The Almighty God of the poor looks down on the defenseless and determines to take up their cause. The wise know that standing behind the small is the giant presence of omnipotent God, so the height of folly, then, is to prey on the weak, small, and poor. We are weaker than the poorest because they have the strongest God as their guard. Likewise, a foolish response to the poor would be to ignore them because they can never return benefit. This, too, is shortsighted, for God delights to bless those who bless those who cannot bless back. The wise look for those who cannot repay kindness or physical help, knowing that their little acts of mercy gladden the Merciful One and a glad God is a generous One. The wisest bless the poor, however, not as an investment in hope of gain, but from the sheer joy of acting like God acts to us.

14.32

Wisdom is never perturbed when the wicked rule and run riot; rather, wisdom mourns their fate in pity. The wise know that ultimately no one can outrun the Hound of heaven. At some point, in this life or the next, the wicked will be caught by the Almighty Judge, and there is no escape, not even in death. Fools cavalierly ignore all warnings, taking false refuge in the hope of this life being all there is to enjoy. What a horror to awaken on the other side of death to face judgment and eternal punishment. Doing wrong things in this life increasingly paints you into a relational corner, and death reveals that corner to be alive with fire and brimstone. There is no refuge for the wicked. Think of the horror of being eternally caught, eternally punished. The righteous, however, can smile from their coffins, for they are now eternally safe.

14.33

The wise don't have to be known as wise, while the fool demands to be known as foolish. Wisdom breeds contentment and a nonchalance about recognition. Folly frantically wants to be noticed, and the narcissism of fools trumps the price paid for being recognized. In other words, the fool wants to be seen even if they are viewed badly, subscribing to the view that there is no such thing as bad publicity. The wise realize that most publicity is bad—virtually all, perhaps—and are therefore content to be unknown and unrecognized. In our age, social media excels at promoting fools. Wise is the one who avoids any sort of promotion and rests quietly, unobserved, happier and safer for the lack of attention.

14.34

What makes a nation great is not its money or military. What makes a people great is not education or earnestness. What makes a culture endure is if it does the right things as a collective. When rich and poor, male and female, young and old, strong and weak combine to do right things, then that nation and civilization rise. When any demographic falters, the whole nation declines. It is impossible for a nation to thrive or even to endure if the poor and the young are righteous, but the rich and the strong are corrupt. It is impossible for a kingdom to endure if the rulers are right and the populace lazy. When all members of a society, mission, or church act righteously, that organization is blessed. When any subset is wicked, all will suffer. This is why wise members of any organization insist that all members maintain and guard doing the right things constantly. To not encourage (and enforce) a common culture of right is guarantee your own corporate disgrace.

14.35

Wise servants make both their leaders, their peers, and their followers look good. It is shortsighted folly to advance yourself at the expense of your colleagues or leaders. That type of self-promotion is always revealed and will always cause shame, incurring the wrath of those you work or live with every day, which makes your service or tenure there impossible. Essentially to undermine your colleagues is ultimately to fire yourself. Leaders love those who are more concerned for the reputation of the whole or the other than themselves. The wise understand that we rise or fall in community and that to build up anyone we are associated with is to rise with them and benefit from their advance.

PROVERBS
Chapter 15

15.1

Foolishness takes a little time to emerge. Most men and women do not display their folly in the first round of conversation or conflict. Foolishness becomes clearer as emotions rise. Anyone can appear wise when they are calm; it is turbulence that exposes both wisdom and folly. Those who intentionally diffuse tension (even when that means swallowing offense and mastering their own emotions) are the sages among us. Those that inflame conversations, confrontations, and communities when angry (even if justifiably so) are fools. How often wisdom can turn to foolishness when anger gilds our words with wrath.

15.2

It's not enough to know the right thing to do; we must apply what we know in the right way. It's not that the foolish do not know things as a person can be incredibly intelligent or informed and not be wise. Fools are fools because they use knowledge wrongly. A mark of wisdom is the ability to distinguish between a principle and an application, to ever retain the principle but vary the application according to context. The wise are wise wherever they go. The foolish are only wise in one place. They can learn and mimic an application and give the appearance of wisdom to an observer, but place them in a context where a dynamic application to a static principle is needed, and their folly will emerge.

15.3

What comfort it is to know that the Lord sees every evil person, every evil act, and every evil motive. When surrounded by evil, we can rest knowing there is constant monitoring of every threat, dastardly plan, trap, trick, and attack. Because the Lord sees every evil thing, we are completely protected from the random nature of evil—we are not immune, but we are protected. The wise understand that omnipotent God sees all. Thus, anything that happens is either purposed or allowed by Him who is both sovereign and good. Likewise, God keeps watch on the good. No secret act of kindness occurs without the Father beaming down His satisfaction in the present and storing up His reward in eternity. We are not saved by works—that is biblically clear—but we will be judged and rewarded according to our works—that is biblically consistent.

15.4

Perversity is depressing. For those whose humor cannot rise above mocking or insult, the sum effect is to drain life from both the speaker and the hearer. Comedians may experience depression, and the more cutting and crueler the comedy, the sadder the interior state of the comic. We do no good to anyone, least of all ourselves, by negativity, including negative humor. Humor is a sugar veneer on an assassinating tongue. Other perversities are also as killing. Death to the hope and innocence of the victim is well documented, but just as deadly is what perversity does to the perpetrator. It is self-mutilation of the soul. By contrast, words of purity, beauty, encouragement, affirmation, praise, love, and blessing have supernatural power to both the speaker and the hearer. Acts of kindness, grace, trust, joy, rescue, and deliverance give life to both the giver and the receiver. The best antidote to depression is words and acts of pure kindness to others.

15.5

The wisest children and disciples receive instruction from those who are near, from those who have feet of clay. Folly closes the ears of those who cannot get past the eccentricities or foibles of their intimate connections. It is the foolish child who, because he sees a parent's frailties and limitations, will not listen to a parent's wisdom. It is the foolish disciple who discovers her mentor has feet of clay and thus, stops listening. The wise can learn from anyone. The wise do not stumble when they discover that every wise man carries some folly in his heart. The wise can learn from the young, from the wrong, from the different, and from the evil. This confidence is knowing there is only One who is good and ever wise, while the rest of us have veins of folly flowing through our character. If we are honest enough to admit our own personal mix of wisdom and folly, we can be lowly enough to mine wisdom from everybody else.

15.6

We must be careful not to confuse money with treasure. There can be much trouble when there is much money. In fact, there almost always is. The increase of money almost inevitably leads to the increase of stress, infighting, and dissatisfaction, especially if the money is illegally gained or improperly worshiped. In the homes, either simple or grand, that see money as a transitory commodity, something primarily to give away or bless others with, there is always joy. Wisdom rules that house, barring money from the throne or even from the family council. Wise families and happy homes do what is right regardless of the implications on finances. Foolish homes vote money into the decision-making inner circle and unleash all manner of unhappy chaos.

15.7

It is folly to keep wisdom to yourself. The wise share whatever they have, for they know that in giving knowledge away there is an inevitable return and an impact on the common good. Fools think that the sharing of what they know will lessen their advantage, little realizing that stinginess with information and understanding in the end affects the miser most badly. The wisest thing we can do with knowledge is to give it away, for the laws of sowing will take those seeds and return a mighty harvest to us. Those who do not liberally sow what they know can never reap back what others add to that knowledge, and all are diminished. The real loss is in the private retention of knowledge to that knower and that knowledge, for it will ever be incomplete.

15.8

What makes a gift beautiful is not what we give, but how we give it. We can present the most beautiful song of worship but do so as a performer and the Father winces. We can preach the most penetrating sermon but do so in the wrath of man, and the sheep are wounded, not won. We can give an immense amount of money but do so from guilt or for glory, and the Knower of all hearts is unimpressed. We must give from the right heart and in the right way if the Lord is to be pleased by our sacrifice. We can please the Lord deeply without having anything material to lay at His feet. When with a pure heart and adoring eyes, we talk to Him simply, guilelessly, honestly, and lovingly. That's a treasure He places on the wall of His heavenly throne room and displays to all His friends.

15.9

It's not where you go, but who you follow and how you follow. Geography, as far as our service, changes. If we fix our value on a place or a position, we have misplaced our value. God is not overly concerned on the where of our service. He is more concerned on the how of our heart. When we follow the Lamb (wherever He goes), when we follow the Lord (who has nowhere to lay His head), wherever we go, He is delighted with us and values us. God loves it when we do right things, pure things, kind things, good things, and obedient things. He hates it when we are unkind, unloving, untruthful, unfair, and unwise. The reality is that the way of the wicked sometimes winds its way into the praxis of the righteous, and God hates that. The wise are vigilant to keep wicked ways, even little "cute ones," out of their repertoire.

15.10

The wise understand that the Holy Spirit both nudges and knocks. As a gentleman, the Spirit whispers to us: "This is the way; walk ye in it." He walks beside us and gives us a little elbow tap and a little indication of the head when we come to a fork in the road. As long as we stay sensitive to the leading of the Spirit, He leads gently. The beautiful and awesome love of the Holy Spirit is revealed when we foolishly step off the path. He loves us too much to let us make a mess of our lives. If we ignore the little nods, nudges, and whispers, He is not above grabbing us by the collar, dragging us by the ear, or knocking us over the head with some two-by-four of pain or disappointment. The Holy Spirit loves us enough to hurt us in order to help us. The stakes are high. Sulk at this loving spanking of the Spirit at the peril of spiritual death.

15.11

God sees what goes on in evil places, including my heart. It is the height of folly to willfully forget that God is present, at my elbow, watching every private act. Humans excel at self-deception and intentional blindness. The wise have such a robust ongoing sense of the omnipresence of God. His literal physical presence, His all-seeing eye is so real to them that they feel the bore of that loving gaze whenever they are tempted. In our folly we act like Peter and betray the Lord because we have pushed His gaze to the recesses of our conscience, but when we are wise, we look across the courtyard of life and see the flashing eyes of God holding our gaze, and looking into those eyes, we can't bear to betray Him.

15.12

Fools lash out at those who lovingly hurt them. Correction is occasionally delicious, but more often it brings shame as someone points out something wrong. When we are corrected, our flesh wants to leap up in self-defense or to distract any observer from our error or flaw by attacking the corrector. If repeated enough times, this action silences the ones who could help us best when we need them most. We must be careful that sarcasm, cynicism, and a critical spirit do not paint us into a corner of moral pride or a helpless state of our own creation because we scoffed at others so often that we no longer think they can help us and they no longer have the will to assist. Even though it stings in the moment, the wise are not dismayed at pain, shame, or correction, for the wise do not dare to silence the surgeon's knife.

15.13

Joy is an insuppressible radiation. When the heart is truly happy, the face sings. This is true for organizations as well as individuals. Happy organizations have core leaders that are joyful. You can tell the private temperament of parents by observing the public demeanor of their children. When children are happy and content, it typically means their parents have true private joy, not just public and forced mirth. By the same token, if leaders at the center of an organization are not deeply joyful on their inside, it doesn't matter how strategic or organized they are, their organization and their field-level workers will operate under a cloud. The greatest gift a parent can give a child, or a leader can give an organization, is to fight for joy in their private, inner life. Unfaked joy at the heart spreads to every exterior countenance.

15.14

Folly is an addictive food. Little acts of foolishness create hunger for larger ones. In this way folly is insatiable and demands greater and greater exposure, particularly through words. The foolish man is the talkative one, no matter how wise or witty his words may sound. For the wise shut up and seek. The wise open their ears and shut their mouths. New missionaries would do well to take a relative vow of silence for their first year. Wise missionaries listen, learn, ask questions, and refrain from expressing their opinions, even if they have great experience. You can usually correlate how wise someone is to how infrequently they engage in trivial talk and by how earnestly they listen and learn.

15.15

A merry heart is impervious to evil. Lock a merry heart in a prison cell, and that cell will be full of singing. Take a shirt from a merry heart, and that heart will seek to give you a matching coat. Compel a merry heart to walk one mile with you, and two miles later that heart will be at your side smiling and humming contentedly. When men and women can truly say, "He has made me glad," nothing rocks their world. Every day is a good day, and they feast on every situation. How opposite for the sin-bound heart—even their victories are losses, their accomplishments dissatisfactions, and their advances retreats. A merry heart (and thus, a merry life no matter the circumstances) is chosen. We chose to confess sin, receive mercy, and walk in obedient trust. In making those choices, Jesus makes us glad, and no sorrow of life ever ultimately prevails.

15.16

The truly rich are those who have room in their heart for only one fear: the Lord. When we only bow to King Jesus, when we only care about what our heavenly Father thinks, when the only advice that has the final say is the counsel of the Spirit, then we become fabulously wealthy, and that wealth can't be lost or stolen. We don't even have to worry about guarding that treasure because no one has access to it unless we let them. How different this trove is to money and physical possessions, which must be guarded, locked, and watched over continually, so vulnerable that one can never not protect them—it's exhausting. How much better then to have so little that demands constant guarding and to have so much that can't be taken from us unless we foolishly yield it up. Spiritual treasure is much harder to obtain than physical wealth, but much easier to keep.

15.17

How sad that so many unwittingly seek sadness. The lie that monetary wealth is intrinsic to happiness has deceived all the world. The lie that luxury can compensate for the betrayal of friends, loss of relationship, and damage to our integrity is tragically believed everywhere. Fools think that possessions will be more satisfying than relationships and so they violate relationships in order to gain greater physical comfort. They eat well but eat alone, even when surrounded by people. How much better off are those who choose relationship over private resources. Those with less to eat but with more loved ones with whom to eat are invariably happier, for they have discovered that love has nutrients that food can't provide. Well-fed, well-loved, well-loving souls are ever more satisfied than selfish, spoiled ones.

15.18

God's character is repeatedly described as loving, compassionate, merciful, and slow to anger. The fact that God is characterized as slow to anger indicates that anger is a vital aspect of His nature— as vital as love and mercy. He is just slow to get there. Wisdom then gets angry over the right things (which happen to be wrong things) slowly. Foolishness gets angry over the wrong things right away. To be a person that lives angry is to be a person that inappropriately extends conflict and creates opportunity for evil. To be a person that angers slowly is to be a person that appropriately uses anger to destroy evil and creates opportunity for good.

15.19

Laziness is not neutral. Laziness hurts and impedes. To be lazy is not to be sedentary; to be lazy is to lose ground. Life is a swim against the current. To stop swimming is not to stop, but to be swept backwards. The foolish think they can do nothing, and nothing will happen. But when we do nothing, bad things happen. Hedges of thorns grow that hurt and impede others, not just ourselves. Laziness is neither neutral nor merely personal. Laziness always damages the common good. Industry, activity, labor, and hard work do the exact opposite. The wise realize that private work adds to common good. The wise rejoice that their hard work opens the way for many others. For hard work is not neutral or personal either—it always does good for others.

15.20

Wisdom brings joy to all, not just the one who made good choices. When we act wisely, it has a ripple effect on those near and far. In this way wisdom is respectful. It seeks what is best for others and it is never self-seeking. Foolishness, however, addresses every question with the lens of self: What is best for me? In God's sovereignty the greatest good for me is always determined by identifying what is best for others. The wise trust the God who gave Himself. They trust that if they make their choices based on what pleases Him and blesses others, they will make the best choices that bring them the most good. Fools cannot see past themselves and make their choices based on what is best for them, finding it is not only worse for them but disrespectful of others. Counterintuitive as it may seem and countercultural as it may be, if you deny self when you make choices and do what is best for others, you will end up doing what is best for all including yourself. Do yourself a favor by forgetting yourself. The gift of self-forgetfulness makes everyone glad.

15.21

There is undeniable fun in foolish things. To take pride in this fun, to continue to feed on it and to feed others on it is short-sighted. Folly is only a joy to those who can't see the future. Those who can see the future know that folly starts with fun and ends with tears and pain. Fools chose glory and end up with suffering. The wise, the ones who understand, choose suffering and end up with glory. Those who don't eat, sleep, or exercise right pay the price in middle and later age. Those who do not reign in their tongues end up reigned by them. They chose a loose tongue and end up bound by their own slander, gossip, cynicism, sarcasm, lies, meanness, or exaggeration. Life contains both hard and easy portions, and we basically have two choices: Either we chose a little bit of foolish fun on the front end and then endure much pain, or we choose a little bit of pain up front and enjoy much long-term joy.

15.22

Wisdom begins in knowing you can be a fool. The wise always ask others for input and counsel, for they realize that humans can be smart enough to self-deceive. The obvious power of self-delusion is our utter inability to see our blindness. A wise person realizes that others are similarly blind and so does not elevate the counsel of one person (or group) to God-like status. The foolish trust either themselves or one person (group/ideology/system) too much. They neglect the reality that full-sighted balance can only come from a sincere consideration of multiple perspectives. Fools recoil at the criticism of their ideas, for they think criticism detracts from their plans. The wise welcome criticism of their ideas, for it can always be channeled towards improvement of the plan even if the motive of the critic is suspect.

15.23

There is such pleasure in being like Jesus. Though we are so prone to pride, there is a legitimate and sanctified rejoicing when we recognize we did something or said something in a way that Jesus would have. When God speaks through us, we can get carnally proud, but we can also beam a holy smile that our mouth was used for good. We can feel the pleasure and pride of God coursing through us when we speak for Him. Double goodness results when we speak the right words at the right time in the right way. From the mouth can flow God's healing, reconciliation, encouragement, and hope. How good it is when in our moments of struggle God uses a vessel to speak life to us. How glad we are when He uses our words to speak life to others.

15.24

Wisdom keeps walking toward heaven. The wise put as much distance between themselves and danger as possible. Courage and folly are cousins, and it is not bravery to see how close to the edge of spiritual danger or sin we can stay. Folly gets a macabre delight in peering over the cliff into hell (or even at what is twisted). Wisdom doesn't even want to look at evil and takes no joy in hearing what is ugly. Wisdom looks away. It walks away from what sounds filthy and winds its way towards what is pure. If we are wise, we will ever be walking towards what is pure, light, good, and kind, and ever walking away from what is vile.

15.25

Very little is what it seems at first glance. The proud seem strong and well-defended, but they are actually vulnerable. The meek seem like easy prey, but they are actually impervious to assault because of the unseen. The proud are so because they have intelligence, beauty, wealth, power, or some obvious natural advantage that everyone can see. The humble and the disadvantaged appear to have no natural gift, talent, or recourse. The wise see what is invisible and the foolish ignore it. The wise see that the towering presence of God looms over both the proud and the lowly. He will strike the proud and defend those with no one to help them.

15.26

Bad "hearting" spoils good thinking. It doesn't matter how smart we are when we live in rebellion or practice wickedness. It is folly to think that God will accept good things from bad hearts. Wicked humor is not funny. Selfish giving is not generous. Unloving counsel is not caring. Leading that is not serving is not helping. Good things (thoughts, gifts, actions) given from wicked hearts are attempted bribes; they are repulsive to an incorruptible God. To God, if our hearts are pure, though our gifts be less impressive, they are more welcome.

15.27

Greed has collateral damage. It ultimately hurts anyone in the relational vicinity, not just the one lusting for more. There are ways to make money quickly outside the laws of the land or outside the bounds of integrity, but those ways never lead to good for your family or friends. Real friends and faithful family call out greed in another. Greed is not a solitary sickness; greed is group gangrene, and its effects hurt all. Wise households do not tolerate greed for gold, glory, or girls among their members. Rather, they love one another enough to mutually stamp it out. The families and friend groups that hate shortcuts to gain and that embrace the labor of the long haul find joy in living.

15.28

Wisdom doesn't necessarily know the right thing to do with alacrity. We should not confuse speed of processing with the best option. Some problems are so complex that we don't find the right action or response until our spirit churns through all the relational and spiritual and emotional data. Foolishness confuses a quick answer with a smart answer and in that mistake pours gasoline, not water, on fires. Good hearts must be intentional about having good tongues, for sometimes a good intention prematurely shared causes damage rather healing. Those who don't care about healing, those who purposely or even carelessly wound through words are children of the devil, the one who uses a golden tongue to bring grievous harm.

15.29

The God who is omnipresent, filling time and space, puts some distance between Himself and those who are wicked. Because geographical distance is impossible, it is a distance of deafness. We do not want to be the fools that God tunes out due to our repeated nonsense or rebellion. What a hellish condition—to have so annoyed God that He will no longer listen to us. Soberly, God's deafness can be developed not just by flagrant wickedness but also by repeated vanity or whining. By contrast how beautiful to have a voice that God's ear carefully tunes to and waits for because those prayers are always selfless and lowly. The wise live and speak in such a way that God is ever eager to hear their prayers and to act on their behalf. Let's not turn God off and have Him tune us out because our prayer life is foolishly carnal or selfishly oriented.

15.30

Demeanor matters. God does not appreciate gloominess or a dour countenance. There is no spiritual badge for dampening colleagues or events because you are either a critic or a pessimist. When we bring joy, energy, hope, and life to those around us, the Father rejoices. God loves it when we spread His life. God loves it when we chose to focus on the positive things others do. God loves it when we repeat testimonies and share praise reports of what the Spirit is doing in the earth. Intentionally dwelling on what God has done, coupled with believing He will yet do good things, make the whole church of God healthy. There are many foes and many concerns, but God doesn't want us dwelling on the negative. God wants us sparkling with hope, speaking of the good, and looking towards what will be good in His time.

15.31

We become wise by having our folly publicly noticed and corrected. Wisdom is not acquired in isolation or through mistake-free living. Wisdom is acquired through the painful and humbling process of rebuke. Therefore, the wise give thanks through tears when their failings are addressed. The wise fight through the pain of shame for the hope of learning. The wise know that life follows accepted discipline. The wise are able to be rebuked by life itself; they don't necessarily need a human to voice the correction, though they submit to that means readily. The wise are hungry enough to learn that they allow events to rebuke them. Fools are too gentle with themselves. The wise are ruthless in self-evaluation without doing self-harm.

15.32

When we don't listen, we hurt our future selves and our eternal soul. The best way to show eternal kindness to ourselves is to listen to others when they disagree with us, correct us, rebuke us, and discipline us. True instruction always comes at a price: Either we labored to apprehend it, or it worked us over for us to understand it. Those who make changes after confrontation are the wise, for true listening includes change. The fools are those who shake their head "yes" but set their heart and will to "no."

15.33

Respect for King Jesus is the wisdom lesson. Genuine appreciation for God's comprehensive authority is the first step in knowing anything. If we want to be wise, we must settle first that we will trust that God is sovereignly good, and we will resolve not to doubt His nature. If we want to be wise, we must determine that when we face a problem, our starting assumption will be that the problem is not with God, and it never could be. Wisdom is not an understanding of every problem; wisdom is an understanding that the problem is never, ever with God. When we have the heart humility of believing that God is always right and always good, then He honors us by helping us understand the dangerous and difficult things.

PROVERBS
Chapter 16

16.1

If the Lord can use us when we're surprised, think what He can do when we're prepared! If God can use us when we're ignorant, imagine what He can do when we're informed! The wise are very seldom extemporaneous. What seems automatic is usually some type of muscle memory, some recall of study or hard-earned life lesson, some public presentation of a privately studied truth. We are not excused anywhere in life, ministry, or mission from the long, difficult, and often secret preparation. When we have been diligent behind the scenes to prayerfully ready our response, remarks, rebuke, or reflections, God stands ever ready to fill in the gaps, to inject His creative thoughts into our mind and His discernment regarding the unexpected into our spirit. We can be confident that if we have been diligent in past preparation, God will be faithful to supply whatever is lacking for the unexpected in the present.

16.2

Not one of us has 20/20 vision when it comes to our own character or person. We are physically and spiritually incapable of a completely accurate view of ourselves. The same is true of any critic or any fan—no one has us completely defined or evaluated. There is an examine of spirit of which only God is proficient. The foolish trust their own self-evaluation, while the wise know that no man (including themselves) fully understands the heart, the motives, and the spirit. We are inevitably prone to self-deception, and we are all an indecipherable blend of what is true and what is false. This is why it's critical to ever return to the only One who understands everything about us in order to ask what He sees. When all think we are pure, He sees where we are vile. When all think we are vile, He sees where we are pure. Only God can truly see—and correct—our motives.

16.3

Sustainable works in life are attained by allowing the Lord to vet them before we establish them. When we launch our visions or dreams before slowing down the process by allowing the Lord to review, amend, improve, or even deny them, we can indeed create something good, but we hardly ever establish something that lasts beyond us. The true wisdom of any endeavor is revealed by its sustained power beyond the life of the initiator. If our heart's desire is good that outlasts us, we would be wise to submit the dream to God before we launch it, not launch it and then levy the Lord for blessing. A commitment of our works to the Lord has the inherent assumption and desire for honest review and refining. The "downside" might be delay and the removal of something of which we were naively fond, but the upside is that unseen flaws will be removed and long-term life assured.

16.4

There is great wisdom in coming to terms with the limiting reality that you are a creature, that you have been made by Someone wiser than yourself for purposes other than you have chosen. This acceptance requires a modicum of humility and yields immeasurable joy. In our foolish flesh, we resent the reality that we've been created, we long for the elusive goal of being self-made. We had nothing to do with our birth and ultimately nothing to do with our destiny. We are not robots. We have will, and effort matters. But at the end of the day and at the end of time, God will be glorified in us and by us eternally no matter what we choose. We all ultimately serve God's purposes. The only question is whether we do so by heaven or hell. God is just as glorified by hell as He is by heaven. God could not be good if He did not punish evil. Hell, to the wise, is an eternal reminder of God's goodness. How tragic that our foolish, rebellious, and confused natures have twisted hell into a rationale that He is bad. Only fools consider righteous punishment evil.

16.5

Pooled arrogance does not mean accumulated strength. Because pride is an abomination to the Lord, its increase makes its doom more certain, not less. Rather than be intimidated by the billowing forces of evil, the righteous wise should be sobered by the impending punitive act of God on all that defy His absolute Lordship. We can be sure that the Lord of glory sees the rise of pride and that He will judge it sooner rather than later. Foolishness either allows arrogance to grow in our own heart or leads us to align with other arrogant people because we have been bewitched by their charisma. Both actions will be punished. The wise ruthlessly resist pride in themselves and assiduously avoid being influenced (through intimate friendship) with those who are arrogant. The more arrogant we are, the weaker we become in spirit. The more arrogant hearts that assemble together, the more certain punishment.

16.6

It is the mercy of God that He forgives us for lusting after lesser joys. It is the truth of God that only His joy fully satisfies. If we want mercy, we must admit we have latched on to lesser, destructive, offensive pleasures. Addictions are only overcome by the expulsive power of a greater affection. Vice tends to have a binding power (through demonic enablement) that we cannot break through sheer effort. We need the delivering power of God to strike the controlling and evil jockey off our laboring back. To prevent its return, we need to desire what is pure more than we desire what is vile. I only overcome my tendencies towards iniquity (the fleeting pleasures that are sinful) if deep in my spirit I take deeper pleasure in Jesus and what brings Him joy. I am not kept from sin by threat; I am kept from sin by a longing for the One who truly satisfies.

16.7

The first step to peace with all is peace with God. Peace with God demands absolute surrender, and we cannot win the hearts of others if we have not submitted to the Lordship love of the Father for us. First, God wins us to Himself, then He wins others to us.

He does not waste energy and time reconciling us to one another if we have not been fundamentally reconciled to Him. Peace with all essentially comes down to making sure our heart is right with God. That accomplished, God woos on our behalf.

16.8

Justice and righteousness make one rich and they are more valuable than money. The tragedy of most who seek riches is that they do so at the expense of the right treatment of peers and the just treatment of the poor. When we seek advantage over those equal to us or take advantage over those weaker than us, we impoverish ourselves. We may gain money, but we lose riches.

16.9

God delights in revising, refining, and upgrading the plans of man. God delights when man takes initiative and exercises the creativity bestowed from heaven. God's reviews of our plans are similar to those of a benevolent editor: He likes that we are creative, He sees the merits of what we propose, He sees the possibilities we have missed, and He sees how our ideas can be improved. It is beneficial to have an editor who also happens to be omniscient. If we are secure enough to allow the Almighty to refine our plans, we will be directed to the best path in the best way at the best time. Wisdom takes no offense when God improves on our ideas.

16.10

Leaders are entrusted with truth, and they should not undermine their bestowed authority through foolish or idle talk. As a young, single minister, I once preached a sermon and afterward several older congregants took me to lunch. Through the course of that conversation, I made several immature comments. I will never forget the shame that coursed through me when one of the hosts set down her fork and quietly said to me: "I can see that you are not who I thought you were while listening to you preach." My foolish conversation around the table undermined whatever wisdom I channeled at the pulpit.

16.11

Truth is non-negotiable, and absolutes are God's protection for all. The integrity of a community is only preserved when law and judgment are applied equally, no matter the offender's prestige, power, or connections. Honor is not particular. We are to reward and advance those whose character is Christlike, no matter their origin, ethnicity, gender, connections, or appearance. But the process of making decisions by seeing past outer layers to the inner spirit does not happen naturally or without effort. We must determine to see as God sees; otherwise, we will default to our natural prejudice.

16.12

When leaders sin, it is a double evil. The more status and influence one has, the more damaging the consequences of the errors. Sin in a leader destroys, not only their moral influence but also the very structural integrity of what they lead. Families, churches, our institutions, and societies stand on the twin (mutually dependent) legs of righteous leadership and sound systems. If either the leader or the system is wicked, the other is infected. It is impossible to have a wicked leader that does not lead the whole fabric to becoming wicked. Thus, it is reprehensible for a leader to live in sin, for that sin will inevitably destroy the whole community.

16.13

Longevity is tied to doing the right things early in your leadership and in maintaining those early principles through all the seasons of life. Right things remain right when they are spoken of, spoken for, and spoken about positively. Leaders have the verbal power of blessing, for followers rise to the expectation that leaders have of them. Followers love to hear leaders repeat the same old tribal stories, the same old ancient truths, the same old time-tested principles. The right thing for leaders to do, the wise speech for leaders to make is not a continuous creation of new ideas, but a steady rehearsal of what is ever true: past, present, and future.

16.14

Wrath is holy, always in God and sometimes in man. Wrath is to be so passionately against something wicked that you determine to spend energy destroying it. When a leader is provoked to such a point that they determine to act with finality, there are two courses of action available to the wise. The first and easiest is to submit to the leader's decision and not keep alive what the leader wants to kill (program, ministry, position, activity). But the second requires discernment that is both gentle and courageous and aims to redirect the zeal of the authority away from killing (ending, stopping, firing, removing) until calming facts (hitherto unknown) can quench the flame. Wisdom is not to always appease, but to know when and how to appease and to know when to stand aside and accept (or even aid) the wrathful intentions of the leader.

16.15

It is folly to behave, speak, act, or react in a way that clouds the spirit of your authority towards you. The favor of our leaders is an atmosphere we are responsible to create for and in them. It is not always necessary to be present to create this favorable posture in our authorities; it can be done remotely through prompt excellence in delegated tasks and responsibilities. The favor of kings relies on secondhand information, referrals, and reports as well as intimate interactions for its sense and inclination. The wise know that regal attitudes toward us are not determined in the moment of interview, but in the quiet days before and prior to meeting with the powers that be.

16.16

What's best isn't necessarily what's most attractive, nor is it always what is most tangible or most immediate. Gold, money, physical resources, and their power are quickly felt and quickly seen. The power of wisdom, on the other hand, is hidden and deferred; its advantages not revealed in the moment and its benefits deferred to the future. Fools choose the power of now, while the wise choose the power of later. The greater power is in the future, and the path to that power today is in choosing wisdom and understanding over silver and gold in the present.

16.17

The natural traffic patterns of heart and society follow the well-worn paths of evil. Fools do not recognize that the broad highways with their popular, convenient, higher speed limits, more frequent rest stops, smoother surfaces, and softer winds lead to destruction, nor do fools realize that life is only maintained if you exit those roads. The wise continually exit the popular path—and not once, but multiple times. The first exit removes us from disaster, but not danger. We must ever choose the higher, more rugged, more strenuous path. Evil living is easy, and upright living is difficult. Upright living is a continual exit from evil, a continual turning to a lonelier and narrower path.

16.18

It was François Fenelon who pointed out that nothing is so offensive to a haughty heart as the sight of another. It is relatively easy to discern a prideful heart in another, primarily because we are so riddled with it ourselves. Fools focus on what is arrogant about others. The wise have the lowliness to seek and find arrogance in themselves. In the mercy of God, there is a lag (of various lengths depending on His variables) between our pride and our destruction, and there is a space He affords us that we might repent and forsake arrogance. But destruction is the inevitable consequence of pride, and it is foolish to see it in others and deny it in ourselves.

16.19

Humility in loss is better than arrogance in gain. The Kingdom works from the inside out with merit determined by heart not muscle, where motive counts as much (or more) than results. We win for King and Kingdom when we get the attitude on the inside right, no matter what happens on the outside. When we win the internal war, external victories are like bonuses; they're nice and we welcome them, but we still have joy without them. When we lose the internal war, external gains ring false and hollow. In the long run, humility always wins, and pride always loses.

16.20

There are different good ways to obey but not all are equal or yield equal results. When we obey with wisdom, we experience excellence. When we obey pragmatically, we find success but not necessarily fulfilment. When we obey begrudgingly, we achieve without joy. When we obey from a core that trusts that the Lord is sovereignly good in all that He allows or ordains, we become and remain happy. If we are going to obey, we might as well do so in a way that leaves us happy, not grumpy. Of all the ways we may interact with God, wisdom discovers that happy obedience is the highest and most fulfilling form.

16.21

How we talk impacts how we listen. How we talk impacts how others hear us. To throw pearls before swine is to present good things in bad ways. When we present truth in a way that cannot be digested, we, not the uncomprehending listener, are culpable. Wise communication comes from a heart that wants to be understood, not from an ego that wants to be respected. When we want praise, we unwittingly try and impress by distancing our intellect from those we speak to. When we want to serve, we take great care to simplify our message so that it can be understood. Sweet spirits lead to sweet lips which lead to open ears and willing wills.

16.22

Wisdom is a renewable resource. When wisdom is applied, it multiplies. Wise acts lead to truth discoveries. When we do the right thing, we open doors to understanding. Treat people as you should, and you will gain deeper insight into human nature. Decide with integrity under duress, and you will see more clearly into the most difficult scenarios of life. Chose the moral path at great cost to your person, and you will have less doubt about what is true and more awareness of what is false. Wisdom acted on renews and grows itself. Wisdom spent is wisdom invested. Conversely, foolish choices make you more stupid, and one wrong choice empowers and propels the next.

16.23

A subtle form of folly is to talk our way to wisdom. Often, we are like Peter who when confronted with something beyond his experience spoke before he thought (Mark 9:6; Luke 9:33). It is unwise to talk when we are uncertain, angry, shocked, hurt, provoked, or surprised. The wise are marked by the patience to slow down their mouths so they can hear their spirits. Rather than talking our way to wisdom, we should listen our way there. It is no loss to lose our voice for a season, if we spend that time listening to our hearts.

16.24

Life-giving words affect both the body and the soul. Integrated as we are, when our souls leap, our bodies straighten. When we dispense kindness from our mouth, vitality passes through the ears (body) into the heart (soul), which strengthen both our structure and our substance. Using words to attack damages not just the spiritual, emotional, and mental aspect of the one we maim, but also harms their physical health. If sticks, stones, and words *all* break bones, then words can also heal them.

16.25

If the arm of flesh will fail us, how much more will the eye? When making life choices, we have to see with spirit eyes, we have to see beyond the broadest path and easiest choice. In life the gaudiest signs and the most noticeable marketing do not always indicate the most valuable product. The persons who most blatantly advertise themselves tend to be the shallowest. Choices that would later kill us begin by seducing us. Wise choices are made through a combination of physical investigation and spiritual discernment. Here the people of God have the greatest advantage: The Spirit Himself bears witness within regarding which choices are the narrow life ways and which are the broad roads to destruction.

16.26

Motivation that lasts must be internal. We don't work the best or hardest if the desire isn't internally owned. Hungry mouths and hungry hearts provide energy that can sustain long after natural zeal wanes. What is true practically is true spiritually. When we labor for more of Jesus or more of His glory among the nations, because deep in our hearts we are ravenous for Him, we can drive on. The person who labors for himself for more of Himself drives on.

16.27

If we have a tendency to prompt our friends to gossip, that is as evil as gossip itself. Itching ears are as wicked as burning lips. Some men are prone to sink ships through loose lips, and others are prone to sink them through eager ears. Passive evil is just as destructive as active evil, and we cannot smugly think we're better than the gossiper if we empower him or her through listening. If we dig up evil by encouraging friends and acquaintances to talk when they should be silent, it is ungodly and unwise. The literal text of this verse says: "A man of Belial digs up evil." In other words, it is demonic to empower gossip.

16.28

If it is demonic to empower gossip by listening to it, it is perverse to pass it on. When we accommodate half-truths, we poison what was once beautiful, damaging friendships that were pure by injecting the venom of lies. Half-truths are lies. The danger in whispering (private conversations that exclude all parties or perspectives) is that partial truth destroys life; it does not give it. The wise are those whose words are in the light, who have no secrets, who allow all perspectives to hear, judge, and season what is said. Open speech is accountable speech, bounded and balanced by exposure. If the words of your mouth cannot bear the weight of public scrutiny and correction, then the wise thing to do is to swallow them.

16.29

There is something seductive about violence. Violence is a manifestation of power, and deep in every fallen human soul is the desire for more power than we presently hold. What makes the Lord Jesus so incredible is that He gave up power. The incarnation is staggering because it flows against every human tendency to accrue. God in the flesh became weak and poor, and there is nothing enticing about either of those. Yet, that sacrifice led to all that is good. It is folly, deep-seeded folly, to desire more power, for it inevitably leads to violence or coercion. It is heavenly wisdom to give up power, wealth, fame, and reputation, for it leads unavoidably to life and blessing.

16.30

When charisma precedes character, evil is born. Winks by nature are private and exclusive. They indicate special knowledge and a bond between conspirators, a bond that leaves someone out. It's perverse to exclude for your own gratification or humor. Godly character always includes others for their own good, and evil character always excludes others for our own convenience. To not act, to not speak, to hold back what could help others for our own convenience is absolutely contrary to the will and character of God. It is foolish, for if we live that way, we will die that way—excluded from the goodness, help, and blessings of God.

16.31

Age is glorious only if it crowns a life of doing the right things. Grey hair does not automatically confer honor. In fact, the greatest folly can also be found in the aged. Those who cling to bad habits and selfish living into their later years are objects of great shame and pity. Experience does not automatically teach us. Unfortunately, we can be the fools who have one year of experience repeated twenty times, for we did not have the humility to learn and change from our experiences. Let us respect all the silver haired for the years of life they traversed but let us emulate only those who learned from their travels, those who acted righteously all along the way.

16.32

The definitive description of God, repeated over and again in Scripture, is that He is loving, merciful, compassionate, and slow to anger. Essential to the nature of God is holy wrath at what is evil; God would not be good if He did not dedicate Himself to the destruction and purging of what is vile. If we are to be good as He is good, then we, too, must be dedicated to the destruction of what is evil. If, however, God with all His perfect wisdom is slow to get angry, how much more should we of imperfect wisdom be slow to destructive wrath. Fools vent their anger quickly, without bounds, and inevitably scorch some of the innocent. The wise get angry, but slowly, in circumspective manner, careful to channel the anger of heaven, not manufacture their own. At the end of the day wise anger is a strength that is compassionate and foolish anger is a venting that only destroys.

16.33

Because God is completely sovereign, there is no such thing as luck. Followers of Jesus are usually not so blatantly whimsical as to hang rabbit's feet from their rearview mirrors or horseshoes over our doors or to knock on wood to keep favor rolling. But we can offer less obvious prayers to the god of chance. We do so by erroneously thinking the unknown (to us) is unknown to God and therefore somehow precarious. Hoping for the best is casting lots without trusting God's eternal knowledge and power. God is outside of time. He is the only One who knows the end from the beginning. He does not only know all that can be known, but He knows all that could be known. He knows every possibility of every choice. He knows every possible ramification of every integrated action—and He knew this from eternity past. Luck makes God small, and that is idolatrous. The wise make God big and will not countenance any practice or doctrine that reduces His majesty.

PROVERBS
Chapter 17

17.1

Poor and simple is better than rich and angry. There is a dignity in simplicity often best displayed among the poor. In the West, poverty is often associated with what is unkempt and uncared for. While there are examples of such un-stewarded poverty in the Global South, there are more plentiful examples of a simple poverty that is clean, winsome, ordered, inviting, and at peace. Resources do not bring dignity and decency; stewardship does. Resources robe us with external order while often cloaking the chaos within. Simplicity exposes who we are and thus is more suitable for accountability and responsibility.

17.2

Wisdom provides heritage, and shame creates orphans. Cream always rises to the top, and character always (eventually) trumps charisma. It might take time for the spiritual order of things to rule the natural, but the spiritual will always win, for the spiritual always endures and grows from strength to strength while the natural always decays. If we will apply ourselves to godly wisdom, we store up for ourselves an imperishable inheritance, no matter how humble our natural gifts or native origin.

17.3

The Lord is very good at getting the dross out of our hearts. In the same way heat exposes what is not pure gold, trouble exposes what is not noble character. God refines us by placing us in difficulty so that what is not of and like Him will be exposed. Just as humility comes before honor, so humiliation must precede holiness. Some evils are so deeply emmeshed in our nature that nothing but a crucible reveals them. In mercy God limits the scope of our shame and exposure to just Him and us at first. But if we do not honestly repent, He is not above spreading our shame that we might be truly freed from our sin. If we will not be humiliated before God, we must be humiliated before men.

17.4

Truth is kind and firm in how it listens, refusing to attend to what is spiteful. True kindness walks away from or shuts down false or damaging speech; free speech must always be honorable. It is a passive evil to empower gossip by listening to slander or to empower liars by listening to tripe. We are liars with our ears before we are liars with our mouths. If we make a practice of being the accommodating listener to complaints, bitterness, insurrection, and bile, then we partner with it and will shortly partake in it. We cannot long listen to vitriolic speech (whether from friends or the media) without soon having that speech inform our thinking, manner, and character.

17.5

Sovereign God makes some people poor and keeps them in that lowly status. Poverty is not always punishment from the God of all resources; it is often a blessing and sometimes a promotion. It is one of the ironies of wealth and its accumulation that happiness is often inversely related to riches. It is also true that only God can rightly apportion poverty and its attending calamities; thus, we should neither desire nor deride those whom God has asked to bear that status. Poverty is only rightly shouldered if borne from the inside out. It is the poor in spirit who steward the range of economic experience with joyful peace.

17.6

We respect our own progeny by staying true to what is beautiful over time. And nothing is more beautiful than the Lord Jesus. The aged delight over the generations that follow, and that delight is reciprocated when the ancestors do not stumble in character or conviction or faith into their golden years. The best gift we can give those who come after us is a legacy of righteousness, running our race well to the very end, loving Jesus more with our grey heads than we did with our younger strength. What glory it is for children and grandchildren to look up to their elders with joy because those patriarchs and matriarchs shine ever brighter until that perfect day. Let us cause no shame to those that revere us and have no unseemly stumbling when all our youthful vigor is expended.

17.7

Character and words should align. We cannot truly represent the King as His royal children if our words do not match the grandeur of our Father. The more we walk with Jesus, the more responsibility He gives us, and the more responsibility we are entrusted with, the more important it is there is no discrepancy between our walk and our talk. If we behave poorly, our lofty words only grate on the ears of those around us. There is an admitted gulf between the behavior of all messengers and their proclamation. What bearer of the gospel can promise they have ever lived up to the full standards of Scripture? Fools accept the gulf, embrace it by excusing it, and in sloth daily broaden it. The wise note that gulf with alarm and ever strive with God's help to narrow it.

17.8

Generosity opens doors. We do not give to receive money, polluting generosity by making it a utilitarian means of selfish gain. We give because God is a giver, and He wants His children to look like Him. We give because God is a blesser, and He wants His ambassadors to dispense His life and favor. One of the twisted applications of the so-called "prosperity gospel" (for nothing self-centered can rightly be called gospel) is that prosperity is primarily physical and financial. Prosperity is primarily spiritual and relational. The wise are generous with their time, affirmation, forgiveness, love, grace, hearts, and humor—not just their money. And thus, wherever they go, they prosper. When we are generous, we increase the circle of friendship, and there is no greater wealth.

17.9

Silence can be a great love act. There are times where silence is hateful and harmful, but there are also times that the wise act of healing love is to cover a transgression. We demonstrate a deep love for others (friend or foe) when the damaging information we know about them dies with us. We love most genuinely when that knowledge of transgression dies within us, so deeply covered that it is forgotten even to ourselves. Covering transgressions that have been repented of and atoned for (when that covering is not injurious to the innocent) not only binds us to the forgiven, but it also empowers the forgiven to be bound to others who need not know what God Himself chooses to forget. We all will at some point need that mercy. Our Lord Jesus absorbed sin and shame for the sincerely penitent, burying it forever in the grave. Only fools dig up what God has buried. Only fools bring to life what God has killed.

17.10

The wise learn the easy way. Fools insist on learning by the most painful means. Because God is so tender in His shepherding of our souls, He first woos, then warns, then wraths. God's initial rebukes are so gentle and kind. He launches them with gentle smiles. If we will not smile back, God then scolds; He need not strike us if we will but heed. He will surely strike us if we persist in scorning Him, for He cannot be good if He has unending tolerance for what is bad. Our good Teacher will surely school the bad out of us. How joyful or painful the lesson is entirely dependent on us.

17.11

God has a very low tolerance level for rebellion and tends to deal with it decisively and forcefully. It may seem cruel to cast one third of your heavenly family away from your eternal presence, but the fault is not in the divine King when His created subjects lusted for His throne. The very nature of a monarchy demands that treason be punished by death. So how much more when the monarch is perfect and sublime! If God is thus intolerant of rebellion, how vigilant should we be of any trace of it in our midst, whether in our heart or any earthly family. It would be unwise to think we are kinder than God by having more tolerance for evil than He does. What God deals with cruelly so must we, starting with ourselves and the household of faith.

17.12

Sometimes the pain we must inflict on our foolish friends is to remove ourselves from their proximity (because their folly never only hurts them; it also affects those who are near). Nature teaches us that not every dangerous situation can be diffused through logic or reason. For example, we don't have conversations with enraged mother bears; instead, we run away. We run away with Joseph from lust; we do not engage it in conversation. We don't try to counsel folly out of a fool. Much as we would love to save fools pain, when those fools are our friends, often pain is their only remedy, not palaver. Sometimes the wisest thing to do is step back and let those we love experience the consequences of their decisions. No friend is as convincing to the fool as pain. Pain can be, as C. S. Lewis soberly reminded us, "God's megaphone."

17.13

Both evil and good are like dominoes arranged in long lines. Neither evil nor good is ever done in isolation; there are always a series of acts, always consequences. If we are the recipient of goodness, whether from God or another, the spiritual order is to pass the goodness on, to continue its chain. If in our arrogance, selfishness, rebellion, or folly, we pollute the chain, and after receiving what is good, we pass on what is evil, we doubly sin—for we not only abort good, but we instigate bad. The terror is that a blatant corruption of mercy chains (by rewarding evil for good) launches evil harm to all those under your authority. Only fools pass on harm to those they love when all they received was good from those who love them. God has no tolerance for the "mercied" who do not mercy.

17.14

Once you start fighting, there is no clean or quick way to back away, and all truncated fights leave messes behind them, all fights have costs and consequences. Only cowards determine never to fight, and only fools fight frequently or unnecessarily. The wise constantly seek to pour water on strife (not gasoline) and they only go to war with great hesitance. When the wise go to war, it is total war, a fight to the death, a battle to the end. Conflict has an energy all its own and once set in motion it cannot be reined in. Maturity chooses when and where to fight and stays at it until the job is done. And so must we approach our battles. We must choose them wisely and stay at them until the war is won.

17.15

God needs no blindfold to cover His eyes, for that protective measure is only for the abominable systems and humans predisposed to justify the wicked and condemn the just. Justice is most helpful when it sees right into the depths of men's hearts, not when it closes its eyes and relies only on its ears. The wise do not rush to judgment and they realize there is always more than can be physically seen or heard. Some things must be discerned in the spirit from the Spirit. Fools do not take the time to let the Spirit help them see.

17.16

Wisdom is not free and it is not gained until every installment is paid. We are not allowed to collect wisdom after one down payment. We must follow through with multiple costly deposits to the end. Wisdom like all great jewels is both beautiful and expensive. Fools think that what is priceless can be secured without commitment to a long struggle. Only those who long to be wise so badly that they're willing to go to war for it, taking casualties along the way, will gain it. Fools devalue wisdom by refusing the long struggle, while the wise realize the arduous pursuit of wisdom only increases its reward.

17.17

True love is consistent; it does not fluctuate with the vicissitudes of life. False love runs hot and cold and tends toward the emotional. True love is kind of boring, quiet, without drama, unfazed by triumph or disaster. False love makes loud demonstrations and frequent boasts. True love is silent, steady, and ever so present it often escapes notice. False love draws attention to the lover, while true love is often unseen, the veiled foundation which supports life and survival. The wise are not enamored with the dramatic and verbal love, for they know adversity will blow it away. The wise notice and revel in love that does not boast nor parade itself, for that love shows up and endures in wartime; it has never left, and it is all that stands when every pretense has been blown away.

17.18

Fools think they are saviors and overextend themselves to help the one, making them unable to help the many. The wise carry no messiah complex and trust God enough to let Him rescue His beloved. It is folly to think we care more for those we love than God does. It may seem like the right thing to ride to the rescue, but only God can continually do that in fullness. We of limited resources are asked to lay down our lives for the community, not for the individual, and we can only do this by giving a little bit of us to all, not by giving all of us to one. If we give all we have to the one, we become incapable of helping others. Wisdom trusts that God loves more than we do, and wisdom lets God be the Rescuer-in-chief. We contribute to God's rescue, but we do not take responsibility for it. That's vanity actually, not charity.

17.19

Loving arguments with your brothers and sisters, and loving winning those arguments leads eventually to your destruction. There is an energy and adrenaline that conflict sourced in being proved right provides—and it is evil fuel. We were created to fight for, not against. We were created to fight for the glory of God in all the earth among every people, not to fight against our own people. Those that love argument and strife among the body of Christ are motivated by demonic powers, even if unwittingly. If you continually lift your head and heart to prove how family members are wrong, you will eventually lose all three: head, heart, and family.

17.20

Actions eventually follow the tone of your words. What you joke about over time is what you become. If your humor is crooked, so will be your walk. If you continually jest through deceit, you will eventually believe your own twisted jokes and lose not only the ability to tell the truth, but also the ability to know what is false within you. A perverse mouth is self-blinding and self-destructive, for you no longer can discern what is truth; thus, you inevitably embrace what is wicked to your own harm. To joke frequently about evil is to play with fire, for it invites evil and deception into residence, and once the light that is in us is darkness, how great is that darkness.

17.21

Few joys compare to the father whose son is wise, and few agonies can match those of a father whose son is a fool. But we do not only beget natural children; we also make disciples. Those we shape and mold not only repeat and adopt our convictions; they also tend to acquire our character flaws—and magnify them. If we err a little, our spiritual sons will develop that error and expand it. If we allow a little sin into the camp, our spiritual progeny will allow a little bit more. Growing sons (physical and spiritual) requires the determination to have Jesus prune from us all that is foolish because a little bit of our folly goes a long way in our followers.

17.22

Health follows joy. Joy makes medicine even better. Joy takes what is naturally curative and adds supernatural boosters to it. The unwise confuse the order and think that to have joy they need to be healthy. It is the opposite: We need to have joy in order to be healthy. Joy gives light to the soul when the body decays. Joy does not have to be lost when physical strength declines, and joy gives spiritual additives to the body when physical strength increases. The joy of the Lord is our strength; our strength is not the joy of the Lord. When we joy, we become healthy, and we are not fully healthy unless we joy. That's why hospitals and wheelchairs cannot keep joy out—health is the weaker partner to joy.

17.23

Bribes are not only incentives to do evil; they can also be incentives to do good—good that the Spirit and others beside you determine. Justice is perverted when we abdicate the responsibility to determine what is right to us by becoming obligated to a wealthy benefactor. The wise will sometimes refuse generous financial support, for that very abundance can become a prison that leads you to abstain from some obedience or in the worst cases practice what you have not been commissioned to do from on high. Financial dependence may provide security, but sometimes that security is maximum, a prison of another human or organizational will. If we are wise, we will refuse the gifts which promise liberation but deliver a gilded cage.

17.24

The body of wisdom is accumulated from innumerable small observations. Wisdom is not a grand monolith; rather, it is a slow and steady composite. Fools search the earth for one truism or one guru in whom the grand total of intelligence is located. The wise find nuggets of wisdom every day—right before their eyes and in all kinds of people. Wisdom is not science; there is no grand theory that unites all truths together. Wisdom is not human; there is no grand personage that unites all the treasures of truth in time. Wisdom is divine; God uncreated and incarnate is truth and we need not travel land and sea to find Him. He is available daily anywhere and always to the one who has the understanding to seek.

17.25

Folly starts with grins and ends with grief. Folly's lie is twofold: that we can enjoy foolishness without repercussions and that those repercussions can be contained. But folly always bruises, and it bruises the ones who love the fool the most. Wisdom determines never to bruise the ones we love, never to cause bitterness to those who have given themselves for our sake. The height of selfishness is to repay those who have invested their best years in us by striking them with our folly when they are old and vulnerable. The reality that our folly will always damage the ones we love as much or more than it wounds us should be deterrent enough for the wise.

17.26

Strong leadership does not treat everyone the same. The easier (and inferior) way to lead is to punish a group for the infractions of a few. This may be simpler, but it is not smarter, for in the long term, when we punish the good along with the bad, we undercut morale and remove the incentive for goodness to flourish. An equal error is to undermine emerging leaders when their character has led them to make honest mistakes. Youthful leadership will occasionally entail the wrong decision from the right heart. In those cases, the wise elder will affirm the prince and quietly manage the consequences without causing or casting shame.

17.27

Verbosity does not prove intelligence. An economy of speech often marks the wise. The wise don't have to speak often or loudly to be heard. Elections and politics don't identify the wise leader; only the reaction of peers can truly do that. When a group assembles in a room, watch for the one who speaks sparingly and softly, yet when he or she speaks, the motion carries, and the point adopted. That one is the true leader, that one is the sage.

17.28

Lengthy speech tends to reveal our folly, not our wisdom. The more we talk, the more we err. Speech reveals what is in our hearts, and the Bible tells us that what is in our hearts is better not broadcast. The wise understand it is better for our idiocy not to be publicized. The only way to guarantee this modesty is by choosing silence. Fools forget that the more they talk, the more they demonstrate their inadequacy. There is a time to speak up, but there is a better chance of saying something wise if we have meditated (prayed) at length and then speak in brief.

PROVERBS

Chapter 18

18.1

Wisdom lays down personal desires and ambitions for the greater good. It is impossible to discover the greater good in isolation. To truly know what is best for others, we must live among them, share their sorrows, feel their pain, and cry their tears. In this sense, the incarnation is the height of wisdom, not just love. Because God became flesh, He did not restrict Himself to atonement theory, nor did He seek His own desire, but having known all our temptations and limitations, He was and is able to judge wisely. Wisdom walks among those for whom it decides, while folly makes decisions from afar.

18.2

We should not only listen more than we talk, but we should also read more than we write. There is nothing new under the sun, and there is much gold in the old. It takes some digging and mining to find what is both priceless and timeless. Fools despair of the effort it takes to re-discover the deep truths that are supra-cultural and would rather express what is in their own hearts, for it is always easier to talk or write (tweet, text, post, or blog) than listen or read. The more connected we are to information, the more careful we must be to cross-reference the data that appears new with the principles that have been proven diachronically. The wise are slow to express what is in their heart, for they know it is abundantly wicked and treacherous. Fools broadcast their stupidity unwittingly, and the wise are intentionally taciturn, for they know that deep within they bear folly, too.

18.3

A critical spirit is a wicked spirit. We twist what is wicked into a positive by convincing ourselves it is noble to be adept at seeing the wrong in other people. Criticism that does not cry veers into what is evil, for it is void of compassion and leads to contempt. Concern that weeps over the brokenness or lost beauty of the errant is legitimate, for it loves the wounded and seeks to lift them up and out, not cast down into a pit of irrecoverable shame. If dishonor brings reproach, then affirmation brings honor. The wise build up by honoring, which is righteous behavior. Fools tear down by attacking and mercilessly criticizing, which despite its intelligence and even accuracy is evil. To say true things without a merciful heart is wicked.

18.4

Wisdom is a waterfall that cascades from person to person. When we speak truth in love, it has a multi-generational life of blessing. The life we speak over others they will pass on. While it is true that hurting people hurt others, it is just as true that healed people heal others, blessed people bless others, loved people love others, and "mercied" people mercy others—if, that is, they have any sense of gratefulness. The way that thanks is best expressed to the giver is to pass on the gift received, which is the intention of our good God for all His benevolent gifts.

18.5

The wise do not let the wicked intimidate or cow them into any unjust decisions or decisions that counter what is right. There is admitted immediate terror in the threats of the wicked, but the wise realize that the benefits of compromise under pressure in the short term are disastrous and damning in the long haul. Fools cave into pressure and pay the long-term (sometimes eternal) price. The wise resist pressure—no matter how pressing, painful, or convincing—for they know that short-term pain is *always* better than long-term disaster and punishment. Folly chooses escape from immediate pain and suffers eternally. Wisdom chooses short-term pain and enjoys eternal pleasure.

18.6

Fights never start without the kindling of foolish or angry words. Many conflicts could have been avoided if one party involved remained silent. Wise silence is fundamentally different from appeasement or cowardice. Wise silence absorbs insult whenever it can swallow it without the innocent being harmed. When innocent ones are at risk, the wise always speak out and take action. When what is at jeopardy is reputation, comfort, or pride, the wise understand that long-term economy suggests the appropriate action is silence and absorption of scorn. Fools do not have the patience to see the long-term benefits of swallowing a little bit of pride for the greater good. Communal life is lost when fools refuse to lay down their personal feelings or conquer their raging emotions. When we lose our tempers, others lose their lives.

18.7

At the end of the day, fools always incriminate themselves. Scripture warns that every idle word will be accounted for or judged. This certainty strikes terror into my soul, for I know how many foolish things I have said. I already stand guilty with the overwhelming evidence against me with no additional aid needed from my enemies or accusers. My own mouth bears witness against the wickedness of my soul. May God have mercy on us all. My past nonsense (words of arrogance, strife, impurity, and folly), I must place under the blood of Jesus. If I am wise, my future sense must be words regulated; otherwise, I will merely inexcusably snare myself.

18.8

False words are seductive. Our fallen natures have become wired for invigoration by what we should not hear. It often requires discipline to steadily hear what will lead us to life, while no effort is necessary to listen to what will damage our souls and others. There is something deep within our flesh attracted to gossip, slander, lewdness, criticism, and junk. It is indeed deep evil calling to deep evil, and it is soft on the ear. The wise take pains to listen to what will bless them and others. Ears that lead to good are muscular, attentive by intent and through effort.

18.9

Laziness loses not just the past, but the future. When we are slothful, the easily apparent destruction is the erosion of what others labored to build before us. We prove our folly when we allow to atrophy the beautiful things created at great cost to others. The less apparent but just as destructive is the future loss. When by our laziness we do not prepare beautiful things for future generations, we have destroyed what could have been, for laziness aborts life as well as euthanizes it.

18.10

Our protection is not in place, position, or power, but in the character of God. The reason the righteous remain safe is because they don't deviate from the nature of God as He reveals Himself in the holy Scriptures. Those steadfastly committed to the sovereign goodness of God in all He does and all He allows are immovable. Death does not scare them; poverty does not trouble them; abuse and pain does not shake them; and sickness does not discourage them. Our emotional strength is based on our spiritual understanding of God's character being an immovable fortress—fixed, sure, good, wise, strong, steady, and timeless. The wise settle the character of God theologically (not emotionally or experientially) and in doing so shelter in a tower immune to the deceitful attacks of the devil.

18.11

If the wise shelter in the character of God, fools shelter in the currency of their own resources. The problem with trusting a purely physical commodity is that it can rust or be stolen or destroyed. Wealth is a double deception in that it tragically leads us to believe that we don't need God (for we can buy healthcare, rest, escape, protection) and that we will always have access to resources. This latter deception is prey to temporal misfortune and eternal judgment. In a moment we can lose family, property, assets, or our very life as many a rich and powerful person in history has. A moment is all that stands between our resources for defense and utter naked helplessness before either the forces of evil or the great force of the Godhead. Only fools live one moment away from disaster.

18.12

Humility is destruction insurance. Destruction should not be defined by physical calamity but by the decay of soul. Destruction is not essentially poverty, sickness, prison, or death; destruction is primarily a damaged soul. In this sense, if we remain poor in spirit and lowly before God, we can never be destroyed. In this sense, if we are arrogant, we are soul dying, and it is only a matter of time before we are consumed. We might still walk the earth wealthy, powered, and admired, but we are the walking dead. The eternal soul is the humble soul, and the soul that will be honored through time is the one wise enough to daily bow before King Jesus. That soul will be eternally among the walking alive.

18.13

There is always another side to the story. The other side may be wrong or both sides may be wrong, but when more than one person is involved, there is always another side to the story. In dealing with humans, it is wise to remember that good friends can have diametrically opposed opinions and that godly people can fundamentally disagree. If we make judgments before we have heard both parties out, we are sure to make a decision that causes shame to all. Wisdom has the patience to hear both parties out, even if the other is younger, more prone to folly, or even an enemy. If it's true that stories always have two perspectives when men disagree with men, how much more so when men disagree with God. After hearing the complaint of men, the wise always go to God to listen to His side of the story and always remember that God alone is truth, never exaggerating, never confused, always aware of all sides and all eternal implications.

18.14

In the holism of our beings, spirit trumps flesh. Certainly, God created the body, a temple intended to glorify Him, but biblically, spirit is always more important and stronger and always prioritized over the physical body. The loss of a physical part of our body cannot compare to the physical loss of a part of our soul. A handicap physically is of far less consequence than a disability spiritually. Humanity glorifies the body and demeans the soul, while God magnifies both but does not equate them. We can have a broken body and a soaring spirit; we cannot have a broken spirit and soar physically. The body matters and physical exercise is of some benefit, but what we really need to guard and tend is our soul, for from it flows the wellsprings of life.

18.15

Lifelong learning is the mark of the wise. True wisdom is signified by enduring curiosity and an awareness of how much we don't know rather than a fixation on what we do know. Fools revel in how much they know about a topic; the wise wonder at how much they don't. Satisfaction with a certain depth of knowledge means learning is lost, while hunger for a deeper understanding of what we know in part typifies the wise. It is not always wisdom to know all things superficially; that, too, can be a cloaked folly. It is wise to be insatiable for more understanding about what we do know as there can be a certain hubris when we are satisfied with what we do understand about someone or something. There is an attractive, appealing prudence about those who are always hungry to understand more. Jesus loves it when we are dissatisfied with what we know of Him—He ever welcomes the familiar seeker.

18.16

Posturing for attention is a terribly inefficient way to be useful. In fact, when we desire to be noticed more than we desire to be effective, we will be seen less and less over time. When we desire to be useful more than we desire to be recognized, the greater good is accomplished, for those who want praise tend to divert energy from service to self-serving activities that don't bless the unseen. There is a delightful irony in this principle: Those who want to be seen will be ignored because their vanity removes them from blessing the community, while those who bless the community draw the attention they don't crave or need. At the end of the day, attention is revealed as an illusory imposter. Those that want it don't get it, and those that get it don't want it. You can tell if your heart is foolish or wise by whether you want attention or not.

18.17

No human arrives at, expounds on, or disseminates truth faithfully without accountability and a corporate hermeneutic. As surely as all truth is God's truth, humans need others in order to understand His truth without personal error. God saw fit to present His Son to us through four gospels, each one helping to interpret the other. God ordained that forty inspired voices would reveal His character to us—thankfully, we have more than just the book of Ezekiel! God sees fit to have different cultures help one another understand the Bible. God uses others to help us see our blind spots, to correct our self-deception, and to hold us accountable to facts. The wise have more than one mentor and more than one cultural coach, for all humans are fallible and limited. Fools can be the super intelligent who are bounded and bound by a singular perspective.

18.18

No human is completely impartial, and no human system of justice is completely mechanical. As a result, both human error and human compassion will always intermingle when conflicts of interest arise. The only way to be completely fair is to be completely dispassionate. Relational removal in decisions has the advantage of being completely fair and the disadvantage of being inhumane. Sometimes fairness or justice must be sacrificed for intimacy when people are involved. Casting lots can solve thorny issues by its dispassion, but it's a secondary solution, for it cannot bring conflicted parties together. If we want relational solutions (and we should), we must be prepared to live with the inequities of human dynamics. Mechanical decisions can keep the strong from killing one another, but only relational decisions can help them interact in intimate love.

18.19

It is easier to keep unity (even at great cost) than it is to regain it once lost. Betrayal is the most common way we lose unity with one another, and hell hath no fury like a relationship scorned. It does indeed take incredible effort to overlook hurts, and the emotion of that moment propels us to break fellowship. If we can remain cognizant of how difficult it is to renew intimate trust, we are much slower to forsake or undermine it. All men and women are wired to betray; we all have a little Judas in us. The wise recognize it and battle it from within. All men and women are created to host the Spirit of counsel who is ever true. The wise welcome Him and ask Him to help them stay true. Only fools forsake unity for small difficulties, and only fools forget how hard unity is to build and how nigh impossible it is to rebuild.

18.20

Wise speech self-nourishes. When we curb silly, pompous, or critical words, we feed our own souls. The less we speak cavalierly, the stronger we become. Wise words are like nutritious foods, a steady use of a modest amount gives life. Too much of any good ingestion causes harm; too many words, even if they are intelligent and articulate, destroy the soul. Moderated words not only bless the hearer, but they also bring good to the speaker. We self-care wisely when we speak sparingly and kindly. Speaking too much leads to a hungry soul, a famine of health, and an abundance of folly. Sowing life through gracious words to others is to reap life in our own lives and souls.

18.21

Sticks and stones will never hurt us, but words will break our bones. Obviously, physical pain is real and should not be sought out or misjudged, but emotional and spiritual pain lasts much longer and is more damaging than physical affliction. In fact, words can do much worse than break bones: They can take life, they can murder. Fools don't realize the power of their own words and wound everyone around them without awareness. Wise leaders are increasingly circumspect with their speech, for they know that those they influence will take what is said in moderation and stretch it to abundance. Wise leaders know that affirmation can spark resurrection, that encouragement can penetrate dark despair, and that blessing can renew vanishing hope. The wise intentionally and carefully use words to bring life.

18.22

There are few ways God expresses His favor and His mercy more than in the spouse He grants us. If we submitted the choice of our lifelong best friend to Him (and not rushed or forced our own will), then God will grace us with the person He specially prepared to bring us to the greatest joy. A good spouse is not a perfect spouse, but even those imperfections will be used by a perfect God to bring us good. Those that choose a spouse outside of the Lord's selection will get the exact spouse they deserve—and it won't be pretty. I believe that Isaac and Rebecca had it right— one man and one woman for life. I believe God's sovereignty in mate selection means He knows the one person in all the world in all of time that is His best good for us. Wait for that spouse and life will be good. Panic and chose other than who God has prepared to "good" you, and life will be badly long.

18.23

As we age, most of us (if we've lived wisely) have more resources than when we were young: a little more wisdom, a little more money, and a little more influence. In worldly advance, though, the accumulation of resources tends to make the possessor gruffer, more austere, guarded, cynical, or just meaner. Godly accruement makes us kinder. The wise stay poor in spirit even as they become rich in life. When we stay poor in spirit, we stay like the God of all—the God who is rich, powerful, and wise beyond understanding, yet full of mercy, gentle, gracious, and patience. If our resources make us rough, it's an indicator that they have taken us from the God who is kind and are leading us to sorrow. If our resources make us meek and lowly, humble and sweet, then we can be encouraged that they are leading us towards Jesus.

18.24

A person must be loved before he or she becomes loveable. And we must love before we demand to be loved. When we love others, we not only see the miracle of God's image in them blossom, we not only give them the confidence to shine because we see in them what life's pain has hidden from them, but we also begin to shine ourselves. We become more beautiful the more we love. We become more friend-worthy the more we befriend. True friendship is spiritual friendship, and spiritual friendship is based on a common commitment to the glory of God in the friendship. A high view of God protects and grows friendship into the highest form. Those that are most similar and most mutually devoted to awe of God will be the closest friends—closer than blood relatives. Our spiritual family will outlast our physical family, so how doubly sweet it is when our spiritual family and physical family overlap.

PROVERBS

Chapter 19

19.1

Wise poverty is better than rich crudity. It is an unfortunate law of the world that wealth primarily promotes wickedness. When the wealthy use their means for the furtherance of the gospel among every people, it is to be lauded both for its sagacity and its rarity. Most wealth is used for indulgence and indecency. Wealth tends to give man idle hours, and idle man tends to be idiotic man, finding laughter in the decadent and degrading. A quick traverse of a wealthy nation's entertainment reveals that money leads us to make fools of ourselves and be proud of it. Wisdom seeks then to be pure, fighting against the natural tendency of wealth to pervert.

19.2

Haste increases the likelihood of sin. For both anxiety and doubt, the solution is to wait in prayer for Jesus to come. Jesus can open doors that we haven't even thought of. Jesus can give peace where the enemy sows anxiety. Jesus can assure doubts and confirm thinking if we will but wait for Him. In the waiting, Jesus can also correct thinking if it's errant, amend or tweak it if needed, or simply remove that passion and replace it with His zeal and energy in a different direction. There is much to do, and night cometh when no man can work (John 9:4). We cannot let this reality rush us into an equal and opposite error of launching out without the blessing of God. Waiting is a gift. It protects, calms, and assures.

19.3

It is foolish to doubt God. The wisdom of man takes pride in being intelligent enough to question everything. Higher wisdom understands that taking Most High at His word is the most intelligent and pain-saving course of study. Intellectual deception follows moral rejection, and the first lie whispered is "God is not good." If we believe that lie, the door opens to all kinds of evil and pain, evil that we twist into good because we twist a good God into bad. It's foolish to doubt what the Bible says about God and man. It may seem enlightened, for example, to think you are better than God, that a God who created hell is bad, and thus your God would never send anyone to eternal hell. It's not enlightened—it's madness, it's idolatry (you reduced God to what you want Him to be), it's blasphemy, and it's folly. This folly is based on the twin foolish premises that God is not good and that we are "gooder" than God. True wisdom trusts God. True wisdom knows that God could not be good if there was no eternal, painful hell.

19.4

Money makes you lonely. When you have a lot of money, you have many false friends. When you have little money, you have few true friends. But either way, a fixation on money makes you lonely. The wise understand that friendship cannot be bought and should not be sold. The wise figure out how to have intimate relationships outside of toys, vacations, homes, possessions, or technology—not without these things, but independent of them. True friendship transcends economy and physicality. True friendship is spiritual and emotional, for these foundations can transcend all trouble and time.

19.5

Lies eventually hurt the teller. In the short term, deceit protects the liar and harms the one being addressed, but this pain is momentary. If unjustly wounded, you will be vindicated. In the long term, the liar wounds himself. First, he loses his integrity, then he loses his conscience, then he loses his reputation, then he loses his friends, then he loses his soul, then he loses his mind, then he loses his dignity. To the one slandered, the cost of lying is significant but temporary; but the cost of lying to the liar is dreadful and eternal. The terrifying costs of lying should drive us to the truth. Truth-telling preserves your soul and blesses others. Lying blasts others and destroys your soul.

19.6

Don't let a person's giving capacity fool you, for generosity's motive is the real test of authenticity. There are many who give (time, attention, flattery, or finances) for their own ends or glory. True generosity is defined by pleasure in the glorification of God. If we give that God be elevated, praised, and made much of, then we have been truly generous. If we give to gain glory, power, or advantage for ourselves, then we have not actually been generous. The wise give to make God great, and fools spend lavishly on their own name. Generosity is not the goal if it is divorced from God's glory. Our goal must ever be to lift up Jesus, and only when we lavishly, extravagantly spend for and on Him are we truly generous.

19.7

Giving, not receiving, is the currency of brotherhood. As a father leaving my university age sons behind in America as my wife and I returned to the Arab world, I asked for two things when they wondered what they could do for us. I asked them to love Jesus and to take care of one another. Few things delight the heart of a father as much as when his children sacrificially take care of one another. The world will truly see we are like Christ by the way we love one another. Giving, not receiving, is the currency of partnership and Christian brotherhood. To approach partnership (union of any kind) from the perspective of what we can receive by joining is a spirit foreign to Christ. Jesus approaches brotherhood, partnership, union, team, the church, and the world from the perspective of what He can give. We give because our Father is a giver, and He wants us to look like Him.

19.8

A pure heart is the best protection from folly. Wisdom starts in the soul, not in the brain. Some of the most intelligent persons in history were fools; their abilities betrayed them because they were not wise in their hearts. A wise heart knows it is limited, and a foolish heart thinks it is self-sufficient. A wise heart fears (is in awe of, trembles in joy before) the Lord. A foolish heart questions God, indirectly thinking God is suspect, putting God on trial as if humans have the capacity to judge His actions or motives. If our hearts are simple, if we acknowledge that we do not know, if we dare not doubt but resolve to trust and honor Jesus, He grants understanding and that understanding preserves us from evil and error. Oh, how foolish is the heart that says, "I know!" Wisdom begins by knowing we do not know, by knowing the One who knows.

19.9

Lies kill in all directions, including the source of the lie. Truth heals and brings life in all directions, including to the source of the truth. Soul healers are those who disburse truth. Soul killers are those who disseminate half-truths or outright lies. When we lie to ourselves, we assault our own health. When we speak truth to ourselves, we swallow good medicine. To do what is wrong, while we are in the flesh, is always easier than to do what is right. One day that will be reversed, and in the new Eden we will only long to do what is life-giving. For now, we must fight against the pull of the easy way of deception and contend for the high ground of truth. It is challenging to speak truth to anyone; it is only the ruthless who speak truth to themselves.

19.10

Outside benefits should match internal character. If we have resources beyond our integrity, if we have charisma without character, we decay from the inside and destroy those outside us. Power in all its form (most simply in wealth, but also in personality) is poisonous if it is not tempered by lowliness. When we give (or are given) power before we know how to wield it, we inevitably scorch our own souls and our surroundings. Wisdom is kind enough to defer benefits until the recipient has the capacity of character to handle the gift. Gifts that wound the receiver or those around them are foolish unkindness. Let us thank the Lord that He withholds from us the good that would destroy us and others. Let us be good enough to be prudent in how we promote others. Let us not lift them up to their own demise.

19.11

The forgiving ones are the true nobility. I remember a simple Sudanese elder explaining international diplomacy to me saying: "It is the responsibility of the greater nation to absorb the offenses of the lesser. Because America has great power, she must hold that power in restraint, unthreatened by the petulance of smaller, weaker nations. Just like an adult does not lash out at a child who attacks them, so the greater forgives the insults and injury done to them by the smaller." Wise glory does not need to defend itself nor seek revenge. Vainglory fights for honor and prestige, and in doing so loses both.

19.12

It is the responsibility of the follower to stay on the right side of leadership. Our ego wants our leader to pursue us, speak our language, keep us informed, and consider our opinion. If we are brutally honest, we want our leader to serve us, for most of us like servants much more than we do masters. In our self-centered view leaders exist to serve us. We hear them talk of servant leadership and misconstrue it to mean that they obey us. We would never put it that crassly. We couch it in terms of service, but deep within we are all bossy and we all want our way. Wise followers are lowly enough (bowing from the inside) to learn to communicate in the style the leader prefers, keep him or her informed, pursue them, consider their opinion, and serve their agenda. Leaders can open doors and close them, so it behooves all followers to study their leaders and make the effort to earn their trust.

19.13

Those close to you can nibble you to death, and vice versa. We can wear down our intimates by our constant fleshly interaction with them. Folly usually isn't stupid. Folly is often informed and articulates dissent too frequently or injudiciously and from the wrong spirit. Sons, spouses, or servants that annoy in small doses over time eventually wear down those around them with unfortunate consequences for all. The fool in the moment of reckoning is surprised and wounded, for they have been blind to the thousand little frustrations they caused those in proximity. Since all have fallen short, all have disappointed and frustrated someone. The wise are self-aware enough to recognize their slip and secure enough to step away and give their loved one (or leader) some space to recover. Too much of anything draining in a row, even if the things are small, can remove any desire for your leader or loved one to help you.

19.14

God bequeaths the best inheritance. It is often given early in life so that it may be enjoyed in elongated fashion. It's not monetary; in fact, it's worth more than money and gets more valuable with every passing year. The bequest is a prudent spouse. Prudence knows you and knows how to balance you. Prudence knows when to encourage and when to exhort, when to smile and when to be silent. Prudence knows when to hold and when to withdraw. Prudence knows us better than we know ourselves. God in His wisdom has determined what is best for us, and for some who are single, divine kindness drapes prudence in garbs other than marriage. The wise, whatever their marital status, seek out the prudent and stick close to them.

19.15

The consequences of laziness hurt the lazy first and most. To not exercise is to act against our own body. To not obey is to act against our own soul. To not learn is to act against our own future. To not bless is to act against our own forgiveness. To not expend ourselves is to act against our own resilience. To not help others is to act against our own rescue. By not doing anything we do so much harm, first to ourselves and then to those around us. It is always the hardest working that have the most time, energy, joy, and satisfaction. It is the lazy who are grumpy, harried, dour, and ever wanting more. The wise realize it is far too much work to be lazy. Fools, by not working, assure they never will have rest.

19.16

Obedience is the opposite of recklessness in regards to the nurture of the soul and body. Those who are fastidious to obey escape the damage that the careless incur. This is true physically and spiritually, and just like in gambling, the house rules always win. If you exercise, you get stronger. Obedience is spiritual exercise, and those who take pains to obey become spiritually stronger. Those who are reckless (careless or selectively obedient) expose themselves to the temptations and terrors of life—and always lose. In some areas physical and spiritual disciplines converge. Fasting, for example, can make one both spiritually and physically stronger. The wise look to carefully obey, and the wisest seek out the obedience that benefits both body and soul.

19.17

We are all in debt to God. But few are they (and blessed are they) to whom God is in debt, for He repays with an interest rate that far exceeds the original gift. The wise understand that generosity to the poor is a loan (not a sunk cost) that God observes with relish and repays with extravagance. The wise then continually open their heart to the needy, even when it is inconvenient. The wisest realize that God's repayment is not limited to goods in kind, or even goods in better, greater kind. God's repayment includes a transformation of character. When we give, we act like God (who is the Giver incomparable), and if we act like Him long enough, we become like Him. Because God delights in what is good (why He primarily delights in Himself), He delights in those who are like Him, and the surge of His good pleasure can be felt in their souls. You see, when we give to the poor, God repays us with His pleasure, which is worth so much more than a mere return on our money.

19.18

To not discipline is to destroy. How foolish the generation of parents who refuse to inflict pain on their children. Discipline is not cruel, not wicked, and not life-taking. Quite the opposite. Discipline is kind, righteous, and life-making. There is no discipline without pain, and pain is not an evil to be avoided at any cost, for the greatest good in life awaits on the other side of pain. Laying aside the folly of unnecessary pain and the perversity of abuse, the wise prudently hurt the ones they love in the short term that they might fully heal them forever. Lessons from pain are restricted to a formative season when spirits are supple. If the lessons are not learned early, then, later in life when we are rigid, pain will only blind, it will not bless. The most loving act of a parent or leader is the willingness to discipline by inflicting necessary pain for necessary growth. To avoid causing this difficulty when it can bless is to ensure the difficulty when it will only destroy.

19.19

Anger unrestrained builds a prison. It is a mistake to cater to an angry person through placation, for you only help the wrathful build their own cage. Unrestrained anger will eventually bind the uncontrolled in an emotional and relational prison, isolated from care, love, and healthy relationships. If we remove the consequences of lost tempers from the wrathful one, we do them no favors. The wise confront the wrathful, refusing to let them destroy themselves while they injure those in proximity. Impunity from the consequences of ire lead to imprisonment in isolation and ignominy. Anger in itself is not evil, for God Himself gets angry. But anger unchanneled and fueled by sin cannot be excused, covered, or rescued; it must be confronted and opposed.

19.20

Learning is a long-term investment that gives a higher yield the longer you live. There are always immediate personal benefits to learning, such as dangers escaped and advantages reaped, but the greatest return on listening to counsel and accepting correction will be down the road when our choices affect others. Real listening changes our character and habits, for real heeding of correction means we alter our behavior, ceasing to do what is foolish and taking up what is wise. If we do this repeatedly, it becomes reflexive, intuitive, and instinctive. As we age, we will more naturally make the right choices and those choices will open floodgates of blessing for others. When we come to the season of our greatest influence and authority, if we instinctively do good (in the manifold times when we will not have time to be reflective), the benefit will cascade and spread. What we learn and live out today will serve many tomorrow.

19.21

God always gets His way over man's ideas. In our hubris we think we know better than God, so we either make plans and then ask for His endorsement *or* we stand in judgment of what He is doing as if He should have asked us to endorse His plans. Folly judges only by results in Machiavellian crudity, but things going right doesn't necessarily mean they were right, and things going wrong doesn't necessarily mean we were wrong. Let us remember we are prophets, priests, and proclaimers, not pragmatists. We do not stand at the foot of the cross shaking our heads saying, "Well, that didn't work!" We gaze up in wonder at the crucified Son saying, "Behold the Lamb of God who takes away the sins of the world" (John 1:29). God's plans are always right, even if they include crucifixion, which they always do.

19.22

The merciful poor are far better citizens than the lying rich. A Pakistani businessman once told me that to register his daughter in a Riyadh school, he had to falsely check a box. He confessed, "Having no one to help me, I lost my moral compass." Lying may grant temporary, physical advance, but it also hastens spiritual decline. It is long-term folly to lie in order to preserve self or opportunity. It is wisdom to make the difficult choices that will cost you financially and practically, for you are in effect showing mercy to your future self. How poor are they who do not have the Holy Spirit within to counsel and empower in times of temptation. How wise are they who listen to the still small voice when the loud shouts of temptation assail.

19.23

Reverence for God keeps your soul free, satisfied, and defended from evil. Man has ever been prone to equal and opposite errors when approaching the Almighty. One error is to avoid intimacy and the other is to disdain honor. Most of us today flippantly accept intimacy with our transcendent God showing only a modicum of respect for His majesty. We have the Father aspect settled, but we have forgotten He is also an awesome, fearsome King. We forget that His being good does not mean He is safe. Unfortunately, a purely casual, comfortable approach to God opens us up to evil. If we have no fear of God's wrath towards our sin, we imperceptibly slide towards less fear of compromise and disobedience and displeasing Him. The wise both run to the Father's embrace and fall at the King's feet trembling. Fools only embrace Him; fools forget to tremble.

19.24

Laziness is slow suicide and quick murder. The lowest form of laziness, the form most repellant to an ever-working God, is the form that doesn't have to work and chooses not to work. To have to work (else you starve) but have no work is despair—another tragedy but not to be confused with laziness. Laziness is when you have the capacity to feed yourself and others, but you are so inconsiderate you do not pass blessings on, nor really benefit from them yourself. The spiritual equivalent are the Pharisees who neither enter in themselves *and* lock others out—in both cases food is wasted. The spiritually lazy do not share what they know of God with others. The physically lazy do not share what they have in kind with others. These kinds of selfishness are abhorrent to the God who epitomizes selflessness; thus, laziness should never be found in anyone who bears His name.

19.25

The wiser you are, the gentler your correction can be. In fact, you can learn from the woes and wounds of others. The wise are corrected by proxy, for they take note of others' errors and punishments and amend their ways before the blows descend on them. It doesn't take much intelligence to learn to keep your head down if the soldier next to you lifts his head up and loses it to sniper fire. Never waste other people's pain. Ever learn from the misfortunes of others. When you see tragic consequences, determine that you will not make the choices which lead to those disastrous outcomes. Conversely, learn just as attentively from those who succeed because their choices were wise. It is no crime to piggyback on the lessons of the wise. Only fools insist on only learning experientially; the wise learn much by observation.

19.26

Those raised in the West would be wise to learn from those in the East, those who know full well that to dishonor your parents is to dishonor yourself. This principle, of course, is biblical before it is Eastern, but it's just that a growing informality with all authority in the West has set us adrift from our respectful biblical moorings. We claim it's the inside that matters (so we can wear shorts and a backwards ballcap and drink coffee in the house of God), forgetting that our bodies and souls are so closely connected that they catch each other's diseases and dignities. Inward posture should always be reflected in some outward synchronism. When we do not respect our forebears (including some traditions, values, and perspectives), we set ourselves up for disaster and destruction. We can be innovative and creative without jettisoning all that is good from those who have learned painful lessons on the harsh paths of life before us.

19.27

Ever listen, ever secure. We cannot stop learning, for to stop learning is to immediately begin to drift towards the shoals of hubris. The older we become, the more intentional we must be on fighting for the lowliness of a teachable spirit. The greatest hinderance to knowing more is knowing some. We so easily become satisfied with what we know, limping along on one good leg of experience, never sprinting on two robust legs of ever thirsty seeking. Fools are content to limp, the wise ever dream of running. If we keep learning, we keep exercising our spirits to stay humble, and it is the humble that are secure from the pitfalls of the pride of life.

19.28

Injustice is demonic. Christians in the West often ask why more demonic activity is seen abroad. Even if sincere, the question is laughable. Is there anything more demonic than the filth pumped into our homes, hearts, and heads through over-available electronic media? Is there anything more demonic than the twisted science and perverted morality taught in our schools? Is there anything more demonic than greed uncontained, violence glorified, prejudice justified, and persons objectified? Is there anything more demonic than crudity proliferated and given awards and acclaim? Wisdom is the forensic dusting that recognizes the devil's fingerprints on all the simple utensils at home. Fools can only see it in dramatic demonstrations abroad. The devil doesn't have to bind us dramatically if he can drug us sweetly.

19.29

Scoffing sarcasm is stupid and self-destroying. It may seem intelligent to have the ability to make fun of others, but that's not intelligence—it's just dressed-up cruelty. The laws of God dictate that pain causers are pain receivers. This is true for the good as well as for the bad. It hurt the Father immeasurably to strike the Son. Parents who enjoy disciplining their children are vile representations of the heavenly Father, for any infliction of pain should pain us. This is the inbuilt safety mechanism God installed to help keep humans from destroying one another. It is only right to cause pain if we know that the pain will bring life (like kind surgeons). Humor is not wrong but killing is. If we use humor to hurt others, we murder their spirits, and it will injure ours in the end. By all means let us use humor but let us wield it to bring life.

PROVERBS
Chapter 20

20.1

Alcohol in the Bible is not sinful in itself. After all, Jesus brewed some. But at the same time, it is not suggested for kings, and pastors are urged to use it in moderation as medicine. Medicine is a two-edged sword. The wise tend to make a wide berth around what the Bible says can destroy them. I'm from a tribe of gospel ministers that have agreed not to drink alcohol, yet we do so without judging those who differ, for we tend to self-medicate with caffeine. We who love our coffee and tea have sympathetic understanding with those who love their wine—yet we all must tread carefully. If we are addicted to anything or anyone other than Jesus, we are foolishly entertaining a mocker, a brawler who will lead us astray.

20.2

Wisdom respects the reach of those in authority and does not needlessly provoke those who rule. There is something in every human that resents authority and desires to test a boundary. The line in this regard is dangerously thin between courage and folly. Foolish behavior calls caution cowardice or cowardice caution, ever toggling back and forth on the wrong side of description. It is just as foolish to be cautious when we should be courageous and courageous when we should be cautious. There are times to provoke the authority, but the wise realize there will be consequences to every provocation—sometimes life and sometimes death, but always consequential. This sober reality doesn't mean we never provoke. It just means we realize we only have so much life to spend, so if it's to be spent, let it be done judiciously.

20.3

The better, bigger man swallows insults and loss in order to end strife. The story is told of some ruffians who attempted to provoke a man on a bus in Detroit some years ago. The passenger refused to take the bait and fight, looking calmly at the youth who wished him harm. The bus approached a stop and the passenger rose. The thugs were suddenly alarmed at his size and stature as he was much bigger than they realized; they had been standing while he had been seated. Without a word he handed them his business card, nodded, and stepped calmly off the bus. Curious, the young would-be fist fighters looked down at the card which read: "Joe Louis. Boxer." Louis was perhaps the best boxer of all time, wise enough to know that any fool can start a quarrel (or end it). Wise men only quarrel when there is no other way to peace.

20.4

There is never a good time for sustained hard work. We are sometimes graced with an environment where everything aligns and work is as play, but this is not normal. The wise understand that most work in most people's lives requires a dedication and commitment that does not demand pleasantry in order to function. The foolish idealistically want to work with only those they like, only in situations to their liking, only on terms of their choosing—and they end up hungry and with nothing. The wise work in all weather, with all people, in all circumstances, tolerating what is unpleasant and uncomfortable, for the joy of harvest. Harvest comes to those who work, motivated internally and eternally, even when they don't want to. Hunger and shame come to those ever waiting for the ideal working environment.

20.5

There is some measure of wisdom in every person, and the understanding one seeks to mine it. All people have the capacity to teach us, some by their folly and others by their wisdom. The most beautiful of the aged are those that can learn from the young. The most winsome of missionaries are those who can learn from the ones they evangelize. The most noble of parents are those who can learn from their children. The most gracious of leaders are they who learn from their flock. Folly is sometimes evidenced by the intelligent and powerful who think they have nothing to learn from those with less education, money, experience, or natural gifting. Wisdom is often demonstrated when the great sit in genuine, thankful humility at the feet of the small.

20.6

The more you boast, the less faithful you tend to be. Talking about our past exploits tends to shift our focus on current or future challenges and we slide into the contentment of living off past glories. Talking about our future exploits can gain us credit and admiration without cost, and soon our flesh realizes that we can be honored without having to do the hard work. Wise men, therefore, talk little or not at all about what they did in the past or will do in the future; they just strap on their work boots and silently press forward. Foolish men talk too much and work too little. Talking is the enemy of working. Boasting is the opposite of faithfulness.

20.7

The unpopular moral act is an investment in your spiritual and physical children. Leaders who defer the hard choices and changes for those who follow them are cowardly. If we are more concerned about our legacy than about a healthy launch of the next generation, then we are foolish. The wise incur pain, misunderstanding, and unpopularity to self in the short term for the initial success and enduring vitality of the next physical and spiritual generation. In the long term the wisdom of those sacrificial choices will be venerated. Wise men love those who come after them long enough to absorb short-term pain in order to avoid long-term problems. Fools embrace their own short-term pain and shove the problems of debt, decay, or difficulty onto those who remain when the selfish hedonist moves on.

20.8

You don't have to speak to be heard. Wisdom sets a climate conducive to wisdom and antagonistic to folly. The wise create an atmosphere that pre-empts nonsense, without fanfare. By posture and demeanor, we can communicate pleasure and displeasure, and when others act in ungodly ways, it is wise to squelch that folly non-verbally first, and verbally as necessary. A wise, righteous father can communicate and accomplish with a mere eyebrow lift what a foolish father cannot accomplish through tirade and fisticuffs. The wise will read the non-verbal signals of the righteous and be corrected or comforted. Fools run past those cautious warnings and expose their folly, having to be verbally rebuked. When a leader shapes a group in godly character, much deviance can be averted by the group culture, much nonsense can be aborted when the atmosphere and expectation is holy.

20.9

No one is self-purified. We all need another one to cleanse us. No one is self-perfected. We all need others to refine us. No one is self-sanctified. We all need the Spirit to preserve us. The wiser you are, the more you realize how sinful you are; the closer you draw to Jesus, the further away you realize you are. The more you press in to know Christ, the more you realize how quickly you tend to wander. It is foolish to be presumptuous about your spiritual condition; presumption is not to be confused with assurance. Wisdom understands that assurance is married to deliberate seeking, holding on to the One who holds on to us. Wisdom has no illusions of goodness or grandeur, but falls daily at the feet of Jesus crying, "Lord Jesus Christ, Son of God, have mercy on me, a sinner."

20.10

God hates cheats and liars. The people of God are to be the people of truth and light, not clever manipulators of facts. To be wise is to determine to live a transparent life that has no duplicity in it. Fools love the games of trickery, misdirection, intrigue, and deceit. Fools become wise in deception, but in the end fool only themselves. There is no place for deception among the wise people of God, and there should be no tolerance for anything that is not true. This is especially true for missionaries who work among people groups and ideologies that allow or laud deception. We cannot communicate faithfully about the way, truth, and life if we have any tendencies or behaviors (including in our identity and nomenclature) that are misleading. It is better to be simple and transparent, navigating the difficulties, than to be cleverly misdirecting and introducing complex half-lies. And always, at the end of the day, our friends and our enemies respect us more if we have nothing to hide, if we have never misled them.

20.11

Our identity comes from what we do, not what we claim. In this sense a label is immaterial, as what truly defines us are our actions, not our words. If this is true for the young who are less guarded about their image, how much truer for the old who take great pains to present themselves as better than we are. Humility is a sober sense of reality about both God and ourselves and a refusal to be lauded for what we are not. Folly insists on our self-description being the measure of our worth, while wisdom knows that we are only worthy if our actions match—even exceed—our rhetoric. Today, some are ashamed of the name "Christian" and use other titles. This is shortsighted, for the problem is not in the name, but in the behavior. Whatever title is taken to avoid offense must soon be discarded as our behavior will likewise spoil the new moniker. Then energy must be spent in reformed action; otherwise, we will need to coin new terms for ourselves in dizzying rapidity.

20.12

We are created to observe before we speak, to listen before we lecture. God indeed made eyes and ears, but in the natural progression of life a child listens for two to three years before speaking coherently. So should it be in our spiritual development. We should listen long before we speak and learn long before we teach. Wisdom has the patience to embrace silence, that we might hear and weigh the words of others. Because all humans carry some folly, wisdom takes the time to hear many counselors. Missionaries who listened to a local cultural coach are wiser. Missionaries who listen to a multitude of cultural coaches, sifting, synthesizing, praying, and reflecting are wisest. A cultural coach is not omniscient because they are local; all men are partially blind. No pastor and no person should only listen to one man, nor primarily listen to one mentor. Wisdom listens to many voices and then takes that chorus to the one true Word for aid in discerning what counsel will stand. Only then does the wise man speak.

20.13

Good things loved to excess destroy. Hard things loved in perspective dignify. Sleep is a good thing, and we have the example of the God-man taking a nap. We also have His repeated example of rising early to pray. Truth be told, we have more ink about His prayer than His sleeping. We can infer that both sleep and rising early are good, but much prayer is better than much sleep. Sleep is about pace and prayer is about power. We are to love prayer; we are not to love sleep. Ashamed, I am the fool who loves my sleep more than I love my prayer. Night is coming when no man can work (John 9:4). Let us sleep enough to have energy to work hard, always trusting that if one must be sacrificed, it will be sleep, and prayer will make up the energy deficit. When Jesus comes, He will not laud me for much sleeping, but He will be pleased at much prayer and diligent work. Let us be wise enough to live out the truth that much prayer leads to hard work and sweet sleep. Much sleep undermines fervent prayer and prevents dignified work.

20.14

We don't have to use false words to gain advantages. In the eternal market of integrity, value is attached to mutual benefit, not to singular advantage. It is human to want to get a good deal for self. It is divine to want, and pay for, a good deal for all. When we use falsehood to gain an advantage over our fellow man, we have fallen to employ the tools of the devil and his demonic companions. When we use truth to put others at an advantage, often at cost to ourselves, we have risen to engage the means of heaven. In all negotiations the wise employ truth, for they are astute to know that in the end truth is everyone's gain and lies are everyone's loss.

20.15

There is little treasure more valuable than right thinking and speaking. As the lips speak from the overflow of the heart and mind, what is more precious than rubies is the knowledge within. Thus, the wise are intentional in their pursuit, saving, accumulation, and dispersion of knowledge—much more than they are in their pursuit of money, power, status, or fame. Fools seek and hoard the wrong treasures, gaining money but living poor. The wise seek and dispense knowledge, rich toward God and generous towards men. Every good steward keeps an eye on their physical future, care for children and parents, recourse for the days when daily income subsides. With how much more diligence should we keep an eye on whether we are growing in Godly knowledge and if we are storing it up by giving it away?

20.16

Godly generosity recognizes that helping can hurt and that gifts without accountability tend to corrupt, not empower. If we chafe internally when accountability is required for the stewardship of gifts we receive, it is a warning sign that pride has a foothold within us. Pride does indeed come before destruction, and accountability best serves the humble and the holy. In our folly we think it is the holy that don't need to be watched. When in reality (because none of us are intrinsically holy), it is being watched that helps us fight *for* holiness. The wise then cry out, "Watch me with the carefully compassionate eyes of accountability! Do not leave me to my own devices! Love me enough to establish clear boundaries far from any cliff and insist that I stay within those merciful limits." Fools resent any limits and all-watching eyes—and they fall and despoil the gift. Gifts without accountability turn into curses.

20.17

Lies are like soul candy: They taste good going down, but within, the extra sugar is harmful. Missionaries and ministers are given the assignment to present the gospel. This necessitates a certain skill in communication and in presenting difficult truths in understandable ways. Those whose vocation it is to win a hearing among people are susceptible to using their skills to win admiration to themselves. Oral communicators can stretch truth (in pulpits, newsletters, or storytelling) to make themselves look wise, witty, or worthier than others. This is especially true by those who are financially supported by other Christians and churches. It's a competitive market (though we all acknowledge it shouldn't be) as churches and believers have many who ask for their prayers and support. If one stretches the truth to win a large (or wealthy) congregation or large (and generous) support base, it may feel good on the front end, but it will be gravel in our mouth, shoes, and soul down the road. We in the business of truth can in no way, anywhere or with anyone, build on falsehood, which includes half-truths, exaggeration, false humility, withholding of confession, and humble brags.

20.18

Ideas are improved and refined by exposure to minds other than our own, especially critical minds. We have a natural tendency to love our ideas and to shield them from criticism. We have a natural pride that thinks we have considered all the risks or that our risk mitigation strategies are comprehensive. We have a natural impatience that resents the process necessary to repeat, explain, and defend the idea over and over again. We have a natural reluctance to allow others to shape our idea as we then must share credit for it, and we love to get glory for ourselves. Wise men embrace the frustration and time required for the refining of an idea or plan because they are more concerned with efficacy than with credit. Fools love the praise that can result from an innovative, courageous idea, but they care less if the idea lasts or blesses others. Because war always means someone will die, it is even more important that many hearts and heads agree before we make decisions that will cause much pain on the path to precious peace.

20.19

Flatterers are not real friends, for their motivation is to mine information from you that they can use to their advantage. Fools use information to gain status for themselves to the hurt of the ones the information concerns. Unconcerned with the wellbeing of others, flatterers use inside information as currency, that they may buy for themselves status in community and society. Beware those who flatter you; they will likely betray you. Those who sing your praise to the heavens will likely shout your follies to the ends of the earth. True friends protect you by telling you the truth about yourself, not telling others about your truths. Thus, if we are to be true friends, we will not flatter and whatever information comes to us unsolicited stays with us to our grave—and no flattery can raise damaging information about others from the dead. In this sense, wise friends are often prudently deaf and mute.

20.20

To dishonor your parents is to sentence yourself to irrelevance. To dishonor your authority is to prove you are not to be trusted with leading. To dishonor your colleagues is to prove yourself unworthy of their friendship. Dishonoring others eventually leads to discharge and isolation. Fools think that criticism of others elevates, but it only isolates. When we criticize those around us, those who have helped us, those that have sacrificed for us, those that have loved us, it angers the Lord, and He judges the dishonorable harshly by banishment. Foolish hearts dishonor their intimate associates under the delusion that making others look bad causes themselves to look good. The wise understand that assassinating the character of others leads to solitary confinement in shame and that the path to honor is paved with acts of respect towards others. Dishonor leads to loneliness. Honor leads to loving community.

20.21

Quick gains lead to quick losses. We want Pentecost without Calvary. We want 3,000 believers added to the church without 3,000 years of preparation. We absolutely believe and pray for miracle accelerations, but we are not foolish enough to believe they happen in vacuums. Breakthroughs in battle result at the end of a long process that includes vision, mobilization, training, learning, deployment, engagement, and struggle. Then, *suddenly*, God breaks through and the tears of years are forgotten in the adrenaline surge of opportunity. Fools focus on that glorious moment, scorning the hidden and mundane glories that made it possible. The wise embrace and enjoy the anonymous years of grinding out daily glory, knowing there is no such thing as sustained gain without a laboriously built foundation.

20.22

God is so much better at revenge than we are. The wisest thing we can do is let God settle old scores. Humans don't have the holiness of character required to appropriately enact revenge. Inevitably, we sully any righteous anger with selfish motives. Revenge in the hands of men is invariably a twisted tool that only maims the user and the other, while unglorifying God and lacking redemptive power. Only God has the wisdom, goodness, mercy, and strength to wield the tool of revenge in a way that is redemptive, restorative, and glory-inducing. We are self-deceived if we think any good thing can result from man-governed revenge. We are self-aware when we release all desire for revenge into the merciful, just hands of the only One who knows how to use that dangerous tool wisely.

20.23

Wisdom is content with measured profit, for godly business does not advance at another's cost. The path to godly wealth is narrow and steep, slow and selfless. Wisdom knows that the real goal of business is not making money; rather, the goal is the glory of God and the good of others. There is a danger of framing our own greed in altruistic language, yet godly business is marked by contentment, consideration, and collaboration, and not by competition. An orientation that looks out for the interests of others will practically grow more slowly, but in that compassionate approach it will spiritually gain a competitive advantage not available by any professional means—the favor of God. When God looks down at His wealth creators and sees that they are legitimately oriented on creating wealth for others (even to their own hurt), He smiles. In the Sovereign's smile are riches and blessing beyond compare. The others-focused wealth creator will find the Lord of heaven's treasure focused on them.

20.24

Following Jesus closely sometimes means that your view of the future is blocked. If we really are intimately walking behind Jesus, sometimes our view of Him will obscure our view of what is coming. The wise are content with not knowing the future if they can but know Christ and be close to Him. His presence explains their difficulties. It is not facts or future that calm them; it is proximity to Christ. Fools strive to see what is coming rather than strive to stay close to Jesus. We must release and repent from our ceaseless desire to know, understand, or figure things out when those desires overwhelm our desire to be close to Jesus. When we get as close to Jesus as we can, we wonderfully realize our anxiety over tomorrow is forgotten in the wonder of being near Him. Who needs to see tomorrow if our view is consumed with Christ!

20.25

Wisdom is slow to offer gifts but quick to follow through on promises made. Foolishly we tend to overpromise and under-deliver. God is the only One who endlessly exceeds His own promises and who overdelivers. God does not give the Spirit by measure— He pours it out. God does not grudgingly mercy—He lavishes unmerited favor. Because we do not have the resources, capacity, or the character of God, we should promise less and deliver more. Certainly, the wise keep their promises, that is academic. The deeper wisdom is simply to promise less than you deliver. That does not mean a retreat into a stingy heart and life. On the contrary wisdom ever calls us to give more; we must just talk about it less.

20.26

Slowly and surely, we must purge those we lead from what is destroying them. A wise leader sifts out what is wicked in her own heart, family, leadership team, and followers. A wise leader is ruthless in self-evaluation and rigorous in review of the character of the ones she trusts. Trust is not a blind acceptance; it is a conscious choice to give power away even as you use authority to correct. God trusts us even as He sanctifies us. God allows us to work for Him even as He constantly works on us, sifting the evil out of us, threshing us as necessary to remove all chaff. It is the cruel (or cowardly) leader who never corrects or cleanses those she trusts.

20.27

God uses our own personalities to speak to us. He uses our own spirit to search us. This is not metaphysics; this is just language and comfort. We know the language of our own heart best. This is why arrogant people most offend arrogant people. They speak the same language, and they see a little further into the motivations of the heart in one another. The humble are less offended by the arrogant because they are wired differently, while the proud understand one another and thus offend each other. The Holy Spirit is fluent in every personality type. He speaks and sees right into our hearts and has the capacity to communicate deeply to us, through us. The still small voice within is God speaking our dialect. We would be wise to listen.

20.28

Mercy and truth are the basic building blocks of longevity in leadership. As they are complementary legs, a short supply of either causes a limp and a long neglect of either cripples both the leader and the follower. The calibration of the two is where fools are separated from the wise. Fools indeed have a mix of both mercy and truth. Unfortunately, they are merciful when they should be truthful, truthful without seasoning mercy, or a confused mix of both that confuses and incapacitates those around them for its instability. Because mercy triumphs over judgment, when in doubt we do err on the side of mercy. But doubt is no lasting way to lead. The wise, in every decision, silently breathe prayers to the only One who perfectly balances mercy and truth depending on Him to help them get it right. Fools toggle back and forth carelessly causing great harm in the inconsistency.

20.29

It is wise and rewarding to assemble multi-generational teams around us. The energy of youth and the wisdom of age are such a powerful combination when the blend is right. We want to avoid both the sin of Rehoboam (who despised the counsel of the aged) and the sin of the "Old Boys Club" (who despise the contributions of youth). If we are wise, we will not shuttle between the two (energy and experience) but allow those spheres of influence to converge and season each other, presenting the most powerful combination for life and service. These principles should be lived out personally. We need to stay young in our heads and ideas and our hopes and our vision even as we age and grow in experience. What weakness and loss when hearts grow tired and heads stay immature, and what strength there is when wise old heads govern young, fresh hearts!

20.30

We should be thankful for everything that hurts us, for there is always a lesson in pain. When pain is incurred because we are foolish, we learn to avoid that folly. When pain is incurred because others are foolish, we can rejoice that we were chosen to absorb that pain, ensuring it's not passed onto other innocents. When pain is incurred because we are wise, we thank the Lord that He is worth all wounds, for injuries in His cause are ever the price to overcome the evil one. The wise are thankful for painful correction, for they realize their own blindness or stubbornness precludes self-correction. We are neither wise enough nor courageous enough to do surgery on ourselves; we need the merciful blows of others to help. Those blows are not always intended to be merciful, but thanks be to God for He uses even the impure acts of others to purify His sons and daughters.

PROVERBS
Chapter 21

21.1

God is King of kings and ultimately always wins, always gets His way. Even when it seems that earthly authorities continually rebel against the Lord and His Anointed, the reality is that even their most heinous acts are turned against them. It must be very frustrating to be the devil and to constantly see how God turns situations to gospel good and God's unique glory. God is so wise that He turns the hearts of authorities without them knowing it. Smug on their decaying thrones, the powerbrokers of this world revel in their supposed autonomy and imagined resistance, never realizing how foolish they look to the angel hosts who are privy to God's unmatched strategic dominance. The wise, therefore, pray for improbable things at the hands of irascible regents, for God turns them easily to His mighty ends.

21.2

No one has completely pure motives. We are all self-deceived to a degree. No one has absolute knowledge of the heart—neither his own, nor that of another. Lowly wisdom recognizes that of all the deceptions we engage in, the most complicated is when we deceive ourselves. The Bible clearly tells us that our hearts are wickedly deceptive and that we cannot know them, but we resist that warning, even resent it. The Lord helps us see our own hearts through the criticisms of others. Granted, most criticisms are not fully accurate, for criticism is indeed the blind poorly observing the blind, somewhat comically. But almost always there is some truth in what others say about us. The wise never discount criticism completely and never believe it fully; they sift through it prayerfully. Fools tend to either ignore criticism comprehensively or swallow it all unthinkingly; both follies ensuring they stay blind.

21.3

God wants us to get it right the first time. Grace provides for mistakes, but holiness is intended to keep us from making them. In His mercy, God does not treat us as our sins deserve, yet His expectation is that we do not sin at all, and His insistence is that we sin less and less. Both the wise and the foolish sin; they just differ in regularity. The wise sin less and less, while fools sin more and more. We know we are growing in wisdom if we are sinning less today than yesterday, and if when we do sin, we feel more sorrow than before. We know we are growing in folly if we sin today and tomorrow at the same pace as yesterday with the same level of contrition. The wise sin less and feel it more. Fools sin more and feel it less.

21.4

Sins of attitude are as wicked and as damaging as sins of action. Attitudes are, in fact, a genre of action, for they have an uncanny aptitude for afflicting others. Demeanor matters. How we sit, how we look, and how we listen all can communicate encouragement, or they can sap life and energy. It is sin to discourage a preacher, teacher, leader, or friend by either a negative or an apathetic look. It is sin to look down on anyone, even if the look is from your heart, not your eyes. The wise remember that the Lord sees all looks, watches all hearts, and demands of His own that they are gentle and meek in their judgments. Fools think that starting from a posture of cynical pessimism, a critical attitude, and a judgmental spirit is enlightened. The wise are lowly enough to have kind, tender hearts which are predisposed to think the best.

21.5

Diligence usually isn't glamorous. From the earliest days in school, we culturally reward those who can answer quickly and unconsciously build into our collective psyche that speed is better than pace. We love to watch the 100-meter race at the Olympics—it's the glamor event. But not many watch the 10,000-meter one. Spiritually, however, in the race of life, haste does indeed make waste and the turtle does indeed defeat the hare. Part of the allure of haste in life is the thrill of being first. The wise stifle the urge to be the first to answer, denying their flesh the craving of recognition. Wisdom has the patience and humility to not need recognition and thus makes better decisions. Fools believe the lie that all publicity is good publicity.

21.6

Lying ends in dark dreams. Of all the damaging lies, the most sinister ones are to ourselves. There are alluring treasures in life beyond our reach. These treasures are not just money and possessions; they also are status and positions. If we strive for these treasures through deceitful methods, we are acting out a death wish. Real life is satisfied with what God choses for our destiny, and wisdom accepts and revels in what God appoints for us. Folly does not trust that we will be happiest with the destiny God chooses for us; we deceive ourselves into thinking we will be happy with someone else's treasure. And if that lie grows strong enough, we do anything (tell any lie, live any falsehood) to gain our goal—and in the process lose our soul.

21.7

There is only One who can handle violence purely and He is divine. In this broken world God has delegated the right to use force to His viceroys (both Christian and other), but we can only wield the sword well if by His constraints and character. A common error is to use violence for selfish gain by destroying others, but that is foolish, for it only ends up killing the violent. Those who live by the sword do indeed die by it. An equal error is to not use the sword, to not stand up for the innocent through appropriately coercive means. To those who have the power of intervention but forsake it will ironically come the punishment of forcible judgment. The Bible does not seem to support pacifism even as it condemns gratuitous violence. Violence is terrible, yet in a broken world necessary. Only those who swing the sword in the wisdom and timing of God are not ultimately slain by that sword. Fools swing too often or not at all. The wise swing very selectively, but very surely.

21.8

Simple, transparent, honest work is long-term protection for the worker. Men and women whose job it is to speak truth should have no lies in their life. Eventually, all lies are exposed and if truthtellers have been "lie-livers," the damage is incalculable. Perversity is usually not all wrong; full wrong we call evil. Perversity is twisted truth. A perverse life is one that stands for holiness publicly (writing, preaching, teaching, mentoring) while harboring secret sins and addictions privately. The wise know that being sweet and kind in public, while being disobedient and selfish in private is perverse. Fools think they can maintain the charade of private vice and public virtue, but God can never be mocked. All those who speak for good speak for God whether they acknowledge Him or not, and if they speak for God but not live for Him, then they (or we) are perverse.

21.9

Constant argument and tension fatigue and then they destroy any relationship. If the default communication style of any partner (or both) is combative, negative, pessimistic, or dour, that relationship cannot (and should not) be sustained over time. Wisdom knows when to walk away from an abusive relationship and does not live under guilt for doing so. In fact, there is biblical injunction not to spend time with "friends" or "intimates" who only drain your soul. It is better to be isolated than to be incessantly assaulted. Robust love does not empower abuse. The wise readily absorb abuse for the sake of Jesus and the gospel, suffering so that souls might be saved; but enduring suffering is not to be confused with empowering abuse.

21.10

Always finding fault in others is the indicator of an evil heart. A wicked heart seeks to find a weakness and then weirdly rejoices in discovering the flaw. Not content to only know where the other is broken, foolish wickedness then shares that unfortunate reality with others. A godly heart is quick to forgive and always seeks to assume the best. If we want to be like Jesus, we must constantly discipline our minds and our emotions towards grace. Kindness starts in our thinking and spreads to our acting. Every time we find fault with another, we shrink a piece of our own soul. Every time we think the best, believe the best, and hope the best, we water not only the other soul but our own.

21.11

Mockers are punished for the benefit of others, for mockers are often the fools who do not learn from their own discipline. The wise are punished for their own growth; this, too, a lesson for the observant, but doubly redemptive because all involved benefit. Simple wisdom does not have to go through the complex gymnastics of doubt or experimentation; simple wisdom observes the pain and pleasure of others. Complicated intellect insists on learning through firsthand pain and often does not survive the experience. How wise we would be to learn from the mistakes of others and grow from the mistakes that are purely our own.

21.12

God does not remove the wicked immediately, even though the wicked always ultimately perish. We do not understand why tyrants are allowed their reigns of terror, even though we can see from history that all tyrants eventually fall. In our wisdom, the best thing to do is to remove wicked powers immediately, especially when innocent ones suffer. It seems foolish to us to live even one day under oppression and injustice. If we were enthroned on high, we would have had one plague on Egypt, not ten; we would have jumped right to death. We all have a little *sic semper tyrannis* (thus always to tyrants) in us, whether we are a Brutus or a Booth. Sometimes we kill Caesar and sometimes we kill Lincoln, and it's not always for the greater good. Wisdom lets God remove leaders in His time as only He fully understands the greater good. Fools rush to assassination mostly because we don't like our leaders, not because they are actual tyrants.

21.13

Generosity to the poor is the best retirement plan. The wicked steward of Jesus' parable rushed to spend his master's wealth by being generous, so he would have recourse when he was made redundant. How much better when the righteous rush not to bless the rich but help the poor, for rather than deceiving their Master, they are aligning with His heart. How the heart of God rejoices when He sees His children acting like Him, passing on His resources because they are twofold wise. First, they realize what they give away now is not theirs and never has been—all comes from Father's hand. Second, they realize that God has unlimited supply and that He rewards those who trust Him to keep supplying. When we give for God, when we act as a channel of His generosity, there is no pressure. We were never the source, and we have no reason to believe the source will ever stop flowing.

21.14

Generosity undermines anger. It is difficult to be angry with those who bless you, serve you, honor you, encourage you, smile at you, and give to you. It is easy to be angry at those who curse you, abuse you, dishonor you, discourage you, frown at you, and take from you. Wisdom understands the prudence of making it difficult for authorities and adversaries to be angry with you. Fools pour gasoline on fire, while the wise pour water. Private generosity has no edge or demand to it, and authority and adversaries never respond well to manipulation. The wise are adept in the discreet de-escalation of tension. Fools miss the signs and make difficult situations worse.

21.15

True justice brings joy to the activist at the micro level. All justice has the aim of macro change and the good of all, but real justice is motivated more by pleasing God than by changing men. When we have acted justly, even in a small way that doesn't seem to have solved the bigger problem, we have acted in the spirit of Jesus. When we act in the spirit of Jesus, that act is its own reward. Great joy surges through us when we do simply what God created us to do: represent Him in the earth. Beautiful is the army that gets more gleeful with the increase of opposition. Charming, irrepressible, and indefatigable is the band of loving warriors when they are glad in their obedience no matter their results. The wise take primary joy in obedience, for unbowed by the demands of conflict they have the wherewithal to press on to the harmonizing joy of success.

21.16

Stupidity kills you, even when it's all dressed up in wisdom. We don't become foolish overnight; we wander there almost imperceptibly. It may be charming to say, "All who wander are not lost," but it's just dressed up folly. When it comes to faith in Jesus, wandering is not a good thing, neither is doubt, distraction, or delay. What is good, life-giving, and life-keeping is a single-eyed devotion—even a fixation—on Him and the expressed determination not to wander off the path. Wandering is based on the flawed assumption that the path to life is broad and that steps off the path are bold and safe. The reality is that the path of life is a knife-edge ridge between two cliffs that fall away to doom. The wise don't wander, the wise don't leave the path, the wise know that those who wander are worse than lost—they are doomed.

21.17

It is the little indulgences that make you poor, both in pocket and in soul. Most followers of Jesus don't murder anyone; we just assassinate with our words. Most followers of Jesus don't commit adultery; we just undress with our eyes or thoughts. Most followers of Jesus don't rob banks; we just rob God by withholding our tithes or by refusing to be sacrificially generous. It is supreme folly to think that because we don't indulge in scandalous sins that we are healthy and rich in spirit. It is the little disobediences that rob our spirits of life and power. It is a little bit of laziness and a little bit of hedonism that impoverishes us from the inside out. Flagrant sins are merely the manifestation of a long, inward decay, a long focus on self over others. No one gets up one morning and decides to murder, steal, or commit adultery; they slide there by a thousand selfish indulgences. We flee those horrors by a thousand private obediences, a thousand little self-denials.

21.18

In the long term, evil is a bad investment; it does not pay. We should be wary of wild promises of instant reward. Those emails that promise ten million dollars, the books that promise languages learned without pain, or those preachers who predict riches if you will give them money—all are charlatans in their own way evil. Evil appeals to flesh, and the most insidious evil is attractive, which makes it even more terrifying than anything Hollywood can conjure up. Most of us are wise enough to know that in real life we should suspect anything that promises gain without pain, yet most of us are foolish enough in our spiritual lives to want that very thing. But it (spiritual gain without pain, work, process, time, and crosses) is illusory at best and wicked at worst. Seeking gain without pain is evil in the short term because it denies the cross, and it is fruitless over time because without the cross there can be no resurrection life.

21.19

If you align yourself with a person that is outwardly attractive but inwardly bitter, the problems will far outweigh the benefits and you will regret that alliance for as long as it endures. Fools marry beautiful exteriors devoid of inward grace. Fools flock to the charismatic while overlooking character deficiencies. The wise seek to spend time and lavish affection on that and those who are inwardly beautiful. When we are smitten with the beauty of character, we experience the miracle of glory transferred. Inside beauty has powers that external beauty cannot mimic. Inside beauty gets greater over time, while outside beauty only fades. Inside beauty makes the outside shine with light; external beauty tends to blind internal darkness. We were made to appreciate beauty inside and out; the wise understand that we seek beauty from the inside out.

21.20

Liberality is based on prior frugality. We only have something to give if we have withheld (over a long period of time) something that is precious. We can only offer to others what we have denied to ourselves. If we have denied credit to ourselves, we have stored it up to lavish on others. If we have denied glory to ourselves, we have a supply to offer up to God. If we have denied pleasure to ourselves, we are well provided to rejoice others in purity and grace. But we cannot give this liberal, extravagant good without a long, disciplined pattern of self-denial. The wise take joy in every moderation, for they know that small, secret savings (withholdings of good to self) will one day lead to great banquets of joy and blessing for others. Fools spend constantly on themselves and then when it is needed most have nothing with which to enrich others.

21.21

When you seek what is right, what is right seeks you. Over time those who do the right things in merciful ways are always ultimately respected, even if resented. If we are wise, we do not react to slander or setback in the moment; rather we let Father God, father time, and faithful action on our part rebut all that is false. It is easy to do what is right when the environment is conducive, but what separates spiritual men from spiritual boys is when we do right when everyone around us does wrong. Wisdom is always farsighted, able to see that dividends are always deferred and always delightful. Fools do not have the patience to let time and integrity do their work.

21.22

Wisdom is brave and tenacious; it is not apathetic. Wisdom is engaged and active; it is not reclusive and withdrawn. Wisdom is developed in the madding crowd, not in the monasteries or the mountains. Wisdom finds a way to directly confront false ideologies and religions without being deceptive. Wisdom scales the city of the mighty, bashes in the front gate, goes over the front wall. If we are to be wise, we must be engaged in frontal assaults on folly. We must attack evil wherever we find it. Let us not confuse wisdom with spiritual pacifism. Wisdom is warlike, fighting open wars with no duplicity or subterfuge. Folly runs from battle or fights with the wrong weapons and in sneaky ways.

21.23

A shut mouth is the shield of the heart. How often we allow arrows to smite our soul because we opened our mouth and let them in! We tend to view our mouth as the instrument of damage to others, an offensive weapon, and it is. It is also a defensive weapon, and a closed mouth can protect us from being hurt as much as it can protect others. So many times unguarded words create more trouble for the speaker, trouble that would have been avoided if the mouth had not spoken. Unguarded words create more work, for they dig holes of suspicion and pain that take time and labor to dig out of. Fools keep creating unnecessary work for themselves through the loosing of unnecessary words. The wise are more taciturn—and less tired.

21.24

Any fool can be a critic. It doesn't take that much intelligence to see problems. Even children can see when the emperor has no clothes. What takes wisdom is the discovery of solutions and the presentation of those solutions in a way that can be accepted. To see what is wrong is easy. To see how to address the wrong in the right way is harder. To present the right in a right way so that right is implemented is hardest. The wise spend very little energy on seeking what is wrong and much prayer on how to implement right rightly. Fools spend all the energy on problems and thus become problematic. The wise spend themselves on gracious, palatable solutions and thus become pleasures.

21.25

Laziness is the first step to starvation. If we do not labor to enter our rest (Hebrews 4), we become spiritually fatigued. If we are not intentional and disciplined in abiding in Jesus, we starve ourselves of nutrients and move from spiritual anemia to spiritual darkness. We cannot be the fools who do not give great care to our souls by the hard work of preparing (and eating) the bread of life. John 15 is accurate when it describes the disciple that does not abide in Jesus, that does not feed on Christ. That disciple withers from the inside out and detaches itself from the vine becoming dry and useless. If we do not work at communion with Jesus, we will starve, and spiritual laziness always results in spiritual death.

21.26

Generosity is the first step to savings. Tithing is the first step to economic recovery. In the economy of God, the steps to abundance are counterintuitive, for they ask us to have the faith in the giving to gain. It is natural to clutch at ourselves when resources are small or diminishing, and it is supernatural to respond to loss by being generous. There are many blessings to the generous heart. When we are generous, others are helped and encouraged. When we are generous, God meets our needs. These are the elemental understandings and results. The deeper blessings are that we look like God when we act like Him (which is sheer joy to the giver) and the discovery that we don't actually need the supply we thought we did (which is profoundly liberating).

21.27

Prayer only works from the inside out as externally based religion fools no one, least of all God. Religious behavior tends to have two levels, both futile and one sinister. At the futile level we sincerely want help (healing, deliverance, rescue, opportunity), so we perform outward ritual as a payment. This is not faith; this only comes from an unbowed heart that is only temporarily humbled by duress. The more sinister form of religion is from a posture of arrogance, a posture that internally only wants to advance self by deceiving or abusing others. When someone is in financial straits and prays to God for a job (with no intention of submission to the Lordship of Christ), that is one level of disrespect, but when a "minister" stands in the pulpit and twists Scripture to leverage money from generous listeners, that is demonic.

21.28

To listen to lies is to empower and spread them, giving them life when you should have killed the ugly menace on the first encounter. Lies and slander are so revolting to the Lord, for they have life and power long after the liar moves on. Paraphrasing Shakespeare, the lies men tell live after them, and the truth is often interred with their bones.[7] Ultimately, all lies are exposed and all truth prevails (shouted from the housetops even!), but in the middle lies do incalculable damage. The wise are intentional about never speaking falsely, for once falsehood is out of the gate it cannot be unheard. Fools are careless with the truth, and that carelessness is magnified by lesser fools with bigger mouths. What gossips hear us gossip in moderation, they will gossip in excess.

21.29

Good men are tender and flexible while bad men are stubborn and confuse strength with machismo. My Arab landlord told me I should take a second wife. When I refused by explaining that my one wife brought me exceeding joy and that the biblical standard is one wife and one husband as long as they both shall live, he curled his lip in scorn and told me several times that I was weak. It is not strength to harden our face and emotions against others and to pursue our pleasures at the cost of their pain. Good men understand that it takes more strength to be kind and faithful than it does to be mean and philandering. The wisest strength is tender and compassionate, and the weakest folly bullies.

21.30

We will never outthink God. How frustrating for the devil with all his intelligence to know by virtue of that intelligence that he is playing checkers and God is playing chess. The One who is the Alpha and Omega, the One who knows the end from the beginning, the One who created our minds and thoughts, the One who knows and sees all is so far above our thoughts, plans, and schemes that all our insurrectionist fervor is laughable. Wisdom, therefore, doesn't try to outthink or circumnavigate God and spends all its energy on pursuing and implementing God's thoughts. Folly wastes time and energy thinking through scenarios, contingencies, and workarounds, rather than embracing and adopting the inevitable.

21.31

Preparation trusts God for miracles. Factored into the equation of all battle plans is the force we cannot see or control. Wisdom takes into consideration the weaponry that cannot be counted. Folly only reckons with what it can oversee. When we go to battle, we do our due diligence. We train, plan, study, strategize, we do all that we can to plan for all we can envision, and we leave space for omnipotence. This means that we always attack forces we have no natural capacity to defeat. The wise appear foolish because they charge giants with slings and small stones, but they are not cavalier. They just prepared themselves to fight knowing that deliverance is from the Lord. Fools don't win battles of consequence, for they never account for their uncountable super weapon.

PROVERBS
Chapter 22

22.1

Relationship and reputation are more valuable than money. The true riches in this world are a good name, not a deep bank account. No matter what others can take from you, be it liberty, possessions, status, or position, they can never forcibly take your integrity. Sometimes our integrity is the only thing we have left, for slander and misunderstanding can even take away our reputation and relationships (even if that's only a temporary heist). This is why the Bible speaks of living at peace with all men with the proviso of "as much as depends on you." We must do all we can to preserve our relationships and reputation, for they are more precious than silver. But what is true gold is our integrity. Integrity can never be stolen; it can only be lost or given away like a despised birthright. The wise never give away their integrity, not for a bowl of lentils or for all the fame or fortune in the world.

22.2

God sees all men as equals, regardless of their financial status. In His sovereignty God has some born into wealthy families and others into abject poverty. He allows some to lose riches and others to gain them, and it's not so simple as the good always become rich and the bad always become poor. The Old Testament understanding (and our experience largely) is that if God blessed you, riches followed. The New Testament shocker was not only God becoming flesh, but God becoming poor, staying poor, and all His apostles following that example. The "I can do all things through Christ who strengthens me" that Paul thunders in Philippians relates to money—living rich or poor. In other words, financial status doesn't matter. God might want you to be Old Testament rich, or He might want you to be New Testament poor, or He might want you to toggle back and forth between them. It doesn't matter, for He will give strength for all, and the focus is elsewhere—on the poverty of a world lost without Jesus and the wealth available to them in the gospel.

22.3

Folly is unprepared, thoughtless courage. Wise courage sees what is coming and takes precautions. In ministry and missions there is no place for a bravado that endangers others or self without gospel glory. Wisdom knows when to duck below the hail of arrows from the enemy and when to rise up from the fortified place to charge. Wise courage does not avoid enemy fire entirely, only selectively. There is a time to risk and a time to wait. Folly always risks and never waits. Cowardice always waits and never risks. Courage has the wisdom to know when to wait (ride out the storm) and when to rise and charge. Wisdom is prepared, thoughtful courage that leads to the rescue and good of others even if self is sacrificed. Folly sacrifices self with no good resulting to others.

22.4

Lowliness and respect for God are the real prizes of life. It is profoundly disturbing that the majority of this world's awards are given to those that promote themselves. There are notable exceptions, of course, but it is primarily before the glamorous that we gather to fawn. We make heroes of those who celebrate themselves, which is folly. God's wisdom makes heroes of those who humble themselves to magnify Him. The results of self-celebration are so painfully obvious in the lives of the rich and famous, for there is nothing in the wake of that pomp but brokenness and devastation. Contrast that to those who only celebrate Jesus, blissfully unaware of self; their lives leave a trail of sweet joy, and their minds and spirits are whole, complete, and satisfied. They may not receive the fleeting honor of foolish and fickle society, but they have the honor and commendation of heaven forever.

22.5

Perversity has terribly adverse effects on its practitioners; it "uglifies" and destroys from the inside out. Chastity and purity have the opposite effect; they beautify and edify over the long term and become increasingly powerful with the passage of time. True beauty increases over time. True goodness amplifies as it ages. A hallmark of evil is that its attraction declines quickly; thus, it must rush to coercion, for it holds no beauty to enchant and hold the will. Beauty, chastity, purity, and holiness need no bonds, for they have captured the will and affections, and as with the winsome, no coercion is needed. Good woos and wins the will, while evil chains it. Jesus sets us free to love Him; the devil binds us up to serve him. Perversity is the devil's chain and prison; purity is the Lord's covenant and palace.

22.6

The foundations we build into our children provide the potential for future strength no matter where or what. We need to be careful to distinguish a principle from a promise. The principle regarding our children is that the things they are taught early on will give them every opportunity for stability later in life. This reality does not guarantee that they will make right choices (including whether or not to follow Jesus); it does guarantee that they have the resource of wisdom to draw on should they choose. The wise parent (like David) stores up vast resources for their children and disciples. The wise child (like Solomon) draws on those resources. The possibility is always there that our children (also like Solomon) foolishly abandon the stored-up resources of wisdom. We cannot control our children (love does not allow that), but we can give them every opportunity to choose life. Whatever their choice, we can rest in the peace that we laid up for them every resource for good. Our peace (regarding our children) comes from what we have done with our heart and resources, not what they have done with theirs.

22.7

Financial power gives leverage and money always changes relationship. If you borrow money, even from a friend, it introduces a power dynamic to that relationship, even if just an emotional one. Seldom are these dynamics positive; seldom is it healthy for one man to rule over another. The wise would rather lack than take a loan. The wise would rather keep a friend than distort a friendship through lending. Sometimes the kindest thing we can do is to say no to a loan and yes to a gift. The wise give loans as if they were gifts, pre-determining that the injection of a money/

power dynamic is not going to affect interaction. The simplest way to keep this relational solidarity is either by avoiding loans and just giving grants or giving the loan with no expectation to have it repaid and no acrimony if that happens.

22.8

Sin will always make you sad, and anger (wrath of man) never satisfies because it can never accomplish the righteousness of God. Sin and anger are similar in that they both deplete: Sin steals joy and anger steals energy. Sin and anger are deceiving, for they promise the opposite in their early returns. Sin promises joy (as fun or pleasure) and anger promises energy (as drive or motivation), but neither can deliver on the promise. In fact, they do the opposite; they withdraw, not deposit. Wise men tend to be farsighted and disciplined, to see past early returns to long-term consequences, to be patient enough to wait for deferred benefits. Fools tend to shun the long view, for the fleeting giggles of lesser pleasures immediately. They are more than capable of seeing it; they just choose to not look.

22.9

Generosity is kindness to your future self. When we give to others, we are actually giving to ourselves, both in the now and in the future. We have been lied to for so long and so consistently concerning receiving, for we have been told that receiving is the highest pleasure. The lie is attractive as there is genuine delight in receiving love, attention, favor, kindness, touch, gifts, recognition, or affirmation. When we are generous, we taste the Father heart of God's deep pleasure in giving. There is an immediate reward in the now, a gladness of spirit that is internal and cannot be measured or even observed. When we are generous, we so delight the Father that He determines to keep blessing us as we can be trusted to pass His goodness along. The long-term reward of generosity is only secondarily that we are taken care of; it is primarily the ongoing delight of being resourced to act how God acts, and thus sense His joy unthinkable and full of glory.

22.10

Healthy teams get rid of cynical members. When remedial correction has failed, it is entirely biblical and Christlike to remove acidic, poisonous personalities from leadership or even from community. Indubitably, there should be a time of grace, loving confrontation, and a reform roadmap, but at some point the most loving course of action ironically is to hand over the sardonic to Satan for the saving of their souls. Saving needs to be multi-directional—the body as well as the member. If the body is suffering, we do not put the feelings (or even the welfare) of one member above the whole. Sometimes the shock of shunning is all the recourse left to us. This extreme measure is oft abused so we must walk softly, but wisdom requires we use all the weapons of health including the dangerous ones. We are neither loving nor wise if for the good of one we do injury to all.

22.11

If you are guile-free and gracious, you will be able to lead both up and down. It can be easier to lead from a position of power (where others have to follow you no matter your character or competency) than it is to lead from a posture of influence. To lead up, to lead those who are under no compulsion to listen to you, nor do what you say, requires character and depth that can be recognized. When we live in purity and speak graciously, those that lead us will reach out to be led by us. The wise, however, do not only lead up this way. They also lead down from a pure heart and a gracious tongue, choosing influence over authority whenever possible. Fools are gracious only when it suits them. The wise are ever gracious to all, for they know it is always suitable.

22.12

The Lord is ultimately responsible for defending truth and destroying lies. Often the best witness is a repetitive one, not necessarily an articulate one. For good or bad, that which is oft repeated is that which tends to be believed. Winsome steadfastness in speaking truth will often be more effective than the occasional erudite eruption. In witness to Muslims, for example, we do not argue into the faith, but we do joyfully testify to who Jesus is over and over again. Articulate apologetics are necessary and helpful, but they do not replace the simple and joy-filled repetition of truth. For as many times as my Muslim friend objects that Jesus is not God, I respond in simple testimony that He has saved me. In time God will defend and prove that truth and in time He will overcome all lies.

22.13

The lazy use danger as an excuse. Wisdom is not an avoidance of danger or risk at all costs; wisdom is the ability to know which dangers to brave and which risks are necessary. To habitually not act because there is the possibility of danger is worse than cowardice—it is lazy folly. In fact, we can hide our sloth behind fear as fear is more socially acceptable than laziness. Jesus accepts neither folly, fear, nor laziness. He castigates them all. Jesus endorses and expects faith, wisdom, and courage. Even if there are lions in the street, Jesus expects us to go outside and to figure out how to either subdue or avoid them. Wisdom never hides from or ignores danger; wisdom engages danger, even if that engagement is management, not conquest. Lazy foolishness is identified by its refusal to engage danger, by its use of fear as a viable reason for inaction.

22.14

Sexual sin will often begin with inappropriate banter, and because Jesus knows where coarse jesting leads, He abhors it. Before we turn our eyes to pornography, we turn there with our jokes. Before we commit adultery, we commit verbal impropriety. Little off-color remarks, a little edge to humor, a double entendre here and a crass implication there, Jesus hates them all. In John 14:30, Jesus said that the evil one has nothing in Him. In other words, Jesus not only never told an off-color joke, He never even politely smiled at one, not even when He was just with the guys. Jesus refused to have any hint of what is not holy, and He expects us to do the same. Let us not open the door to immorality by clever words or even remotely suggestive jests. Jesus considers these little indecencies perverse, for He knows exactly where they lead.

22.15

We are so twisted up, foolish, and self-deceived. We need our childish foolishness beaten out of us with the rod of difficulty. It would be easier if we were astute enough to repent of our rebellious nature without the rod of difficulty, but the steady record of humanity is that we cannot in our own strength regularly rise to even this level of wisdom. Difficulty is God's patient way of teaching us anyway what we declined to learn from Him painlessly. Difficulty in this sense is remedial only, in that we could have learned the lesson an easier way, yet even in our stubborn decline, Jesus loved us enough to teach us the hard way. Human history records that all men occasionally require the rod of learning. What separates the wise from the fools is that this is the only way that fools can learn. The fools learn from the rod less and less while resenting it more. The wise need it less yet embrace it more.

22.16

The only way to retain wealth is to earn it honestly. When money (or any asset) is gained dishonorably, it is never retained through the generations. The wise do not look at the short span of years or the brief breath of one lifetime but at the generations. Ungodly gain might endure to the death of the earner, but usually not much longer, for indeed the wealth of the wicked is stored up for the righteous. The principle extends far beyond mammon. A reputation unjustly earned will not linger; all will eventually be exposed. It is folly to think that wealth or honor dishonestly acquired can be preserved. It is wisdom to know that the Judge of all the earth will do what is right and He will broker no fraud.

22.17

The wise seek out the wise and allow God to speak through them. Fools think that wisdom is expressed through speaking, teaching, writing, and expounding. The wise, however, are identified by how well they listen and how diligently they seek and by their persistent questioning of others. We tend to show off the knowledge we have gained and synthesized, while sages tend to cloak that they know much (unintentionally) because they are by nature inquisitors, not exhibitionists. If we are to be wise then, we should talk less and seek more, teach less and study more, answer less and ask more. It is the ever learning that have the most to teach. It is the ever teaching that have the most to learn.

22.18

Retention is the better part of experience, for there is no true learning if we have not appropriated that truth into our praxis and in turn passed it on to others. It does no communal or gospel good if we are ever learning without coming to a working knowledge of the truth. We do not come to truth knowledge through theoretical accumulation, but by practical application. We learn most when we have to teach, and we teach best when we do so from our personal action of that truth. Simply put, we must ever learn by acting on what we have heard and then teaching others to act on it also. Real learning then is both personalized and "generationalized." What we have received from the faithful we do and pass on to the next generation, teaching them to train others. When truth is active through four generations, it will endure (2 Tim. 2:2).

22.19

Wise teachers refuse to be the answer. They refuse to allow their pupils to trust them more than they trust the Bible, the Spirit, the Father, or the Son. In every age there are cycles of personality cults in which charismatic leaders and ministers gather large crowds to themselves because of their charisma or even because of their sound theology. While charisma and sound doctrine are not evils, neither are they transferable, and thus they must be personalized. It does not help me in the long term if I memorize truth or mimic how to present it. I must know truth and I must know how to discern truth for myself within the constraints of my own being and limitations. No one else's knowledge, piety, or gifting can serve me in the long term. No one but Jesus can be my answer, and the best teachers use a pedagogy that includes both teaching and discovery, pedantic and parable. The best teachers both feed us and teach us to feed ourselves.

22.20

Some of the most profound discipleship is posthumous. "Old Dead Guys" pack into one page what many modern authors spread over whole chapters, and in some cases whole books. While it is true that "of making many books there is no end" (Ecc. 12:12 **NIV**), it is also true that not all books (thoughts/insights) are of equal import. The wise keep reading; the wise keep mining the wisdom of the ancients; and the wise labor through means of old communication to dig out diamonds and nuggets that never grow old. The wise understand that there is nothing new under the sun and that brilliant men and women have gone ahead of us in everything that can be thought. Good stewardship then requires we revisit what they have painfully discovered and faithfully recorded for us. The wise look back so that they can clearly see forward. Fools only look forward and thus end up far behind the times.

22.21

Wisdom is always a costly purchase and a trust received to be passed on. There is no human who is naturally wise or who inherently reverts to truth and goodness. The fall has felled us all, and we are mortally marred in our ethics and conscience. Wisdom is not hidden within us, latently waiting for discovery and extraction; wisdom must be sought outside ourselves and purchased dearly. We only become wise (and grow in wisdom) through diligent, painful seeking. The source of all wisdom is God, but we can purchase at a secondhand (but good as new), discounted rate from those who paid the high price before us. We need not pay as high a price as they did if we are willing to learn from their pain and if they are willing to share their treasure. We would be wise ourselves to pass on those riches at a price both affordable to the sincere purchasers and dear enough that they treasure them.

22.22

Do not think the poor are weak and defenseless. Respect the God who stands behind them observing all interactions between the powerful and powerless. Folly is a little smug in its self-righteousness, never considering evil to be resident within, quick to see it without. We congratulate ourselves on not being wicked, forgetting that almost daily we act wickedly, forgetting that judge Jesus is ever present and that every idle word, every selfish act, and every callous refusal will be held in account. Jesus notes every time we could give (food, money, time, attention, grace, kindness, forgiveness, mercy) and choose not to. He also notes every time we sacrifice convenience, comfort, or cushion to give.

22.23

God is a formidable opponent whether in war or in court. No one in their right mind would choose to fight against God, not on any ground, not for any reason. The reality is, however, that when we oppress others (not just the physically poor, but any who are weak and over whom we have a natural advantage), we actually are insulting, offending, and attacking God. The character of God is to defend the weak, to lay down His life for the small, to absorb insults and accusations, to do what is right even if unnoticed, unappreciated, resented, and attacked. God expects all characters who bear His name to do the same and He becomes quickly angry and opposed to those who do the opposite. Fools press natural advantages for their own gain; in doing so, they gain God for an enemy. The wise lay down their natural advantages to serve the weak and in that loving act gain God for a friend.

22.24

Anger destroys the angry and is a contagious disease. There is a Satanic spell that attaches itself to the emotion of unrighteous anger. The devil is a furious beast who knows he is vanquished and has but a short time left to drag others into his assured destruction. Driven by anger, he not only feeds on it, but he also feeds on those who are angry. Godly wrath drives away all evil while devilish anger attracts all the demons of hell. When devilish anger is unleashed, it overcomes the user and compels them to heinous acts that in their right mind they would never consider. This twisted rage sweeps others into its madness like an uncontrollable virus. The wise recognize this wicked wrath early and have nothing to do with it—or its carriers.

22.25

Bad company does indeed corrupt good character—when the good character is in the minority and bombarded with vice and sensuality over time. When the bad character is the minority, the effect can be the inverse; a godly group of men and women is a force difficult to resist for the individual bombarded with love and truth. Missional living, however, is at odds with being the holy majority as far as numbers go. We are to leave the ninety-nine and live among the unreached. This holy living then can only be sustained if we primarily spend much time abiding in Jesus (for as missionary stateswoman Mary Slessor said, "God plus one is always a majority") and have faithful, godly accountability. If the majority of our influence is Jesus Himself and a godly co-worker, companion, or team, we can victoriously spend the majority of our time as a minority light in lands and contexts full of darkness—and the darkness will not overcome us. If we live in the dark without abiding in the light, we will eventually be overcome.

22.26

We need to studiously avoid being the answer, for there is a temptation to want to be a little messiah. If we are the primary source (as opposed to merely being the channel), if we are always rescuing others, we are in double jeopardy. The first jeopardy is towards pride, towards the lie that we are the solution for others, that we should be praised, for we have intervened as a little god. The problem with little gods is they are never content with staying little. The second jeopardy is the harm we inflict on others when we rescue them from any pain the Lord intends to use to help them. In our rush to be thanked or appreciated, or even in our shortsighted compassion, we can undermine the good God is patiently working. In that sense our good is actually evil, for it resists the wisdom, love, and transformative lessons of God.

22.27

We need to carefully avoid being a debtor to any man. We are under the power of those from whom we take loans, and we were not designed to be under the power of any, but Jesus. When we borrow constantly (without reciprocal lending), when we are always on the receiving end of a one-way giving street, a damaging dynamic is released into the relationship; it's fatal, in fact, to any long-term healthy interaction. Relationships are only sustainable and pure when they are reciprocal. Reciprocity does not have to be in kind, but it must be in spirit. There must be a mutually beneficial and rewarding give-and-take if bondage is to be averted and blessing is to be gained. The wise are never debtors in the grand scheme of life, for always giving more than they receive, they never are bound and ever are free.

22.28

The traditions, customs, and boundaries of our fathers protect us; we cross them at our own peril. Indubitably, when tradition becomes king, it is a tyrant, but when tradition serves, it is kind. We should be careful to let tradition guide us and slow to abandon what has proved wise for generations before us. Fools chaff at what their ancestors have cherished and quickly want to discard the accumulated wisdom of their elders and discover their own truth. The wise cherish what has been preserved for them, viewing it as a priceless inheritance, seeking to understand what seems restrictive, ever preserving the principle, even if contemporary context necessitates a unique application. Fools refuse the hard work of retaining the principle while laboring to an appropriate personalized application. The wise don't move boundary stones.

22.29

When we work with excellence and promptness, that diligence is the best advertising. The simple undergirding of advertising is honest quality. The slickest campaign cannot long support an inferior product; eventually the product itself is called to the witness stand of public testimony. In the same way, ministry makes way for itself without a marketing strategy. If we are authentic ambassadors for Jesus, there will be a quality (depth, anointing, truth, power) to what we say and do that will be verified by all we minister to. Fools give more energy to marketing themselves (appearances) and less attention to timely, quality ministry. The wise pour all their energy into appropriate, life-giving service and they find they need not sell themselves at all, for what people want to buy is authentic Jesus.

PROVERBS
Chapter 23

23.1

The trappings of power are full of traps. Whenever we are invited to dine (commune, parlay, interact) with the power brokers of society, we should do so soberly and prayerfully, as a lion in a den full of Daniels. This is true for both godly leaders and wicked rulers. There is a blinding aspect of power that can overwhelm us and seduce into saying or doing things against our convictions. Into the presence of great men, we must carry the presence of our greater God. Fools forget whom they serve when summoned to the halls of earthly power. The wise never forget that God alone is supreme, including when they are welcomed to the councils of godly men, for even there can lurk delusion and danger (i.e., flattery and matters with non-evident layers).

23.2

The wise man does not deny his appetites; rather, he holds them at bay and soldiers against them all lifelong. There is no man or woman immune from temptation. There is no person who is ever invulnerable to good things becoming bad things because the spirit did not regulate the flesh. A litany of good things (touch, rest, food, leisure, reading, company, exercise, etc.) can become harmful or idolatrous if we do not put the knife to our indulgent appetites for them. One reason critics don't mortally wound the godly is that no critic can accuse the righteous of what the righteous continually present to God for His review. One reason why good men and women fall into sin is because they never put a knife to the throat of appetite when the longing was yet pure. Appetites must be tamed when they are little cubs, for when they grow into lions, our appetites will always eat us.

23.3

Beware the raging thirst for power and recognition that lurks in all of us—no matter how meek, mild, or humble we appear to be. Deep within all human hearts, ingrained in our fallen and depraved will, is the desire to rule and to be respected, honored, and thought well of. The delicacies of power (honor, respect, influence, acceptance, vindication) are tasty indeed, like sugar to our souls. We want and crave it, and though it's not intrinsically bad, it's not automatically good either. These delicacies that can be granted if we're invited to associate with influential people are deceptive, for they are never freely given—they are always dearly sold. No grant from an earthly power is given without some debt owed, some liberty surrendered. We must be careful that we surrender our liberty to Jesus alone, for He alone is wise and good enough to rule us.

23.4

It is not without consequence that human history ends with God judging the god of mammon, Babylon the great, who is characterized by her love of money and sensuality. Whatever the religion and its veneer of piety, a little revelation shows that the god of this earth tends to be money, sex, and power. The misuse of money and sex is always a power play over others. It is always man on the throne, indulgent. In this context the wise carry a certain holy skepticism (and even justifiable fear) about the power that money provides, for money does inevitably give us power over others. Money gives us a voice, a seat at the table, an opportunity to influence, and the power to make changes, whether or not we have the holy character that alone can guide those opinions to truth and life. Folly makes wealth the goal and overworks to have it. Wisdom makes character the goal and is satisfied with whatever standard of living is compatible for their character to deepen.

23.5

We must learn to depend on God no matter the state of our finances. Wealth is deceptive because it leads us to think we don't need to depend on God; or at minimum we take care of what we can and when our money can't save us, we then turn to the Savior. The rich are drawn to viewing their capacity and resources as their primary insurer and God Almighty as their emergency and catastrophic re-insurer. Only when their organized insurance (their capacity) fails will they look to the Lord. This may start out humbly (God has made me a responsible steward), but it so subtly drifts to hubris (I can take care of myself ninety-nine percent of the time and Jesus is my get-out-of-catastrophe back-up plan). How different the wisest One of all who, though being the God-man who was given all authority, repeatedly said (and lived) that He could no nothing without the Father.

23.6

We should not over-try to please potential donors; we will just end up disgusted with ourselves. In antiquity, to be a miser was synonymous to having an evil eye. An evil eye in the Middle East is a jealous eye—an eye that wants what others have or that doesn't want others to have what *you* have. We should not seek hospitality or generosity that is begrudgingly given. Because God loves a cheerful giver, there is blessing attached to a cheerfully given gift. If gifts are given begrudgingly, there is little spiritual blessing attached. Whenever we give a gift, let us remember that to give cynically is to undermine the power of our own gift and to give begrudgingly (in the spiritual realm) is actually to take. Fools give by taking, with jealousy soiling whatever they pass on. The wise give cheerfully, with pure hearts adorning the gifts they bestow.

23.7

Groveling is always undignified, even in its most refined forms. Begging and abject desperation are heartrending, but not necessarily without dignity. To grovel, however, is either to discard the image of God in ourselves or to injudiciously project it onto an unworthy human. No person should reduce themselves so low as to grovel, and no person should be elevated so high as to be groveled before. Even God does not desire groveling. Repentance, awe, respect, humility, contrition, of course! But groveling is disrespectful to self and unappreciated by authority, increasingly so the purer and higher that authority may be. When we are offered charity that obviously does not come from the heart, it is wise to refuse it. Insincere condescension and groveling are ugly partners—we should despise and avoid both.

23.8

Regret always follows flattery, especially if the flattery works. The laws of God dictate that reward is only sweet if it is honestly earned. Any illicit gain turns sour over time, and lusts fulfilled are always disgusting and dissatisfying. The wise reject inappropriate paths to pleasure and prosperity, for they know those paths end abruptly in a cliff. Fools do not understand that the adrenaline attached to ill-gotten gain is not only inferior to the joy from honest labor, but it's also actually poisonous to the soul. Paths that lead to life are usually silent ones, stringent enough to allow no wasted breath or words, challenging enough to give the deep satisfaction only derived from hard, honest work.

23.9

Just because some men ask counsel doesn't mean they really want it. Many times, we ask questions because we want to hear ourselves speak. Our questions are really soliloquies, and we have no interest in the answers of others. The wise know to not only hold their peace if their heart is not really interested in answers, but they also know to hold their peace when the heart of the petitioner has no genuine desire to learn. Sometimes the kindest thing we can do is to let others discover by painful experience what they would not heed gently. To grow in wisdom is both to talk less and to answer less. To grow in folly is both to ask much (with no intention of hearing or changing) or even to answer much when the petitioners have no real desire to hear.

23.10

Ability does not equal authority. Just because we have the power does not mean we have the right. In the Kingdom, might does not make right, and boundaries are determined by God, not by man's strength or by his wisdom. The image of God in man requires that all men are treated with a respect not derived from wealth, age, health, gender, status, or ability. God has established boundaries of personhood and dignity that no man can cross, no matter how powerful the authority and no matter how depraved the other. Authority does not equal ability. Just because we have the right does not mean we have the power. In the Kingdom, God is ever careful not to endow all the elements of interaction in one person or entity, for He knows that no human and no institution can manage unrestrained resource. The wise find the situationally correct calibration of authority and ability, and they do this in concert with others. Fools both abuse the mixture and try to concoct it alone.

23.11

Don't underestimate the power of the poor and weak, for their Redeemer is mighty. There is always more happening than meets the natural eye. There are always more forces engaged than the physical beings we can see. Just as the righteous should be encouraged that angel hosts surround the godly, so should the godless be alarmed that the poor and weak have an eternally, fearsomely strong bodyguard. In the 1950s in Kenya, the missionary kid school I would later attend was to be attacked by Mau Mau warriors who were violently opposed to the British colonial power. Closing in on the school to kill and destroy, they saw it surrounded by massive angel warriors and so fled in terror. The weak and powerless are never alone, and those who attack and harm them will eventually face the wrath of God.

23.12

Everyone can teach us something, especially enemies and critics. Those who don't like us can help us the most (if we're strong enough to bear the barb) because they have no worry about hurting us. Often the concern for our feelings from those who love us limits them from telling us the unvarnished truth. Those who don't care about our feelings or who even intend to harm us can actually do us great service. If we have the mindset and resolve to learn from everyone, we no longer fear insults or criticisms, for we know there is some value attached to every arrow, some benefit to every blow. Sometimes what we need most is truth unfiltered, and ironically our opponents are usually more willing to serve that up than our friends. Wisdom doesn't choke on the bones of criticism when there is some nourishment to be delicately ingested.

23.13

If we truly love others, we intentionally cause them pain at times. To be an authority figure that does not discipline or correct is not only to be a corrupt leader, but it's also to be corrupting. To not discipline is to sin against the future of your charge. For discipline to be real it must always cost the errant and the enforcer. Leadership is pain, and we must both absorb it and cause it if we are to be loving, faithful leaders. We know we are approaching the heart of godly correction when it costs us to discipline. If we enjoy causing pain (and again true discipline must cause pain), then we are far from godliness. If we grieve what we must do to bring life now and later to the one we love and we do it anyway though it hurts both them and us, then we are close to the heart of God.

23.14

Limited punishment now is always better than eternal punishment later. Pain to the body now is eternally better than unending hell for body and soul. Wisdom believes in an eternal hell that has eternal pain and eternal agony of soul. Wisdom so unshakingly believes in the reality of hell that it will do whatever it can to evade that lot and to ensure all others likewise escape it. How foolish it is not to pain self or a loved one now and as a consequence suffer forever. Today's wisdom says it is hateful to believe in and preach about hell, while eternal wisdom says it is more hateful not to. Hell is as real as heaven, and the wise tenderly inflict whatever pain is necessary on others now for the hope of the pleasures those beloved ones may enjoy of pain-free eternal life.

23.15

Few joys match that of parents who learn from their children or teachers who learn from their students. I listened to my son preach a sermon, and he cautioned against treating Jesus like a dumpster. We can tend to bring all our problems, sins, sicknesses, fears, and difficulties to Jesus, but not give Him our joys or our very selves. Jesus is willing to take our trash, but He surely deserves our treasure, humble as that may be. Listening to my son, I had the twin pleasures of being taught by my progeny and of benefiting by what he taught. Having my son help me see more clearly is a greater joy than any clarity I have helped him see. Wisdom is of such a humble composition that the bearer does not think to rejoice in its private possession but rather rejoices fervently in its dissemination and expansion in others.

23.16

Our greatest joy is when our disciples start teaching us. Because the goal of teaching and preaching is not inspiration but transformation, we have only truly succeeded when those we teach surpass us in both understanding and application. Subtle are the shifts in our hearts that lead us to strive to inspire rather than long to transform. Teaching that inspires tends to be centered on man and erudition. Teaching that transforms is centered on God and application. If men and women are not changed as a result of what (and how) they hear from us, we have tickled ears, but we have not bettered the future.

23.17

Don't long for what sinners have; long for what God has for you. Wisdom overcomes the slow panic that life is passing us by, that we are overlooked, that we will miss out on what others enjoy to our detriment. Wisdom relaxes and trusts that God makes better choices for us than we do for ourselves. Folly strives for possession and place. Wisdom never self-promotes but waits with eager joy for what God will give and assign. Zealous is the opposite of jealous. Jealousy leads to anxious coveting, while zeal ironically leads to relaxed releasing, letting go of wanting anything others have so that we can have a single-eyed devotion on God's assignment, God's gracious choice for us.

23.18

How wise it is to long for heaven. Wisdom lives with eternity in view. It is folly that foments or flounders over something that will not matter ten years from now. It is wisdom that is zealous about and focused on what will last forever. Wisdom is concerned about trees but zealous for souls. Wisdom is concerned about cancer but presses towards the eternal city where there is no curse. Wisdom is concerned about the poor but remembers no suffering compares to eternal suffering. Wisdom is concerned about the elderly but focused on the land where there is no death. Wisdom is concerned about the broken but longs for the time there will be no more tears. Folly lives like there is no hell. Wisdom remembers there is no life like heaven and spends life here getting as many people as possible there.

23.19

Wisdom does not come from within. The first realization of wisdom is that we are not inherently wise, and we do not become wise by either contemplation or by listening. We become wise by obeying. In the Bible hearing always assumes action. To hear Jesus is not to listen and be impressed; it is to listen, be convicted, and change. This is why intelligence and wisdom are vastly different things. The intelligent understand, often more deeply and quickly than most. The wise obey even before they understand. Wisdom always leads to intelligence, but it is a knowledge undergirded by action and experience. Intelligence does not automatically lead to wisdom; disobedient intelligence just makes you smart about being stupid.

23.20

The wise person makes friends with those who are disciplined. Greed and laughter are quickly divorced. Whenever there is excess and a yielding to appetite, there is short-term pleasure and long-term pain. The consequences of giddy greed are never worth the momentary indulgence. Folly is attracted to noise and revelry. Wisdom is attracted to work, for work leads to joy that never stops smiling. Celebrations that crown labor are slower to form and longer to live. Celebrations without sweat equity are frivolous and ethereal. The wise choose the deferred joy that will last over the immediate, momentary gratification. The wise choose friends who know how to work hard at joy, and they shun those who scorn joy by refusing to work for it.

23.21

Heaven will be full of work. Work and rest are not results of the fall. God takes much pleasure in work and so should we. Fools think that work is the problem and the enemy. Fools think that appetite and gratification are friends, but they are not; they are slave masters who in the end will make you work beyond limits without nourishment. Appropriate work is measured, includes sabbaths, and strengthens. Wise work is regular, in rhythm, and seasoned with refreshing. Foolish work is irregular, unmanageably heavy because we were not prudent, and destructive. Those who work hard with the most regularity under sabbath principles rest most. Those most lazy work most hard with no reward in the end. Let no one be fooled: Work is inescapable, both now and eternally. But only the wise will benefit from their labor. Heaven will be adoring service, work with joy. Hell will be agonizing servitude, work without reward.

23.22

We must never forget the difference between wisdom and knowledge. The wise retain wisdom, even as they no longer remember information. We are wise if we remember that in the end wisdom is more valuable than knowledge. Wisdom is principle-based;

knowledge is factual, specific, and application-centered. When we understand principles, our knowledge can travel and transfer. When we journey with only knowledge or familiarity with an application, sans understanding the principle on which data and actions are based, we often lose our way and become overwhelmed, incapable of adjusting to new circumstances. Fools discount and ignore the elderly for their obvious attrition in knowledge. The wise sit at the feet of the aged, gratefully mining the wisdom that deeply resides and endures.

23.23

We are wise if we pay the price to get and keep true wisdom. True wisdom is not free; it is earned, hunted, searched for, saved up for, treasured, and guarded. We do not become wise by accident; rather, we become wise through disciplined intentionality. A strong spirit, godly character, and blameless morality are gained and kept in the same way as a strong body—through consistent exercise. The sober warning is that our wisdom can atrophy if unattended, just like our muscles. We are stunned when a leader or minister who once was true and authoritatively wise stumbles. We think that once wise, always wise, which is foolish and cavalier. Wisdom must not only be worked for, but it must also be guarded and grown. We must work as hard to keep it as we did to gain it, especially as we age.

23.24

Wisdom is the legacy from children to their parents. We often think of the inverse: how wise parents bless children, which is also true. But the greater joy and more lasting legacy is when children turn out wiser than their parents. If parents are ever wiser than their children, society is doomed as the world becomes more and more foolish. Wiser children are a communal joy then, a blessing not just to the nuclear family, but a boon to the community and society at large. Indeed, parents rejoice at wise children, yet churches, cities, and nations are the broader beneficiaries of children who excel their parents. How rare this is! How unusual for a family tree to grow in wisdom from generation to generation. When parents are wise and lowly enough to raise children better than themselves, the whole world sings.

23.25

The kindest gift children can give their parents and elders is to make them proud. The deepest wounds are when we bring our parents, in life or in faith, shame and dishonor. Our elders can shuffle off this mortal coil glad if they are at rest in their souls that their children are godly people. Our elders don't really want or need us to be rich and famous. They don't even insist we are healthy. They just need to know deep in their souls that our souls have integrity. No parent expects or demands that their child be perfect, but all parents are at peace when they know their children have Christlike character. This parental longing is altruistic at its core, for the wise know that power, money, and fame are no real guardians; only integrity can walk us through the valleys and tests that are sure to come. Assured that we are armed with integrity, our parents can step into eternity at rest.

23.26

Wisdom never forgets that we are sons and daughters of the living God while never becoming satisfied with bloodlines, never content with being family legally. Wisdom determines to be wholeheartedly intimate. We can be family without being close, but that is foolish. How heartrending it is to be related but disconnected, an all-too-common pain of earth. Wisdom determines not only to stay close to God, but to fix our eyes on Him, that we might continually learn from His actions, posture, demeanor, emotions, and passions. The truly wise watch Jesus more closely as they age. The foolish watch Him less.

23.27

The best way to clearly see treacherous ground is by keeping our eyes on Jesus. Deep pits and narrow wells are avoided by looking up, not by looking down. In our human folly, we grow to want what we watch most or strangely what we watch out for most, no matter how vile it is. We do not escape impurity by fixating on it; we stay pure by fixing our eyes on Jesus. Human history repeatedly circles the shrine of immorality. We resist this constant gravity not primarily through fear of falling, but through love of watching. Being enraptured by Christ the King keeps us from being captured by anyone or anything else.

23.28

The most dangerous enemies to our faith and faithfulness are those we do not see coming. Evil is cunning, subtle, and patient. It comes at us at inconvenient and unexpected times and through unexpected people. We are more adept at resisting the temptation we see coming and less equipped to reject the temptation that seduces us when we are hungry, angry, sick, lonely, or tired. The demonic powers that strive night and day to wound or destroy our faithfulness know how to attack and then withdraw, waiting for a more opportune time. Wisdom is ever vigilant when it comes to the possibility of attack. Wisdom never worries while never lapsing. Wisdom stays far from any cliffs and safe behind multiple hedges and constant disciplines.

23.29

Bad is often simply the exaggeration or inappropriate excess of good. While there is nothing inherently evil about a grape or a glass of wine, the Bible is repeatedly clear that from these good things often come woe, sorrow, contentions, complaints, and wounds. The wise extract the principle: Too much of a good thing is a bad thing. Fools are those who get drunk on food, games, sports, travel, reading, study, learning, singing, music, gardening, cars, friends, service, adventure, nature, ministry, or any other good thing. The wise preserve good by ingesting it in appropriate amounts. The only good that cannot be spoiled by excess of attention or ingestion is God Himself. Being full of the Spirit is the only unadulterated intoxication.

23.30

Wisdom has the discipline to not search for pleasure, but to wait for the portion our good God sovereignly determines. Fear and folly lead us away from trusting our heavenly Father to mercy us with joy. When we become impatient with the measure of gladness God has apportioned to us, dissatisfied with our portion, we set out in search of more of the good things He has granted us. This search always ends disastrously—not because we do not find pleasure, but because we find too much of it in portions and persons detrimental to us. The wise trust God to give them pleasure in the portions that are good for them. In seeking pleasure according to their own determined limits, fools find it and lose all.

23.31

Activities and pursuits, goals and ambitions are like coins; they have two sides. One side is their appearance before engagement, and the other side is their appearance post-experience. Swirling wine and seductive women have one look before they are indulged in, and a very different look afterwards. Wisdom sees both sides; folly is blinded by the spark and swirl. Wisdom is neither blind to nor blinded by initial appeal but has the discernment to weigh opportunity by final consequences. If the final look is beautiful, the activity or choice has the approval of Jesus. If the final look is ugly, the choice is demonic no matter how beautifully it prances before us when it first catches our eye.

23.32

Our first thought should ever be to the last day. Fools never think through to the ending, while the wise never stop thinking about it. From the ultimate end of the beginning—when Jesus comes back in power and glory—to the daily opportunities presented us, wisdom always focuses on ending well. Deferred gratification is obviously wed to patience, and patience is the early indicator of the wise. Rush and haste are not to be confused with urgency and purpose, for rush and haste quickly mark the foolish. Cost counting takes time, counsel gathering requires multiple voices, and exit strategies demand clinical thinking. The wise appear slower, but in the end arrive healthier—and faster.

23.33

Any unrestrained influence other than that of God's Spirit and Word will ultimately lead us astray, including alcohol, tobacco, caffeine, sugar, books, teachers, philosophy, education, friends, and a litany of others including parents. While it is true that all God created is good, God from the beginning decreed all created things which influence us are to have limits. The only unlimited good is the uncreated God. The only way good is unlimited is if it is used in ways God prescribes. Love, for example, is only good if God is in it. Homosexual love is not good; it is perverse. Parental love that never disciplines is not good; it is corrupt. Creation love can waltz right into pantheistic idolatry. Any unlimited influence outside of God Himself is ultimately corrupt and strange.

23.34

When we allow good things to have mastery over us, we have empowered evil to bind us, and our personhood is lost. We are to only have one Master—the God who is good. If any other person or thing controls us, we lose our God-given identity, swallowed up by a perverted good, which is just a synonym for idolatry. If exercise masters us, for example, over time we will lose both our freedom and our identity to this once good thing. Rather than being the God-created being we are intended to be, we become an exercise-created (centered, identified) being bound in idol worship of the body. The wise do not scoff at drunkards or addicts, for they are humble to know their own subtle propensities to bondage. The wise ruthlessly evict from their heart any good thing that encroaches on the Lord's mastery, whether alcohol, nicotine, sleep, caffeine, applause, calories, or fame.

23.35

The insidious nature of evil is that it feels so good until it hurts so bad. Addictions are demonic because they please us as they destroy us, they feed us as they starve us, and they delight us as they dismay us. There is an aspect of wisdom that embraces pain before pleasure. Folly is always the reverse—pleasure before pain. The Christlike pattern is suffering before glory, and the wise are ever wary of advertising (in or out of church) that promises only pleasure and denies any pain. It is ever wise to choose the pleasures of God that wait on the other side of pain. It is foolish to choose the pain of man that lies on the other side of pleasure.

PROVERBS
Chapter 24

24.1

Evil is insidious because it has attraction. There is a bluster, a confidence, a swagger, and an excitement to evil that draws our attention and, because we are fallen, sometimes our envy. The evil one tends to be powerful, rich, privileged, and apparently happy. The happiness is surface level, of course, and yet the broken part of them appeals to the broken part of us. The wise see through the allure of evil to its agonies and want nothing to do with evil, no time to spent socially with evil men. We are mandated to speak prophetically to evil persons, not engage in banalities. Loving the lost means inviting them into our righteous orbit, not unprotestingly circling what is false with them.

24.2

Violence and trouble stirring are typical marks of evil. Cultures, civilizations, and empires that gratuitously celebrate fighting for fame, entertainment, and money are decadent whether they're called Roman, savage, or American. Violence is remarkable in the Scriptures because it's the last resort of a gentle Sovereign.

Yes, Jesus cleansed the Temple, and yes, He will one day destroy the current elements with a fervent heat, but His day-in, day-out nature is meek, merciful, tender, loving, gentle, peaceful, and kind. When this flicker of earth's history is snuffed out, we will eternally live in the peace and calm of eternity. There will be no violence in our forever. When a culture or context has a day-in, day-out norm of violence and antagonism, it is wicked, no matter how educated or affluent that society may be.

24.3

The mark of wisdom is endurance and strength. If particular thinking lasts and adorns, we judge it wise. Folly tears down, "uglifies," and has no staying power. Foolish ideas never linger, for they are exposed as destructive. Wise ideas abide, for they prove themselves by adding strength and durability to people, relationships, organizations, and society. There is no rush to wisdom, while folly is always in a hurry. In our decision-making then, we are wise to slow things down, to pray, to listen, to study, to wait. Foolish decisions come from emotional reactions, panicked fear, and impatience that would not solicit input from multiple counselors.

24.4

What makes something precious is its degree of pleasantness. Gems of stone or character are desired for the effect they have within the attender or observer, not for their appearance, size, or even length of exposure. When we are around someone pleasant, we feel better inside, and we sense peace, joy, hope, or love. Knowledge that is pure and godly has the same effect on us; it grants us an injection of pleasure that lasts. Knowledge that is evil may grant power or even gratification, but in an elusive manner. Ungodly knowledge and pleasures are marked by their transience. We cannot build on the transient; solid lives are built on godly, goodly pleasures.

24.5

Wisdom is the real muscle behind great fighters. The best champions are strongest in their hearts and heads. It is not unusual among athletes or soldiers to have strong or beautiful bodies; what is unusual is the combination of strong heads, wise hearts, and nurtured bodies. We are created to fight, and we fight best when we fight sagely. In this life we are to fight for the glory of God among all nations, but we do not fight aimlessly as beating the air. We do not fight brutishly with no regard for context or culture. We do not fight selfishly with undue regard for our status or recognition. The forces arrayed against us are too imposing to be overcome in our natural strength. Only the power of the Spirit guided by the wisdom of the Spirit will overcome the powers of this present evil age.

24.6

Jesus carried His cross, not ours. We have all been instructed to carry our own cross. We all must struggle with our own sin. We all must make our own disciples. We all must bear our own load and carry our own grief. For all the important willful aspects of life, we must fight our own war. No other human can choose for us. No one can surrender to Jesus for me. I must force my own knees to bow, and I must bend my own stubborn will at His feet. Fighting our own war and making our own choices, however, is most wisely down in consultation with others. To fight our own war without the input of others is foolish. We best fight what we alone can war when we take the time to listen to many other battle-wise voices.

24.7

You can't be a wise fool or foolishly wise. Any strain of folly undermines influence. Folly is like ink to a clear glass of water; it spoils and changes the whole. There can be no room for "a spot of folly" in the wise. A lifetime of wise ministry can be undone and undermined by one moment, one foolish act. Wisdom is not a percentage; it is not a majority position. Wisdom is a posture of the heart, a continual status. It is character forged by countless decisions and shattered by one false act. It is the most painful folly to deceive ourselves into thinking that a body of wise choices can survive one foolish choice unscarred. If we make one immoral choice, all our prior wisdom will avail us naught, and no one will listen to us when we open our mouth to speak at the public gate.

24.8

Evil is not spontaneous, at least not at the beginning. Initially, it takes hard work to be sinister; "final solutions" are usually carefully planned. What is sobering is that evil starts as a servant but ever intends mastery. In our folly humans think we can use evil for our ends, so we open the door to its employment. Inevitably, evil grows its influence; it possesses and rules tyrannically. All who plot evil are eventually overthrown by their own schemes and end up possessed by demons. At that point evil is spontaneous because the human is now the employee and Satan has a soul through whom he acts with hateful harm. Therefore, the wise never open the door to evil, for they know it cannot be governed or limited. It will always dominate and destroy.

24.9

It is a sin to be stupid, and stupid is as scoffing does. Stupid is not inferior intelligence, for Solomon with all his learning did stupid things. Stupid is not lesser experience, for Solomon's greatest folly was at the end of his life. Stupid is a spirit that becomes cynical, a heart that becomes bitter, and a mouth that becomes constantly negative. Wisdom is a spirit that stays tender, a heart that chooses joy, and a tongue that speaks life, affirmation, and praise. While the mouth reveals the heart, the mouth can also affect the heart. The wise discipline their mouth to speak what is good, even when their heart leans towards what is bad. This is not hypocrisy; this is external obedience until we can bow from the inside.

24.10

Go down fighting fear; don't let fear abort the fight. Anything precious is worth fighting for, and nothing is more precious to God than the soul. The wise recognize before the fight that adversity will come and therefore are not surprised by it. The wise recognize in the fight that adversity is a formidable foe and thus steel themselves for a long, hard struggle to the death. The wise recognize after winning a fight that the war is not over and so never let down their guard nor release their weapons. In the grand fight for the eternal soul (the only real fight worth the cost war demands), we must have a tripartite resolve to not give up: before, during, and after. Our greatest strength is in the will, not in the body or mind. Great fighters are not the strongest; they are merely the most stubborn.

24.11

Christ the Savior demands that we join Him in His focused work. He came to seek and save sinners, and while saving power is completely and uniquely His, all His children share the responsibility to rescue. It is foolish to think we will be liked for our saving efforts. Those drawn towards death or stumbling towards hell will often resent our rescue efforts as clumsy or bigoted. Some are blindly convinced they see, while others angrily despair and their pain drives them downward. Still others are arrogant in their broad thinking, not realizing their inclusion has excluded them from heaven. The wise steel themselves the castigation that comes for loving souls, and they press through the scorn in the hope of rescuing those who least want and appreciate it (at least at first). The great irony of the Christlike life is that we will be hated fiercest for loving most.

24.12

If we do not rescue the perishing, we will be judged for it. We cannot pretend to not know what we know. The Keeper of our soul has required that we would save other souls. His loving nature insists that ours be loving, too, and that we love eternally by spending every ounce of life on rescuing from eternal death. The word and witness of Christ is so clear that no one will be able to stand before Him on that great day and say: "We didn't realize that our one priority on earth was soul-saving." The Soul Saver, our Savior, will look through us with penetrating eyes and render (that is, reward) each man and women according to their soul-saving deeds. While we are saved by grace, the Bible over and again warns and encourages that we are rewarded by works, by the great work of obeying Jesus and following His example to save souls.

24.13

The wise intentionally ingest into their mind, spirit, and bodies that which brings life. Wisdom is integrated, and the one who feeds the mind well, but does not physically exercise is part fool. The one whose body shines, but whose spirit shades is part fool. The one whose spirit soars and body runs, but whose mind dawdles is part fool. Father, Son, and Spirit expect us to care for soul, mind, and body. The profit is not equal, but the expectation is that all our faculties will be stewarded well. Rare is the fool who neglects all three components. Sadly, common the fool who neglects one of them.

24.14

The search for godly knowledge is ever fruitful; it always ends in joy. This is because the end of all true knowledge is Jesus Himself. Science, mathematics, art, travel, nature, etc., when explored to their deepest extent, reveal the simplest reality in their complexities: All knowledge, truth, and beauty is sourced in Christ. The pure heart that genuinely seeks the truest truth will ever and always be rewarded, for she will find Him. Jesus is the truth standing at the finish line of all wise journeys, whether that path be through the stars, the woods, the oceans, the microbes, or the library. True Jesus is the Omega of all Alpha searches. We start with seeking truth and we end with finding hope because we find Him.

24.15

It is not wise to be a fault finder. Fools look for faults in their friends, colleagues, leaders, and spouses. Fools lie in wait, seek what they can disagree with, search for errors, and examine for flaws. Fools find pride in the discovery of frailty in those who are lauded but human. This is jealousy in the guise of purity, hate in the disguise of truth. The wise cover faults, not sins. The wise speak truth, even if not all the truth. The wise bless without condoning. The wise hold their peace and thereby keep it. When the wise see trouble or blemish in those with whom they are intimate, they take that blemish to the Lord in prayer and leave it there. Let us not be hasty to find fault; let us be quick to take what concerns us to prayer. This is simply the mercy we would want others to grant us.

24.16

God mercifully reveals our blind spots to us, and He does this so tenderly that we are motivated towards reform. The way humans point out errors in each other is invariably cruel. This roughly starts among children and becomes refined, not reduced, in its cruelty as we age. The falling of the righteous is never permanent if their nature is steeped in repentance. Righteousness is not the natural state of any human, but repentance can be. David's ongoing state was not righteous, but it was repentant. His reflex in failure was to turn from sin, not cover it. The wise live in repentance (the desire to uncover their own sin and turn from it) and thus can rise every time they fall. The foolish live self-righteously (desire to hide their own sin by uncovering that of others) and thus are incapable of recovering from calamity.

24.17

To be glad when evil happens to the evil is evil. Nothing in the heart of God rejoices when He must punish the wicked. His heart ever bears hope that pain will bring restoration, and He always holds back pain as the last resort. Hell's greatest agony is borne by God. The One who is outside of time so suffers even now over those who have and will reject His mercy. If God suffers eternally every time someone scorns His grace and chooses hell, if God suffers every time harm happens to one of His children (even an evil one), we dare not rejoice at his suffering. God feels all pain, including the pain suffered by His fallen ones; they are still loved and cried over in heavenly places. Only the fool laughs when God cries.

24.18

A sure way of distancing ourselves from God and thereby entering the cold shadowlands of His displeasure is by laughing when He cries or by rejoicing when He mourns. Our emotions are based and birthed out of the image of God, and the wise base their emotional reactions on those of the heavenly Father. Fools are the self-absorbed who are neither self-aware nor God-aware. Fools are out of step with the divine emotions. The wise carefully study the mood and measure of their God and mirror it. In that conformity they find richness and life in the range of emotional response; their emotions glorify and represent the Father, and thus do good not harm.

24.19

Worry is sin. Worry about evil people is folly. Worry is the opposite of prayer; for when we worry, we cannot pray, and when we pray, it is impossible to worry. Worry is sin because it is doubt that God is sovereign. Worry is sin because it is fear that God will not prevail. How foolish it is to stop trusting God. The wise do not worry, for they do not take their focus off God's great goodness. Fools concentrate on the trouble, and God's power moves to the periphery of their vision or is even lost to their view. The wise keep the concerns (real, valid, and dangerous though they may be) on the periphery, gazing longingly and devotedly at He whom they can trust. Worry is sin because it ignores God. Faith doesn't ignore problems; it just focuses on Christ.

24.20

Fret originates in forgetfulness. The Bible is so clear that suffering comes before glory and that glory wins in the end. We are promised suffering, and we are promised triumph. Fools forget both promises, fixate on the temporary trial, and lose sight of the ultimate vindication. The wise keep their gaze on eternity—no night, no curse, no death, no tears, all of Jesus forever—and are not unduly concerned by present pain. This is not to say there is no pain, but the wise refuse to dwell on what is now and they refuse to forget what is coming. We fret when we forget how it all ends and how long the goodness lasts. Wisdom lives with eternity in view, knowing the lamp of all that is wicked will soon be snuffed out. Folly darkly focuses on momentary troubles, forgetting the light that will soon dawn.

24.21

Rebels and rebellions never last; they always self-destruct. Wise sons are not enamored by change outside of context, the context that authority is in essence good, not bad. The wise realize that new is not always better and that authority always has less problems than autonomy. The ideal of autonomy, when divorced from authority, always decays into anarchy. Authority preserves life while anarchy destroys it. Fools think that autonomy can be managed without authority; but it cannot, for the forces of evil within every man always manifest in selfish ambition. The wise know they are only free when they are governed and so come to terms with their need, their desire, and their good to be under authority.

24.22

Rebellion has a very short life. The intoxicating delusion of freedom sweeps fools into systems and situations where ungoverned abandon leads to dissipation and death. The lie of rebellion is that internal self-rule is more accommodating than external authority structures. This lie goes back to the first man, first woman, and the first angel to fall from heaven. Satan thought and convinced humans that self-rule was better than God's rule—and we have all suffered the consequences ever since. The day we eat of the fruit of rebellion we die. We may live on, and we may even rule, but all that is precious is killed and all that endures is cursed. The wise stay under authority and have nothing to do with anyone or anything that rebels.

24.23

The literal Hebrew translation for the phrase "show partiality" is "recognize faces." Wisdom remembers that we should not and cannot judge by outward appearances. The richest looking man may be the most impoverished of soul. The most beautiful woman may be the ugliest within. The oldest looking may be the youngest thinking. Partiality is greedy, for its end desire is accumulation to self. Wisdom remembers that we do not bless or love those who will bless or love us back and we do not essentially give or honor in order to be given to or honored. In self-centered manner, folly scans the crowd for who can help "me" or "us"; wisdom scans for whom *to* help. Wisdom looks to give, while folly looks to receive.

24.24

Be just no matter the cost, for in the long run justice is always less expensive than corruption. Wisdom speaks truth, even when it causes pain to both speaker and hearer. Wisdom denounces evil, even when the evil can lash out. Wisdom knows that global good depends on local justice. Worldwide stability depends on common people in hidden contexts consistently making the brave choice to do what is right rather than what is easy. Folly tends to be cowardly, refusing to speak truth to power; and that fear is based on the harm power can do to prophetic voices. Wisdom knows it is much more dangerous and damaging to incur the condemnation of the nations and the ages than the wrath of the passing principality.

24.25

Because the righteous are tender and lowly, they are much easier to rebuke. Any charlatan or coward can castigate the humble people of God. What takes real courage is rebuke of the arrogant wicked. The wicked strike back, are not humble or kind, and do not hesitate to use violence, whether of tongue or tank. The righteous yield power and coercion; the wicked wield it. To rebuke the wicked will always exact a toll, a cost, a price, a pain. The wise realize, however, that the cost of being a prophetic voice is worth the casting of any scorn or stone. There is a delight when truth is told, a delight within the truth teller that comes from the Truth Maker. The blessing of speaking for the Righteous One is the joy of partaking in His character, a reward no amount of abuse can plunder, for they cannot access it.

24.26

There is something sweet about truth in all its forms. Truth is so powerful. It can cross metaphysical boundaries and give soul-surges of joy and sensations of peaceful happiness. When truth is spoken, it has a physical effect on us. We laugh, we settle, we rejoice, we rise to action, we viscerally improve when truth is spoken. Lies, on the other hand, cripple, eviscerate, discourage, maim, restrict, detract, discourage, sicken, and kill. Indeed, there is the power of life and death in the tongue. The wise use truth to heal and call forth life. Fools twist truth and take life. There is a direct connection between spoken truth and physical health and life. Truth that sickens is just a clever lie in disguise.

24.27

Necessity is always a priority over comfort. Civilizations that falter do so after they begin to prioritize luxury over industry, spending over saving, and entertainment over sacrificial service. The same is true for churches. When churches turn their steadfast attention from the priority of saving souls to the indulgence of growing the flock, they begin to falter. There may be a lag time between their physical and spiritual demise (some churches keep growing long after they began dying), but dying they are all the same. To stay spiritually alive, churches and Christians must constantly choose the hard work of making disciples over the busy work of creating departments. To stay spiritually faithful, churches must save their wealth to send it to the nations, not spend it on themselves or their buildings. To stay spiritually relevant, churches must choose death daily over entertainment Sunday.

24.28

If heaven is summed up by loving God and neighbor, then hell is the opposite: hating both. Hate is simply to be so against someone or something that you wish to destroy it. Hate is not intrinsically bad. There are some things God hates (divorce, abuse, injustice, deceit, etc.). But when the evil heart wants to destroy the God who is everywhere or the human who is near, it is folly. For you cannot destroy God or the human near you without ultimately destroying yourself. Love of God and neighbor then is wise, and hate of them is foolish, for it is futile in the former case (God cannot be destroyed) and suicidal in the latter (harm to those near you will always entail harm to self).

24.29

Wisdom does not hurt the one who has hurt you. Wisdom breaks the pain cycle by being the hurt swallower. Folly thinks there is remedy in passing on hurt. Wisdom knows that hurt extended is pain multiplied, that hurt does not diminish with dissemination. Wisdom knows that the way for hurt to be healed is by absorption. Someone has to choose to swallow the pain rather than to pass it on. Ultimately, no one feels better through hurting others. Revenge is strangely unsatisfying; in fact, revenge tends to be soul destroying. Fools think revenge will help them, but it only hurts them. The wise know that forgiveness is the only long-term freedom from the pain caused by others.

24.30

Laziness is the sin of activity misplaced. The obvious form of laziness is lack of any industry or effort (right actions replaced with sleeping, eating, or unrestrained leisure). The subtler form of laziness is labor in the wrong direction, labor spent in unfruitful ways. Obvious laziness does not work; subtle laziness works in the wrong way, or the wrong place, or the wrong time. Outright fools work at play. Wise fools work at the wrong things. The foolish wise work at the right things in the wrong way or time. The wise work at the right things in the right way at the right time.

24.31

Laziness is a series of small choices. Decay and death do not happen overnight, whether to teeth, a field, a building, or moral character. Most decay, due to deferred maintenance, is hidden in the early and middle stages and only becomes evident when matters turn drastic or in many cases too late. Such is the case with moral failure. Neglect of the little things quietly and secretly accumulate, and then it invariably manifests after sin has been committed and lives are destroyed. The wise realize that souls and ministries deteriorate in hidden manner; thus, they do not wait for the material evidence but discern the decay before it is obvious. The wise confess before they are caught. Fools think what is hidden is manageable and are deceived to their own destruction. The wise bring their own decay into the light; it is the only way of escape.

24.32

There are two ways to learn about moral decay: One is experience and the other is observation. Far, far better and wiser is the one who learns through observing from the lives of others. One of the reasons God in His wisdom decrees that punishment be public is mercy. He wants us to profit from the pain of others (through consequences of their own foolish choices, not as God's capricious object lesson) that we might escape that pain ourselves. This is why the Scriptures are so candid about the limps and liabilities of the heroes of faith. This is why elders and leaders in the church are to be disciplined publicly. This is why confession is intended to be public with consequence, not private with no remedial punishment. God's people are openly disciplined for their own good (for healing and recovery) and for the good of the community (to be sobered into avoiding a similar sin).

24.33

Moral poverty sneaks up on us with a thousand quiet steps. It is little sleeps and slumbers at our post that allow the enemies in. Quick moral poverty is as mythical as quick riches or sudden sterling character. Even as wealth is accumulated slowly and through great diligence, so poverty is fallen into by degrees, by consistent negligence. It is the passivity of a thousand days that leaves us wretched. It is a thousand nights of staying up too late that we sleep in too long which ultimately shapes our character and then our destiny, including our finances. We do not usually slide from safe to vulnerable (whether spiritually, relationally, morally, or fiscally) overnight. Outside of calamity, we are impoverished by a thousand little decisions or acts in our power to make that remain unmade or undone.

24.34

Until Jesus comes, we are at war. Because our enemies are not human but demonic principalities and evil powers, there is no abating their attack; they know no night and they need no rest. The wise then realize we can never be unguarded, and we can never lay our weapons down. We never take a sabbath from praying. We never take a vacation from abiding in Jesus. Fools forget that hell burns with agitation, unresting now in its dreaded anticipation and horror at eternal wrath. Demons prowl, armed with fear, hate, and deceit, ever circling, ever searching for a chink in our armor or a slip in our shield. The wise realize demonic forces don't have nuclear bombs; they have but thin, little spears that look for thin, little gaps in our armor.

PROVERBS
Chapter 25

25.1

Wisdom is preserved by writing, or at least by communication. Wisdom must be shared if it is to be kept. Undoubtedly, there are illiterate or deaf-mute wise people who live and have lived exemplary lives, but their impact in communicating wisdom might be limited to only those who know them intimately or to a few scholars. Great wisdom is lasting wisdom, and lasting wisdom must be recorded. This is why the Bible was written. This is why Jesus was the Word. This is why Paul was a preacher and a letter writer. This is why Solomon's proverbs were collected and recorded. This is why David's songs were memorized and passed down through the generations. Vanity veils itself as humility, though it's actually cowardice at best and selfishness at worst. If we don't record our wisdom for future generations, then we are foolish stewards.

25.2

Wisdom is earned; it is not given out all at once. We can gorge ourselves on information, but wisdom can only be ingested and digested over time. God knows that a central part of wisdom is the process of discovery, and that wisdom given painlessly is wisdom lost and wasted. This principle is true for all ages and all statuses. We never achieve a level where wisdom is either gained easily or given gratuitously. The learned, the aged, and the powerful acquire wisdom in the same way as the uneducated, the young, and the weak: slowly, painfully, and gloriously. Wisdom earned is wisdom respected. Wisdom toiled for is wisdom cherished. Wisdom purchased dearly is wisdom guarded carefully.

25.3

Discretion is a most necessary part of leadership, and wise leaders know when to reveal or not reveal what they know. It is possible to be transparent without being indiscrete, even if it is not easy. Wisdom tends to be slow to declare an opinion. Wise leadership is even slower. As leaders we are watched carefully and listened to closely, and whatever we do or say in moderation others will emulate to excess. Followers ever try to manipulate their opinion into the mouths of their leader, and leaders must be diligent to be above sectarian squabbles. Spiritual leaders, who to a degree represent God, must then exercise double discretion and be sure never to insert foolishness, dubious opinion, or sectarian opinion into the mouth of God.

25.4

Purity precedes pounding—though we would have it the other way. We think that once we are pure, once we have arrived, once we are "good," the pounding should cease. God's good holiness operates otherwise. First, God uses fire to remove our dross, then He hands us over to sovereignly empowered smiths to hammer away at us. The closer we grow to Jesus, the more we are like

Him, the better we know Him, and the more we will fall on our knees and beg for mercy. Clearer views of Jesus proportionally horrify our view of ourselves. First, Jesus removes the obvious flaws, sins, and brokenness, then He hammers out the subtle ones. Getting pounded does not necessarily mean we have sinned; it just means we are not yet as lowly, beautiful, or serviceable as the Master intends.

25.5

Wisdom does not allow evil ideas access. Wisdom has an inherent humility which recognizes that no human is impervious to sophistry. Some evil is a siren so intelligent and so alluring that the best thing to do and the most intelligent thing to do is stop up our ears, or even run away. It is folly, not courage, that lends a listening ear or eye to what is evil. We do not need to know or experience evil to shun it, not if we are wise. Delusion can start with an unguarded mind and undefended borders; it can also start with cavalier exposure. Fools think they can be exposed to lies or temptations and remain unaffected. The wise know that not all thoughts should be considered, nor all options be allowed a voice. Wisdom liberally chooses the narrow path without ever being narrow-minded. It is the broad mind that chooses the simple path.

25.6

We should never presume that honor once earned should always be extended. There is a subtle delusion that whispers to the ego that since we are good at one thing, we should be respected for all things, and since we are praised by some, we should be praised by all. While we should never relinquish or undermine self-respect, we should never demand that others respect us, never think we are entitled to ongoing honor, and never hold on to the praise of others as our ballast. The wise are not fueled by the respect of others. They have eyes only for One, and they rise and fall on their obedience to the Lord Jesus and never on the opinions of fickle men or their activity in the spotlight. Fools' self-worth is based on how others value them, and they need attention in order to retain value. The wise are content when the King is exalted, long after their few seconds of fame have flickered away.

25.7

Wisdom conserves energy by wasting no effort on trying to be seen. Fools spend so many physical and emotional calories on being noticed that the quality of their work suffers. Fools inspire in the moment, while the wise transform for a lifetime. When your focus is on making Jesus look good and seeing men and women discipled, you have no time for self-absorption. When you are consumed with self-glory, you cannot make disciples that last, nor can you honor the King, for glory is one thing He does not share. False wisdom humbles itself in order to be praised. True wisdom never seeks glory and is always genuinely surprised by it and uncomfortable with it, unloading it quickly at the feet of Him who alone is worthy of all.

25.8

Haste to dispute never ends well, and haste in dispute makes things disastrously more complicated. The wise studiously avoid quarreling and are adept at defusing tension. At their worst, fools relish unnecessary conflict and at their best bumble their way into it. Conflict is inevitable for both the wise and the foolish, but what distinguishes the wise is their serenity and composure under pressure. Intelligence devoid of wisdom is quickly exposed in tension and conflict. An intelligent person can be cynical, cutting, and demeaning, but that very demonstration of sharp wit is a revelation of a foolish heart. The wise man slows down when events speed up and cools down as temperatures rise. Fools heat up before it's necessary and cool down when it's too late.

25.9

Fools can talk poorly about friends, yet the wise don't talk poorly about enemies. It is always wise to be discreet with any damaging information you have on your enemies. Fools think knowledge is a weapon to wield in revenge against those who hurt them. The wise know that revenge never brings life, and that knowledge is a burden to be carried, swallowed, absorbed, and covered. Knowledge about others, when damaging and shameful, is not to be used against them; it is only appropriately exposed if it can work to bring peace, healing, solution, resolution, or justice for them. Fools unleash and spread pain indiscriminately thinking it will make them feel better. The wise bear pain so that another's lot improves, even the lots of their enemies.

25.10

To break the confidence of your confider is to lose the confidence of your hearer. If I tell you the secrets of another, you can be certain I cannot be trusted with your secrets. Folly thinks we gain the trust of the present by breaking the trust of the absent. The wise know that trust is only gained by demonstrated faithfulness to the ones who are not there to defend or represent themselves. I prove my fidelity by how I treat the absent one, not by what I say to those present. Faithfulness is a lifestyle. Trust is built slowly over time, and it can be lost in one brief, unguarded moment.

25.11

Beautiful words spoken in the right way at the right time are profoundly valuable because they are so rare. The double beauty of words spoken perfectly well *and* in perfect timing is unusual. What is normal is the wrong words at the wrong time, and what is common is the right words at the wrong time or in the wrong way. What is precious is just the right thing said in just the right way at just the right time. The wise speak. Following the Living Word, the wise open their mouths and do not hide behind silence, for self-muting truth is merely a high form of folly. What distinguishes wisdom from the many disguises of foolishness is the elegant blend of content, tone, and timing. To be wise, you must master and blend all three.

25.12

The decorations of the wise, the medals on their chest, are how well they listen and how well they give reproof. As hard as it is to listen well and to accept reproof, it is even harder to give reproof well with the needed blend of grace and truth. When we listen well, it is beautifying both to ourselves and to the one who corrects or instructs us. When we reprove well, it is beautifying to us as well as to the one being corrected. Reproof well done is a skill uncommonly found, and because it is rare, it is precious. Even as it is foolish to not listen to correction, it is foolish to not give it. The wise realize they are liable if they do not reprove. To not reprove leaves both parties ugly, both the one not being corrected and the one not reproving.

25.13

What is more refreshing than good news is true news. Over time we are designed to be lifted up by truth, not by what is most pleasant to hear. This is particularly true when we commission the message. We do not want messengers to distort the message to make it more palatable or to make themselves better liked; we want them to simply, lovingly, and faithfully pass on exactly what we entrusted to them. As messengers of God Almighty, we most refresh and please Him when we are faithful to His content and His character. Our fallen reality means that the message that refreshes God is the message that results in our rejection and scorn. The wise choose to please Jesus, not the hearer or themselves. Fools dilute, diminish, or distort God's message in a vain hope to refresh others, ultimately disappointing everyone.

25.14

There is something profoundly disappointing and draining about boasting. Boasting is being profligate with emotion, not stewarding our own or others' emotions well. When we promise what we cannot deliver, we unnecessarily waste the precious emotional resources God graciously grants. We don't ordinarily place the resource of emotion in the same rank as time and money, or strength and relationship, yet the reality is, emotional depletion takes longer to recover from than spiritual or physical fatigue. When we boast, it is a double loss: There is the spent emotion of escalated hope and the larger spending of hope deferred or dashed. And all that spending is in vain. The wise do not unnecessarily and vainly force others to spend emotional energy. The wise deliver their gifts without fanfare or promotion, and in the joy of that reception any emotional energy spent is fruitful.

25.15

We don't usually get our desires by whining, needling, nagging, or arguing. Counterintuitively, we usually have our requests granted by saying less and by concentrating on presence, not volume. Leaders do not necessarily need to hear to be reminded, but they do need to see. The persistent, non-abrasive presence of the supplicant is more convincing than the loud, demanding appeal. It is the quiet, steady appeal that moves the heart of kings. So then, the wise find ways to bring their cause visibly before the authority without being annoying. This is subtle art; it is not manipulation. This silent plea communicates to the leader a determination and resolve that appeals deeply to their conscience. Fools make themselves annoyingly heard; the wise make themselves dignifiedly seen.

25.16

The respect of boundaries is what differentiates the wise from the foolish. Folly simplistically assumes that if some is good, then more is better. Wisdom knows that anything can be corrupted if unbounded. The reality is, you can indeed get too much of a good thing; good and moderation are wed. Bad is essentially too much of a good thing as much as it is a little bit (or more) of a bad thing. What a tragedy when we lose the beauty of an act, food, experience, or even a relationship when we approach it without boundaries. We ravage what we do not self-guard against, spoiling forever what is pure. Only what is guarded and bounded remains beautiful.

25.17

Asking for help is not always a good thing, for an undisciplined approach to grace is detrimental to the soul. The wise restrain themselves from constantly asking for help for three reasons: to avoid idolatry, to save injury both to themselves and others, and to not unduly frustrate their friend or benefactor. God made humans with the capacity to work towards the solution of their own problems. When self-help is skipped, the soul itself suffers. God made humans with the capacity to help others, but He never intended humans to be the source—that is His place alone. Asking for help too often makes the asker both lazy and idolatrous. We are ever to go to God, our source. We are most often to wrestle the problem ourselves, and we are to occasionally ask for help from others. Fools invert the order—ever going to others first, occasionally working on it themselves, and only turning to God when all other help fails.

25.18

Lies do the most damage, and truth brings the most blessing close to home. When we lie to those closest to us, we end up hurting them and everyone else. When we walk in truth and light with those nearby us, we end up not only blessing them but blessing those far away. It is folly to think that a lie away from home will not do damage within the home. Lies and truth both come home to roost, and it is in proximity to home that they both have their greatest power. Wisdom knows that a truthful life away from home will always result in life to family and neighbors. Fools forget that lies far away from home come home with us quietly and devour furiously, as they are attached to us. We cannot be a false witness on the outside without destruction on the inside.

25.19

Faithlessness is not revealed in the good times. We are not proved faithful by our reliability when all is well. We are proved faithful by being steady in crisis, joyful despite loss, patient when under duress, and consistent when all affirmation, reward, and recognition have fled. When we demonstrate our commitment to others, it instills in everyone around us the confidence that we can be trusted. When others hear and see us defend the absent one, they know we will defend them in their absence, and thus, they know we are trustworthy. Faithfulness is demonstrated in the dark days as it is pressure that reveals what is truly within us.

25.20

Fools often mean well. Fools often say the right things, just in the wrong way or at the wrong time. Wisdom, therefore, is so much more than information or intelligence. Wisdom is knowing how and when to use information in a way that will give life. Folly doesn't have to be mean; sometimes it is well intentioned but untimely. The wise are prayerfully intentional about doing well, not just meaning well. The "I meant well" defense can sometimes be an indicator of foolishness. The wise take the time in prayer to discern when and how they should communicate what needs to be said. The wise realize that sometimes you need to stop singing or speaking. Sometimes you just need to sit quietly and let your tears or presence be your eloquence.

25.21

We must never forget that those men and women who oppose us are like us, and of us. We have more in common with our enemies than the heat of conflict allows us to remember. Even when faced by the harshest critics, wisdom dictates civility, hospitality, generosity, kindness, mercy, and compassion. Fools fight, abandoning their principles and common decency. The wise fight without surrendering morality or principle. The biggest wars are within—to do what is Christlike as opposed to what is fallen human nature. Goodness to those who oppose us while they oppose us keeps us fighting in God's way for God's glory. Meanness, harshness, or evil to our opposition means we have lost no matter if we win.

25.22

In the unavoidable contentions of life, the wise never lose sight of the fact that more is at stake than the current contention. Fools are shortsighted and focus only on the immediate battle, lusting to win it even if it means they lose the war. The wise keep a clear eye on the overall goal of the Lord of hosts and realize that pleasing Him is the big battle, and if apparently ceding ground in the now gives glory to Him in the then, then they cede. Fools confuse personal vindication with God's glory. The wise see it as vain to win a private vendetta if it brings public shame to the name of Jesus. The wise would rather be dishonored and gain the Lord's reward, than honored now and shamed forever. The wise are good to those who are bad to them, so that the good Lord will be gracious to all of us who are bad.

25.23

Every action has a consequence. We will be judged for every idle word. This is one of the most terrifying guarantees of Scripture. We will be held accountable for everything we say, including what we have said in our hearts. All will be revealed, all will be brought into the light, all will be broadcast. If in our spirits we backbite against the Lord, if we complain, disbelieve, whine, worry, or judge Him, it will evoke His anger. We cannot think that errant thoughts and injudicious words will go unpunished. The wise measure every word, even the unspoken ones, ever aware that all will be revealed and judged. Fools are cavalier and disrespectful in what they think and say, forgetting that every idle, idolatrous word and thought will face the wrath of God.

25.24

In the long term, isolation is better than unending contention. No husband can endure without withdrawing (whether physically or emotionally) from a wife who is constantly negative, critical, demanding, or pessimistic. No wife can endure a husband who constantly demeans, insults, criticizes, or blames; she will eventually leave whether in body or spirit. A contentious spirit will eventually isolate the one who always looks to bicker. You may enjoy being around others and may see your banter as harmless or as a personality trait, but those others will not enjoy being around you. They may be near you, but they will not be with you. You will have their guarded attention but not their intimate warmth. To fight, to tear down others, is satanic; to fight for them, to build them up, is Christlike.

25.25

Francis Xavier encouraged his friends to write long letters full of good news. This was back in the day when news from afar arrived once a year. Infrequent news full of goodness trumps hourly news full of despair. The spirit of our age is ravenous for news that is sensational and slutty; dramatic and threatening, and our news cycle is based on the dramatic spiking our emotions to starve our soul. News that feeds the soul is simple and elegant, common and cleansed, gentle and personal. Good news is kind, does not brag, is not provoked, rejoices in truth, believes all things, and hopes all things. The gospel is good news, a proclamation of all the good God has done in Christ. The wise emulate this in their daily broadcasting. The wise make it a discipline to pass on simple, common, uplifting good news.

25.26

The tragedy of a good man corrupted is far more damaging than the tragedy of a bad man exposed. When a man or woman has been used of God to bless, feed, and refresh others and then that person falls into sin, double damage is done. Not only is future good aborted, but past good is marred and spoiled. Great is the harm good men and women do retroactively when they fall into sin. The wise guard not only the future, but also the past. The wise refuse to give into internal or external temptation, for they know the damage spreads backwards as well as forwards, and they refuse to harm in the present the ones they helped in the past. Fools abuse the ones they helped previously and abdicate helping future ones when they choose momentary indulgence.

25.27

What makes a material thing bad is too much of it. The only good that increases in value with unlimited volume is God Himself. Too much water, bread, exercise, reading, sleep, washing, people, etc., though all good things, are in fact bad. Moderation, balance, and harmony between the goods of life keep them good. Immoderation, imbalance, and dissonance between the goods of life make them harmful. This can also be true of immaterial glory. Seeking to increase your glory is shameful. Others praising you (in moderation) is good for you and good for them. God was pleased with His good work and intends for us to be pleased with ourselves when we do well, but that pleasure must be centered in doing what we do well for the glory of God, not for our own glory or for others' praise. Pleasure in good work is purest when deep inside we do it for Jesus, no matter what others think or say.

25.28

A lack of self-control is a lack of self-defense. Outbursts of inappropriate emotion on the surface seem to harm others, but in reality, they harm the unharnessed. The lie of the age is that we do damage to ourselves if we repress passion. The truth of the ages is that the greatest joys lie on the other side of the greatest discipline. The unrestrained glutton does not enjoy food more than the disciplined athlete. The promiscuous is not more sexually gratified than the faithful spouse. Boundaries make life beautiful, and Satan has always tried to twist boundaries into bondages. The wise refuse that lie and embrace God-given boundaries; they are both protected and enriched by that trust. Fools have no boundaries and thus have no protection, and all their beauties are broken.

PROVERBS

Chapter 26

26.1

Good things can be sullied by bad people. Authority is a good thing, but when authority is given to evil people, the authority becomes corrupted, not the evil cured. Giving honor to someone who does not deserve it does not make that one honorable; it corrupts the one giving honor inappropriately. It is foolish to think that good is good regardless of context. The wise know that a good gift given at the wrong time can cripple or wound. The wise know that certain measures of maturity or character are needed in order for good to be good and not become bad. Fools indiscriminately or naively scatter good, even to bad effect. What makes God's good *always* good is His wisdom in when and how to dispense it. Our good can corrupt if given in the wrong spirit, time, or place.

26.2

Curses undeserved cannot invade; they can only be invited in. Spiritual attack is real and indeed can buffet our souls and minds, but the promise of Scripture by the indwelling power of the Spirit is that such attacks cannot take up residence. Certainly, we are not ignorant of the devices of the enemy, and just as certainly we are not alarmed by them. Sons and daughters of the living Lord do not fear the threats, curses, lies, and attacks, neither from demons nor detractors. Curses with cause, however, are a different matter. They have legitimate, sinister power when the cause is a disobedience, a sin, an unsaved and unprotected state of the individual. The wise stay under the protection of the blood of Jesus, the protection of a righteous and repentant life. Fools are unprotected, made vulnerable to cursing's power by being unsaved or unholy.

26.3

The Lord is so tender in His merciful discipline. He starts out with quiet rebukes and measures. If we will respond to the little corrections of the Spirit, there is no need for Him to take more drastic measures. The more tender and responsive we are to the Spirit's conviction and correction, the gentler His discipline. The wise welcome God's tender tap and have no need for the bridle or rod. Fools ignore the simple, less painful corrections of God and can only be helped by more drastic measures. The great love of God is willing to be severe, but it is not His preference. How sweet or sour our path to correction depends on how quickly and thankfully we respond to God's initial care. If we are supple, our discipline will be sweet. If we are stubborn, it will be stringent.

26.4

Fools are not transformed by hearing wisdom in the spirit of their folly. They must have truth fall on them and break them under the authority of the Spirit of God. To answer a fool in the same manner as he speaks reduces us to folly. To answer a fool with the anointing and authority of God is the fool's only hope and the speaker's only recourse. Faith comes by hearing if and when the Holy Spirit empowers the speaking. The wise then do not depend on eloquence or the natural reasoning mind (though they employ both); rather, the wise depend on the insight and unction of the Holy Spirit. The wise never talk down to others; neither do they stoop down to the cynicism, exaggeration, or bitterness of foolish talk.

26.5

Foolish talk must be exposed and resisted. It is neither wise nor appropriate to give free reign to speech that is detrimental to self or society. We cannot hide behind the enshrined right of free speech when that right is used to demean or dishonor others. Free speech in both the civic and private spheres means we have the right to speak what is true and edifying, not the right to speak what is vile and destructive. Unresisted folly is empowered, corrosive folly, and it is incumbent on the wise to publicly demonstrate where folly is false. Central to that demonstration is the spirit in which folly is exposed. Wisdom is more than content; it is also posture and attitude. How we push back against public foolishness matters. The wise answer fools as they deserve—by resisting their spirit, not matching it.

26.6

The primary ingredient in good leadership is wise followership. Humanly, wise followers can make a poor leader appear clever. It is much more difficult for a wise leader to make their foolish followers appear prudent. Good leadership then is essentially supported and maintained by wise followers, as it is the body not the head in any organization that implements policy. If a leader has foolish messengers and practitioners, his leadership is doomed. Much longer and more fruitful is the life of an organization with a poor leader fortuitously staffed by the wise than one with a shining leader without wise followers. Obviously, folly on either end of the equation spells doom for the organization while wisdom on both ends brings life and blessing. Wise leaders invest primarily in making their followers wise and in learning from their followers who are wise.

26.7

Wisdom is not found in words, but in lives. Two persons can form the exact same sounds, but from one mouth there will issue notable power and from the other simply noise. What gives words power is the authenticity, purity, and humility of the heart that said them, not the wattage of the brain that arranged them or the skill of the lips that spoke them. Wise ears then listen to hearts and watch lives before being smitten by or enamored with words. English as an international language has improperly ushered young, less-wise men and women into the limelight while older, sager Africans, Arabs, Asians, and Latinos (who are not as articulate in English) are not as quickly or easily heard. Fools think intelligence and fluency automatically grant a public podium. The wise know their lives and experience must build the platform from which they will one day speak.

26.8

When we praise those who don't merit it, we push them to injure another. Wisdom does not confuse love with flattery. Love is kind enough to speak the truth and finds a way to do so in a manner that brings life. Honor does not "life" a fool; it merely helps her wound and kill others. Honoring fools lengthens the shelf-life of the damage they do to themselves and spreads it to others. Therefore, it is irresponsible (from misguided pity) to do anything that lets folly survive and spread. Loving wisdom is intolerant of folly in self, friends, followers, and even leaders. Loving wisdom finds a kind way to silence and stop what is foolish and destructive. Loving wisdom is brave and does not cower behind compliments.

26.9

It is not wise to let truth spoken by knaves set a trap for fools. Wisdom does not allow the sword of truth to cut or wound when it is improperly swung. This is possible because truth is ultimately located in a person, not in a principle or the pronunciation of sounds. Truth is centered in the Word, not in the words. Therefore, when true words are wielded foolishly, they lose their truth, and we are released from the need to heed them. Words are authenticated not by who uses them, but by how they are used and why. The father of lies is very good at truth, or at subtly twisting it that is, and we are by no means required to listen to him. It is wise to ignore truth foolishly spoken, for manipulated truth only deceives.

26.10

There are numerous Old Testament anecdotes which remind us that the wrong kind of help only hurts. Wisdom would rather go slower, win less, lose more, and suffer longer than exchange one problem for a greater one. Wisdom determines that long-term solutions are worth short-term trial. Fools do not have the patience to weather small storms and thus sail imprudently into rash ones. When we go to war (for souls, for the fame of Jesus among all nations), we must march with those who know how to fight the enemy without killing their colleagues. There is something worse than having no or too few team members and that is having the wrong ones, the ones that devastate from within.

26.11

A mark of wisdom is the increased span of time between sin, particularly the same sin. Thankful for justification, which is immediate, all of us, including the wisest, still sin. Fools then are those who commit the same sin repeatedly and frequently, while the wise are those who infrequently repeat the same sin. Folly and wisdom in this sense are not connected to natural intelligence but spiritual determination. Wisdom willfully abstains from selfish indulgence to please God. Folly willfully indulges self while intentionally wounding God. The frequent repetition of the same sin is worse than eating our own vomit; it is purposefully vomiting on Christ.

26.12

The greatest folly is to think you are something, to think you are someone, to think you are wise. The great tendency for humans of all ages and in all ages is to think we know, think we can, or think we are something. The greatest wisdom in eternity is to be nothing that Christ be all in all. Being nothing is not a divestment of personality or a perverted annihilation of what God has created good; rather, being nothing is fully trusting that God's will for us is best, fully happy in His knowledge, His strength, and His person. Deep within every heart is a rebellion against God being all in all. Every one of us in our fallenness resents at some level the supremacy of God in all things. Every rebel resents at our core

God being all in all. We want to be some, even if He is most. But the wisest One who ever lived, the only One worthy of grasping equality with God, refused to do so and made Himself nothing. It's foolish to do anything else.

26.13

Laziness is the secret partner of fear. We are more afraid of hard work than we are of danger. We prefer adventure (with all its adrenaline which results from risk) to adversity (with the blisters we accrue from boring, strenuous labor). We tend to blame our lack of work ethic on danger, which to us is a less shameful excuse. It looks wise to avoid harm, while it never looks wise to avoid hard work. So foolish hearts avoid hard work by pretending to avoid harm, which is simply a manipulation of truth. If laziness is paired with fear, then labor is paired with faith. Faith works. Faith roles up its sleeves and sweats, and hard work dispels fear. Fear renders you immobile. Faith fires you up to action.

26.14

The lazy work hard at not working and end up working more feverishly than the wise. A sluggard tosses and turns on his bed, lingering there long after sleep has risen and left. Poor planning and procrastination pile up and force frenetic action in condensed periods that do little more than breed ulcers. Steady, disciplined, intentional labor by contrast cultivates health and strength, and the hardworking end up with more time for true leisure than the lazy. It is an exorable law of nature that those who work hardest sleep best and play most. Those who work least have less rest and less joy. Wisdom then sees hard work as a friend, a blessing, a gift, a freedom, and a joy. Beware the lazy path, for it leads only to sadness and slavery.

26.15

The more you have, the greater the temptation to sloth. Industry motivated by selfish increase is simply the marriage of greed and laziness. The indulgent rich may indeed work hard, but to what end? Merely so they don't have to work unless they want to, which is in itself a perversion of the sanctity of work. Work is sacred when it has God's glory in mind first and others' good in mind second, beautiful in and of itself. We will work joyfully in heaven. Work that prioritizes self, work that accrues abundance without sacrificial sharing is the sluggard overfed and the soul wearied with abundance, starved by lack of generosity.

26.16

Laziness makes you talkative and gives you the energy to speak needlessly and thus foolishly. Work conserves words and empowers what is necessary and stifles what is frivolous. Those who work best talk least, and those who talk most have too little of importance in hand. When those who work best then talk, their words have weight and moral authority. The few words of the workmen are of greater gravitas that the garrulousness of the idle. Spoken wisdom is life impacting when it is the gold laboriously mined through a disciplined life. Gilded speech unattended by faithful and hidden deeds has power to inspire fleetingly but never to eternally transform.

26.17

Strife is not to be sought nor is it to be avoided. It is foolish both to meddle in a quarrel not your own and to avoid the quarrel that only you should take up. Quarrels require emotional energy when engaged in through the flesh; thus, to quarrel in the spirit requires our full attention and devotion. The wise quarrel well, which means they get tone and tenor, time and content, ways and means all aligned in a manner that represents Christ. This demands prayer, attention, diligence, focus, and devotion. It is folly to think we never will quarrel, and it is wisdom to give quarreling the righteous attention it deserves and demands if it is to be resolved in a way that makes Jesus glad.

26.18

Needless, destructive violence is always a sign of madness. The sane only resort to violence that corrects, protects, and redeems. The cross of Jesus Christ was bloody and violent; it was resorted to as it was the only means of redemption and new life. The crosses of Nero were flaming testimonies to his evil, profligate wickedness. Violence itself is not wicked. In fact, when violence is wielded rightly, it is the last restraint against wickedness. Sometimes the only way to stop what is wicked is with violence. It is a sword we must fear, for it is so difficult to swing it appropriately; yet there are times when it must swing. Only one cross in all of history has justification, though thousands were planted in pain.

26.19

Deception is always demonic, no matter how much initial delight it brings to the deceiver. The intoxication of clever lies (which indeed have a strange allure) always ends in drunken death. Discretion is valor, and deception is cowardice. The deception manufactured through withholding truth is as damaging and wicked as that which misinforms. Godly men and women are brave enough to tell the truth, even to their own hurt and the hurt of others. To hurt others through withholding truth, or twisting it, is the practice of the perverted. Until Jesus comes, life will include pain, and the folly of deception is that it seeks to avoid pain through lies, which only magnifies pain in the end. The wise choose the lesser pain and the greater good by sticking to truth.

26.20

Wisdom is a gossip swallower. Fasting words and starving slander are how dissension is doused and how damage is mitigated. Wisdom pours water on angry words, while folly pours gasoline. Wisdom knows that the more you talk, the more evidence you provide to the listener that you are not wise. Folly prattles itself to shame. Our ears do so much more to provide healing than our lips. Poor memories make better friends than minds that recall every error. Contention conquerors speak slowly, forget quickly, and by their restraint spread peace quietly and surely.

26.21

Contention is a fire carried within the fool. The fighter in nature carries the sparks within and constantly looks for wind to fan his flame into folly. The flesh carries the fire of conflict into every conversation, community, and covenant waiting for someone to give it excuse, fodder, or opportunity. Wisdom recognizes that selfish ambition flickers in every human heart and takes the personal responsibility to quench those flames from the inside out. The washing of the Word has quenching power, and the embers of sin and strife smoldering in our hearts must be watered every day, for it takes just a gust of selfish indignation to ignite them.

26.22

Wisdom refuses the sugar of slander. Wisdom knows that the healthy, plain fare of the ears is stronger and more nourishing over the years than the sugar of scandal. It is counterintuitive in that the sensationalism that excites us also damages our spirit, while the old stories of virtue and ancient words of truth that bore us give us life. Fools tire of the meat and potatoes of simple truth because it is known; instead, they are beguiled by what is wrong simply because it is new. God is able to renew old, faithful truths, beautifying them to us even as a beloved spouse becomes more attractive even as they age. Wisdom finds new levels in the old and true. Folly flounders into old traps disguised in new trappings.

26.23

The sweetest looking Christian can actually be a murderous soul assassin in disguise. Evil has learned that it can often hide best in the open halls of the church. The most twisted lies can garb themselves in clerical truth. Sweet language from a twisted heart has a peculiar odor and is most poisonous to the soul of both the hearer and speaker. Pious acts and words in public which cover abuses of deed in private are more damaging than the blatant evil which openly mocks holiness. When those that represent the Healer do the hurting, the devastation is crippling and almost irreparable. The wise are ever vigilant not to do harm in the name of Jesus who is only good. Fools take no vigilance, shake with no fear of this unfortunately common trespass, and run the risk of driving God's flock from the range of their Master's voice. When the holy mock the Holy, there will be all hell to pay.

26.24

False representation of self is disguised hatred. When we don't have the integrity to march our wayward hearts to the cross and instead cloak what is dark within by words of light without, we end up hurting and hating both ourselves and others. The soul was not meant to live at odds with itself. We were designed for union and harmony between heart and hands, between will and words. When we feel one way and speak another, we breed within ourselves hostile civil war. We do not make peace by giving verbal vent to every evil thing that lurks within; rather, we make peace by repenting for what is within. Evil within is only excised by the blood of Jesus, not by bloodying others through our hateful words and actions. It must come out, but Jesus must remove it from us; otherwise, we vomit on others without being free from that venom within.

26.25

Words are sharp weapons. True words can kill and maim as easily as false ones, just as in an operation, scalpels can do much harm as well as much good. Kind words can damage if they are spoken at the wrong time or in the wrong spirit. Wisdom goes beyond knowing what to say; it also knows how and when to say it. Right words spoken at the wrong time are, in fact, wrong words. True words spoken from false hearts have no power to transform outside of God's intervention and will not be long tolerated by God's benevolence. We are wise if we remember that good, true words can wound and that they can even deceive. Wisdom wants no part of wounding or deception and takes pains to say kind things from a kind heart at a kind time.

26.26

Hate masquerading as wisdom will eventually be exposed. Wicked wisdom is often dressed up piously and is always manipulative. This falsity is easiest to spot in the self-proclaimed religious, but it is just as prevalent and more insidious in the self-proclaimed humble and secular. Because God is truth and loves truth, He cannot stand deception and guile anywhere they are found. Because God is light and hates darkness, He will assuredly expose all who deceive and will shout clarity from the rooftops. There is coming a time when every thought, motive, and duplicity in our hearts will be made known. Exposure of our evil is guaranteed. The wise choose to expose their own sin through repentance privately. Fools who do not expose their own evil hearts privately to God will have what they hide broadcast publicly to the globe.

26.27

We always reap what we sow. Always. Good and bad, we will reap what we sow. Setting a trap for others ensures we will be hunted and trapped. Betraying others ensures we will be betrayed. Rebelling against others ensures we will be overthrown. Lying about others ensures we will be slandered. Believing the worst ensures we will be doubted. Gossiping ensures we will be criticized. We always reap what we sow. Always. Give and it will be given to us. Love and we will be loved. Thank and we will be thanked. Obey and we will be obeyed. Trust and we will be trusted. Affirm and we will be appreciated. Forgive and we will be forgiven. Pray for and we will be prayed for. The wise consider the good of others and in doing so will harvest good in return.

26.28

Flattery is subtle hatred, for it actually intends to crush, destroy, overthrow, replace, relegate, or remove. Flattery is more spiteful than open lies and is but a disguised form of covetousness. Flattery is cousin to lying, one destroying and the other ruining. Flattery is more painful than lies, for flattery comes from those who are near, from those who pretend to empathize and understand. Lies come from those who do not pretend and in that sense are more honest. Flattery is a double deception and therefore a double pain. Fools flatter and cripple. The wise speak truth and heal, even if they hurt.

PROVERBS

Chapter 27

27.1

The Christian prayer "Maranatha" is content to be discontented. Simultaneously, we both live for today and long for tomorrow. God intends for us to rejoice in little pleasures. In fact, He grants them to us as little deposits of eternal joy. The best way to get ready for heaven, the best way to yearn for the trumpet to sound and the Lord to descend, is to relish the goodness of God in simple joys today. We truly best represent the King of eternity by embracing Him in this time, by reveling in little graces. Satisfaction in small, passing joys today prepares us for unending bliss when dawns the eternal day.

27.2

Self-praise is self-defeating, accomplishing the opposite of its intention. When we try to build ourselves up by drawing attention to ourselves in word or deed, we actually make ourselves small. When we make much of ourselves, we actually hyperinflate our being, stretching it to a capacity it was not designed for, making it more vulnerable and weaker. Self-praise is the vanity of too much hot air forced into the thin shell of our character, which just like a balloon leads to explosion and disaster. When we praise ourselves, we lose the capacity to endure opposition.

27.3

Folly wears other people down, makes those around you fatigued, and thus weakens the community. Folly is never isolated to one individual. In our interdependent lives (for we all were made to live in relational community), one fool diseases the whole family. Wisdom then does not think that a fool is harmless, nor naively think that a fool's harm will only affect the fool. Folly must be removed from the body kindly and firmly. Wisdom seeks a way to remove the folly from the fool without removing the fool from the family. Only as a last resort is the fool handed over to Satan for the destruction of the flesh.

27.4

Human jealousy is an indefatigable virus, wearing down both the one who is jealous and the one who envies. No marriage or relationship can survive human jealousy, for it is a multilateral destroyer, a black hole that sucks life from both parties. Human jealousy destroys the very honor it seeks to protect. Godly jealousy protects the honor man seeks to steal. Human jealousy clings to hidden perverted love, clinging to and smothering others. Godly jealousy preserves and demonstrates sacrificial love, sharing, releasing, and elevating He who is pure above all others.

27.5

Love concealed is damaging to loved and lover. God never hides His love; He always demonstrates and displays it. To hide or hold the love you have for others is to hate them. It is to deprive them of that which would "life" them, thus denying them life, which is indeed a form of hate. Loving correction is a form of life as it keeps the one loved from self-destruction. So, to conceal love by withholding correction is a selfish, cowardly apathy, a mild if still murderous form of hate. If we love one another, we will display that love by correcting one another. The wise are separated from the fools in how, when, and why they love and correct.

27.6

Friends hurt one another for good. Enemies love one another for evil. Dentists, doctors, and daddies hurt without harming, as do the wise. Loving ones know that pain in the short term is often necessary to avoid agony eternally; thus, they have the courage to choose the lesser "evil" to gain the greater good. Fools do not have the strength of character to hurt others in order to heal them. They only have the baser instinct to hurt in order to harm or to bless in order to curse. Faithfulness is demonstrated by our willingness to wound others for their good at cost to ourselves through mutual pain. A litmus test for helpful hurting is who shares and bears the pain—if the healer bears no pain, then his hurting was but harm.

27.7

Hunger can be a gift as appreciation grows in moderation and tends to wane in abundance. When we have much of a physical something, we begin to despise, forget, or regulate its importance. It takes a respiratory disease to remind us that we should be thankful for every breath. It takes throat cancer to remind us we should be thankful that we can swallow. It takes a cavity in one tooth to remind us we should daily thank the Lord for painless chewing. Absence leads us to appreciation. When we have a modest amount of any good item, we are more aware of its value. Wisdom thus embraces moderation, for moderation enhances appreciation. Folly loses pleasure by abandoning moderation.

27.8

Wisdom stays grounded no matter what accomplishments are gained or lost. John Newton, who wrote the hymn "Amazing Grace," was aged when he confronted loss of memory, energy, and capacity. He responded by saying, "Although my memory's fading, I remember two things very clearly: I am a great sinner and Christ is a great Savior." These two pillars grounded Newton through the ups and downs of his life, and the waxing and waning of his strength. When we wander from simple truths, we fall prey to complex lies.

27.9

Truth adorns and beautifies. You are more at peace with yourself when you listen to godly counsel. To see yourself as others see you helps you to see yourself as God sees you. Godly counsel grants a revelation of self, rooted in God, thus rooted in redemptive love. This vision is both honest and healing, blunt and beautifying. Only God and those that represent Him faithfully have the capacity to removes illusions while inspiring hope. Only God blends just the right amount of truth with love, varying the mixture as context and character require. Wisdom marshals the courage to see ourselves as we truly are, so that we catch a vision of who we can and will be in God.

27.10

Loyalty is always rewarded by God, if not by man. We are wise to make loyalty deposits both locally and eternally. Because loyalty is such a God-like attribute (He remains faithful even when we are faithless), God delights when His children evidence it, even to less than worthy leaders or friends. David and Jonathan were united even in this; they both were loyal, and God delighted in that friendship, and they were able to delight in one another. In friendship, leadership, and followership, loyalty is an armor that grants great confidence. We can face most any foe and any odds and any devastation when we know our friends are loyal. Without loyalty even our wins are losses.

27.11

Reproach is lifted over time by our long-term fruit. Steady, wise, godly action over time can overcome all slander and false judgment. It is often fruitless to defend ourselves with words in the short term. Only sustained righteousness overcomes the prejudice of the human heart. The wise do not demand quick vindication; they do not even insist on it in their lifetime. The wise do not defend themselves emotionally or verbally. They just silently build a legacy from the foundation up that no white lie can blacken. Fools rush frantically and vainly for vindication. The wise let their long godly life, and death, do the talking.

27.12

Courage is prudent, knowing when to hide, wait, and remain silent. Sometimes it takes more courage not to act, more wisdom not to react. There can be a fine line between courage and folly, a line as thin as that between wisdom and cowardice. What distinguishes the wise is that they are both brave and disciplined, heart and head in harmony. Fools can err in either direction, either with the heart or the head. Fools don't lack courage or intelligence. They simply don't understand how to blend them and when to adjust the blend, and thus pay the penalty for their misappropriation and their imbalance of the virtues.

27.13

The naïve need external boundaries for their own protection. Growth in wisdom empowers society to give you more liberty. The biblical progression from law to grace provides the basis for human maturity. When we are foolish and young, we need more rules. As we mature, we can be trusted with extended boundaries. The wiser we are, the more we appreciate those boundaries and the less they offend us. Offense at law, accountability, hedges, and boundaries is an indicator of immaturity. The wiser we are, the more unafraid and appreciative we are of those who hold us to account.

27.14

How we communicate what we know and feel is just as important as what we know that burns inside us. Good content is lost or scorned when the delivery mechanism is not appropriate and timely. If we place the truth that we're passionate about before those who desperately need to feed on it in a way they cannot comprehend or receive, we are the guilty ones, the fools who have cast pearls before swine. It is not the pigs' fault that they cannot be nourished by our gems. Wisdom does not waste what is precious in the attempt to transfer it in a way that cannot be comprehended. Wisdom has the diligence and discipline to learn the heart language of the receiver, that no treasure may be lost through ways and means of communication.

27.15

Big battles exhilarate even as they exhaust, for the accomplishment or even hope of great victory compensates all costs. Little battles that never end and promise no victory only exhaust. Steady, small, ceaseless negativity, criticism, or discouragement is more damaging than the gross casualties of greater wars. We were designed to charge giants and have anointed adrenaline course through our veins, carrying us through danger and challenge. We were not designed to bear the constant dripping of internal dissent or negativity. The wise do not allow their mouths or attitudes to be the small, ceaseless enemy within the family, team, church, or body of Christ.

27.16

Do not let the satanic voice of negativity use your mouth or demeanor as its megaphone. Negativity of spirit is nigh impossible to wrestle with as it is so subtle with an appearance of wisdom. Negativity is a cancer that kills from the inside out. The wise do not allow themselves to mimic the devil's voice. They refuse to play that poisonous sound inside their heads, and they refuse to utter it with their mouths. Faith does not deny facts, but neither does it delight to point out errors. Faith also speaks into being what does not yet exist. Faith joins love in believing the best about others and hoping for all good things. Faith silences negativity and vocalizes and prophesies good.

27.17

We need one another to be honest, different, pointed, and appropriately cutting. No one wants the surgeon's scalpel to be blunt or the dentist's drill to be dull. If we are going to hurt one another for good, let us do it with the least pain possible which requires strength and a no-nonsense approach to mutual health. Weak warriors are not made strong by weak colleagues or instructors. Strong Christians are not kept strong by weak friends or spineless leaders. We need the prophetically edgy. We need the fearless teacher. We need the courageous leader to call us out for what we are not and to shape us into what we can and should be. We are better together when we are different kinds of mutually beneficial strong and sharp.

27.18

Submission is always rewarded, particularly in heaven. The order within the Trinity displays the strength of submission, the honoring of others through the humbling of ourselves. There is such a beauty in God the Son submitting to God the Father and in God the Spirit glorifying God the Son, that when glimpses of that beauty are evidenced in broken human relationships, our triune God beams down upon that effort with blessing. We are asked to submit to our authorities because God is perfect, not because our leader is. We are asked to demonstrate the health and hope of perfect union as it exists in heaven even though we serve imperfect rulers here below. When we submit despite our discomfort, we are caring for our heavenly Master, and He who sees in secret will one day reward openly.

27.19

We don't see ourselves as we really are. The human heart is so depraved that we inevitably see ourselves as better or worse than is factual. In order to see into our own hearts, we need to borrow the eyes of others, particularly the Lord's eyes. The "Johari window" is a technique designed to help people better understand their relationship with themselves and others. The window has four quadrants: known to self, known to others, hidden to self, and hidden to others. Both friends and enemies can help us see ourselves clearly if we will allow their encouragement and criticism; and yet even they are half-blind. The Lord alone sees us perfectly, both for who we really are and for who He will make us into. The foolish rely on their perception of self and are limited. The wise look at themselves through the lenses of others and rely on the insight of God, and they are therefore limitless.

27.20

Binging is never good. It is a sterile term we now use for unholy dissatisfaction. Bad stuff, evil stuff makes us hungry and leaves us hungrier. God stuff, good stuff, beautiful and pure things create hunger and then deeply satisfy us. The Bible tells us that lusty eyes and lusty hell are never satisfied with their unholy appetite. Wise men master their appetite and better appreciate natural things through moderation, giving them fuel to feast on Jesus. Fools let their appetite for unnatural things smother their hunger for Jesus leaving them without spiritual energy, lean of soul, emaciated in spirit. The wonderful thing about being hungry for Jesus is that He is so satisfying and filling. The tragic thing about all other hungers is that they are empty and disappoint.

27.21

Praise is our constant examiner. It ever reveals our hearts. In this sense praise is more ruthless than criticism. Praise has a greater capacity than criticism to lay bare the motives, ambitions, intentions, and quality of our character than criticism does. Counterintuitively, criticism often makes us stronger while praise makes us weaker. Praise in and of itself is a good thing, and we should be quick to praise God and others, while slow to seek praise for ourselves. The test of praise is whether we devour it for our own glory or direct it to God for His. When we steal praise that belongs to God, we are weakened by it. When we accept criticism because we belong to Jesus, we are strengthened by it.

27.22

Honor is unfitting for fools because it hurts them rather than helps them. God's truth does not make exceptions and is double-edged. When a wise, strong, or powerful man sins, God's truth rebukes him. When a foolish, weak, or broken man sins, God's truth rebukes him. Real truth is impartial, and it is just as much a lie to speak what is false over the weak and foolish as it is over the wise and strong. To give honor where it is not due is to lie, and whenever we lie, we destroy and damage. The wise do not hurt the foolish by honoring them. Misguided kindness is cruel, for it perpetuates lies and leads to harm.

27.23

Stewards are good at details. Shepherds are good at leading people. And all missions is essentially like all politics—it's local. The best ministry visionaries are those who personally evangelize and disciple. We can have all the strategy in the world. We can be brilliant in precept and principle. We can be unsurpassed in knowledge of culture and language. But if we don't deal well with persons, we falter. It's not enough to be a people person in general, charming crowds and inspiring the masses. If our grander strategy is going to transform, we must be a person's person, knowing and loving hidden individuals. Shepherds are good stewards when they know why the littlest lamb bleats.

27.24

Wisdom plans ahead by investing in kindness and mercy. Unjust stewards think they can buy friendship through favors and benefits improperly granted. Wise stewards do not use corporate power or wealth to make friends, for the inevitable loss of power and riches will lead inevitably to the loss of friendship. Wise leaders, wise people love and give personally and genuinely from a storehouse that does not get left behind when a position is vacated. Kindness and mercy do not require title or talent, just a humble, gracious heart. Power tends to overwhelm grace. But the wise never allow that hollow victory and thus ensure they will be the recipients of grace long after illusory power has abandoned them.

27.25

We cannot enjoy the rapture of resurrection without the reality of the tomb. New life will always require death at some level. Having two kings, two popes, or two heads never works out well, and even good things that age must be removed or replaced with new good things. "The king is dead!" is always followed by "long live the King!" Wise old kings die graciously in the hope of wise young ones to follow. When folly is disguised as nostalgia, we hold onto what we should bury with honor, and in so doing lose both the old and the new.

27.26

Our fruit (both character and disciples) is our retirement provision: the fruit of our lips, the fruit of our hands, the fruit of lives lived well, the fruit of character developed, the fruit of disciples made. As strength ebbs and minds cloud, there is no comfort like a clean conscience. When bodies wear out, we can yet enjoy the vitality of others running with our inherited baton farther and faster than we did. We can sit back in our rocking chair and smile. As our old world winds toward the narrow gate, we can be content, for we carry no baggage, writhe under no angst, and the memories we can remember warm us. Looking back with unclouded joy sweetens the anticipation of crossing the threshold of death into eternal life. Waiting for us, smiling, are those who passed us their baton, and we go to join that happy throng, lingering as the final runners bring the baton home to glory.

27.27

Faithfulness is a legacy that blesses multiple generations after us, for multiple layers of people around us. God is so gladdened by godly children and by obedient disciples that His blessings emanate from them far beyond what they know. God is so giddy about those who serve Him faithfully that He rewards not just them, but any they touch. God is so generous in grace that when He graces, it is impossible for that goodness to be contained by the receiver. There is overflow in all directions and even across time. The greatest gift you can give to those around you, whether family or friends, is to be faithful to your Father in heaven. For when we are faithful to Him, God delights to bless them by making your cup overflow.

PROVERBS

Chapter 28

28.1

Wickedness is married to cowardice, and righteousness both justifies and enhances boldness. Courage is the domain of the holy only. The demonic cannot be brave; they can only be thugs. When the wicked are brave, it is not to be confused as courage, as the motivation is either fear, selfishness, hate, or some other broken impetus. Courage requires the right motivation wedded to the right action at the right time. When we are in the right as God defines it and we act despite risk, we are courageous. When we risk because of wrong, we may be brave, but we are not courageous—we are just wicked. Cowards are those who refuse to do what is right just as much as they are those who do wrong.

28.2

The more wicked one is, the more that rules and rulers are needed. Wisdom allows for fewer rules and rulers, as righteous longevity brings health to every body politic. God always gives us the leaders we deserve; thus, wicked people eventually are ruled by a succession of evil rulers. Godly people engender longevity in their rulers or leaders. We see this in everything from churches to nations. When you are a delight to be ruled, you ultimately bless yourself, for that posture empowers others to lead you long and well. When you are discouraging to lead, you doom yourself to a succession of poor leaders. In this sense, everything rises and falls on followership, and it is godly followers who can make bad leaders good while evil followers often turn good leaders bad.

28.3

It is a double disaster when the oppressed turn on one another, as civil war is the most devastating. From the time that Satan attempted his coup in heaven, tyrants, usurpers, invaders, colonialists, and even apostles have used this divide-and-conquer principle. Paul was not above driving a wedge between Pharisees and Sadducees when under pressure. God Himself often deals with large enemies by turning them into smaller combative factions. This battle tactic is so common it's foolish of us not to recognize its use against us. The wise discern quickly when enemies attempt to divide families, friends, and teammates, and do not allow that simple yet oft successful strategy to subdue them.

28.4

God cannot be good without being violently against the bad. It is not enough to be passively opposed to evil. We must follow our Lord in being intolerantly, aggressively against all that is wrong. Hatred of evil with intent to destroy is essential to being good. It is a good God who created hell and eternal punishment. It is a good God who gets angry enough to destroy what is wicked. Fools announce God cannot be good if He punishes in eternal hell. Normal living and natural justice show God could not be good if He didn't. A good God by essence must remove bad things, and who of us has the wisdom to quibble with how He does that!

28.5

Understanding comes from a macro view of God, not a micro view of the problem. Injustice must be addressed from a gospel perspective. Otherwise, cures become curses, equal and opposite errors. If we do not have a high view of God, we will have a low view of justice, and in our blurry vision we will make our world worse not better. The only hope for the world is if we accept God as He describes Himself and man as the Bible reveals him. Some mysteries and tragedies of life will not make sense until we go into the presence of God. Some truths are too painful to us until we linger in God's home and heart. Problems get our attention but do not explain themselves to us. We must gaze long at Him who is right before we can expect to understand that which is wrong.

28.6

Poverty is neutral while corruption is partisan. It is never appropriate to be crooked, but it is often freeing to be poor. Rare is the person whose character is improved by abundance, and common the one who grows in stature through loss of status, position, power, finances, or privilege. The depravity of man is nowhere better evidenced than by the frequency with which wealth corrupts us. The sufficiency of God is never better displayed than by how often the impoverished evidence satisfied joy. Man's folly is displayed every time God's blessings result in a wayward heart. God's wisdom is revealed every time His severity leads us home.

28.7

Wise men know that their actions always affect others, inevitably including their secret acts. No secret is eternal when we live under the reality of an omniscient God; thus, fools err when they think that any action will be long unknown. Secret sin will always eventually lead to public shame, and public shame wounds in radiating circles from the sinner through his loved ones out through the community to the world. Wise men further know that their secret acts of surrender and service also bless the world from the hearth to the heavens. Wise men are content to toil unknown because private obedience is ever seen by Him who will one day reward publicly, by Him who cannot bless only the obedient but ever blesses all those in proximity to their faithfulness.

28.8

God through Father Time and fate always intervenes when one individual or institution amasses great wealth and power through greed. The wise intentionally participate in the generosity of God, remembering they are stewards and act like it. Fools either flaunt and waste or hoard and hide money and either way lose it all—either by passing into eternal death without it, having those who follow them squander it, or spending it on themselves to a lasting dissatisfaction. For those who were selfish, futile is the power of money when we cross into eternity. Powerful is the effect of money, then, if we generously use money now to make friends with God. We befriend God not by bribing Him (He needs nothing), but by giving generously all we can to those whom God has compassion on, to those who need the basic gospel or the simplest grace.

28.9

Disobedience is the primary denier of prayer. Prayer is denied not just when we disobey God, but when we disobey our authority. Because prayer is indelibly linked to authority, we can't at once violate the principle and plead for the principle to work. We can't resist the authority under which God has placed us and plead for God to exert His authority in that very situation. God does not ever ask us to disobey His authority, and that ask includes us obeying leaders who are not wise, kind, patient, affirming, understanding, or good. If we do not want our prayers to be hindered, we must submit to every authority God has authorized, even the broken ones, wherever this can be done without breaking His laws. Only those answerable to authority have *the* Authority answer their prayers.

28.10

Our ultimate inheritance is based on how we treat others. God will reward with good those whose legacy includes consistent good to others. God's laws of sowing and reaping are inexorable, and He will indeed do good to those who do good. This principle is lived out in temporal life and in harmony with the eternal laws. It does not mean that good people are rewarded with heaven outside of Christ, for the unrelenting truth of the Bible is that there are no good people outside of Christ. If we want the good of eternal life, we must do good to the eternal God. This can only be done by admitting we are infernally bad and only Christ's goodness can cover us, save us, and work in us to do good. We do good to God by what we do with Christ.

28.11

Wisdom trumps riches. We need wise friends more than we need powerful friends. Wise friends are powerful friends, no matter how little money they have. Foolish friends are weak friends, no matter how much money they have. Foolish friends make you weak and wise friends make you strong. To be rich and foolish is to dilute your soul, to be thin in character and heart. Money tends to make you vulnerable, not strong, especially if you are foolish. Character makes you strong and stout, wise enough to depend on God, for you cannot supply your own. This is why poverty tends to build more character than it does wealth. This is why there are more wise people among the poor than among the rich, for the rich think they do not need God, which is the greatest folly of all.

28.12

The victory of one good, righteous person benefits all society. When one wicked man ascends to power and influence, all society is cursed. The world has yet to see what can happen globally when one man is fully possessed of God, but it has seen over and over what one man can do when influenced by the devil. In the same way that the first Adam brought death for all and the second Adam brought life, there is now unharnessed power for good available. If one righteous person can do wonders, think of the gospel impact on the lost if many would be filled and possessed with the living God. If the righteous are filled with the Spirit to the degree that fools are inspired and influenced by evil, the contest will be over, for He who fills the wise is so much stronger than he who fills fools.

28.13

All men are broken, but only those who hide their faults are lame. When we limp on the inside, spending extraordinary energy to appear whole, we accelerate our dying. When we bring our sins into the light, which breaks most of their power, we extend our living and our quality of life. Confession is part and parcel of the sin-defeating process. Confession is the catalyst for sins to be removed and lifted off us. That which we fear (being known as broken) holds the key to our liberation. As we confess and forsake that which binds us, we receive mercy and experience compassion: from those around us who are similarly broken and from He who was broken for our iniquities and bruised for our diseases.

28.14

Time and success war against reverence. When we stop feeling sorrow over our embedded sin and its consequences, we start hardening our hearts to overtures of grace and we are in mortal peril. When we forget that secret sin will destroy us, that it will manifest at the worst time to expose us in the most horrific way, we are foolish and careen towards destruction. Periodic failure is good for the soul. Not sin, just failure: being thought foolish, losing respect, being worse than others, trying in vain, experiencing rejection or subjection. All these can be gifts in disguise. Their minor pain keeps us humble, and humility keeps us from harm.

28.15

Selfish wickedness stupefies us and others. Evil's main weapon is fear, for evil is ever a pretender with more bark than bite. The roar of a lion and the rush of the bear intimidate; they do not injure. It is the threat of injury that tends to immobilize us. No lion and no bear have the capacity to inflict all the doom they promise, but who needs to attack when your prey imprisons itself? Because evil leaders and powers use fear as their primary weapon, the primary way to defeat them is for the righteous to be fearless. Fearlessness is as contagious as fear, and in the end much more powerful.

28.16

We spread life by giving power away, and we influence most deeply and enduringly by releasing control. Foolish leaders strangle the breadth of their influence through the fearful refusal to take risks by making themselves vulnerable. Wise leaders extend their impact by courageously and generously giving power away, even when it's risky. The human spirit was created to follow and lead. We lead best when we trust others to follow, and we follow best when we trust others to lead. The best leaders love to be faithfully led.

28.17

Human life is precious, and to hunt it or take it is to open yourself to demonic terror. Murder trespasses into the domain of God and assumes a responsibility that no human was designed to bear. To take life is to enter an arena populated by powers that are beneath and beyond us, and it exposes us to a harshness and spirit with which we cannot cope. Small murders of reputation, innocence, opportunity, and joy have comparable consequences. When we take that which is not ours (are not stealing and coveting subtle forms of killing?), we open our souls to be plundered and slain by all that is not holy. The wise want no part of the terror that must accompany taking life that is not ours to take.

28.18

Innocence is an enduring condition, a finishing place not a beginning. To be innocent is to be proved right over time, to endure unshakable until the final verdict. No matter the accusations and how tenable they may seem, the innocent one is the one left standing on Judgment Day. The wicked is the one who appears to fall suddenly, while the righteous is the one who surprisingly endures. In fact, no fall is sudden; its causes were merely hidden. No man stands at the end of a tempest without likewise having hidden strength, hidden roots, and hidden springs. It is the hidden things of character and integrity that matter, not the things we display vainly of ourselves or cruelly of other people.

28.19

God always smiles upon hard work. It is its own reward and ample provision. No hard work done from a clear heart will be in vain. The God of creation loves work, and when He sees His own product, He smiles and breathes out good. When His creatures work hard, the One who never stops working, the un-resting and un-hastening, takes note and breathes out good. Even if thieves steal, calamity destroys, or earthly supervisors ignore, God the Worker sees and smiles. When we work hard for right reasons, for others, for dignity, or for good, we are granted the favor of heaven. And He who sees all works all for good, for those who love Him and are called according to His purposes (Rom. 8:28). Let us work hard. God will honor that someway, somehow.

28.20

Faithfulness brings blessings beyond prosperity, blessings more precious than wealth. Shortcuts punish the one who takes them.

In seeking gain before it is due or by means other than it should be granted, we go backwards. Moral shortcuts are long quests that result in loss, delay, and pain. What is good only remains good if it is acquired in the right way and time, if it is conferred as well as earned, if it is given as well as received. The wise do not reach for what will be given one day. They do not strive for what will be bestowed, for in taking it too early they lose it entirely.

28.21

Leaders have the responsibility to keep evil out. Government is incapable of making men and women moral and, in fact, it is not given that assignment, for it does not have that power. God grants government the right to make laws to hold back the power of evil, for only the church through the gospel can help men and women be good. Conversely, leadership and government can do much harm if they, through injudicious application or partial enforcement of law, let evil in. Government cannot make people good, but it can certainly make them bad. We need leadership and government to build barriers against what is wrong, but neither leaders nor external human powers can usher us to what is right. Only Jesus, full of grace and truth, can do that.

28.22

In Hebraic thought, the "single eye" combined the concept of a simple purpose and a generous heart to help others. A single eye full of light was also full of love, brimming with the intention to share God's good with a broken world. The "evil eye," by contrast, was a covetous eye, a jealous eye, a mentality that brought harm and curses through desiring what belonged to others. Covetousness can only extend want; it can never placate it. The jealous are never satisfied and their cravings are relentless. Generosity is surprisingly elegant because the more you give away, the less you want. Generosity is beautiful, for the more you give away, the more you look like God and the more room you have in your spirit for His fullness.

28.23

Strong leaders respect and need "no" men. It is weak leaders who surround themselves with the ever agreeable. Unity requires honorable disagreement. Otherwise, you don't have unity; you just have uniformity. Uniformity is limiting and weak as it only consists of one perspective and wisdom trove. Strong leaders desire a greater database of ideas than their own limited supply and respect those who refine their thinking and decision making through counter points. The strong leader recognizes his weaknesses and limitations, and surrounds himself with those who are better, wiser, and stronger. It is the fool who rejoices in the chorus around him that only sings an echo.

28.24

If generosity does not start with our intimate friends and family, it is only self-serving hypocrisy. If we do not give our best energy to our Lord through abiding, to our spouse through constant communion, to our children through nurturing discipleship, and to our friends through mutual accountability, then we are just performing clowns and giving our best to those who are furthest while we rot away at our core. No matter how strong we appear, we ultimately will topple over, exposed as hollow fakes. Stinginess at home in time, love, attention, affirmation, grace, and goodness sullies benevolence abroad.

28.25

Humility makes peace at disadvantageous terms to self and it trusts the Lord to balance the ledger. The spirit of competition drives us to win every discussion, to triumph in every encounter, and to view satisfaction as a limited supply. In competition, we must strive for our own way, which we conflate with contentment, for there is only so much prosperity to divvy up. Humility employs God's higher math of multiplication, knowing that satisfaction is not limited by yielding our way and will. In fact, the wisdom of humility is that it experiences so much joy in submitting to God and even to others. The one who must always have more than the other (rights, resources, respect) is the one ever dissatisfied. The one who is happy to let others have more is ever prospered by the Lord and rests in strain-free blessing.

28.26

Wise men know that they have foolish hearts and are prone to wander from what is good and true. Fools have a misguided self-confidence about their character, trust themselves too much, and are blinded to the limitations of their natural reasoning mind. The mind and the body were created to serve the spirit, and when we favor either mind or body over spirit (our conscience, will, soul), we careen towards disaster. The wisest acknowledge that the Holy Spirit can use the mind (and usually does) and that He can also trump the mind and communicate God's thoughts to us in ways we can't always explain or articulate. In the needed blend of mind and spirit, the wise trust their spirit to final discernment, and fools rely ultimately on their mind.

28.27

It is just as wicked to ignore the needy as to take advantage of them. The rich man had not abused the poor; he only neglected them (Luke 16:19–31). But God hates inaction. God is angered when we do nothing, for He commissioned us to attack evil wherever we find it. Neglect of attacking evil will bring curses on good men. The only ones who need to fear curses are those who deserve the curse. If you have done evil, you are under a curse and you will pay for it. If you have not done good when it was in your power to do so, you have done evil. God is not mocked, and God has used and will use evil men or powers to bring curses on good men who do evil by not doing good.

28.28

Leadership matters, for when the wicked rule, evil is unrestrained and it prevents good people from thriving in their field. When wicked leaders rise (and they often begin as articulate, charming, educated, clean cut, charismatic, convincing, and impressive in the appearance of solutions), the ones who could help the community the most are systematically driven into hiding. The sign of godly leaders is a proliferation of empowered and entrusted leaders around them. Great leaders are surrounded by great men and women who are free to make decisions, make mistakes, and fix those mistakes. Good leaders become great by seeking and keeping the good and the greater nearby, giving them influence and legitimate power.

PROVERBS
Chapter 29

29.1

There is no sudden judgment of God that is not first preceded by His patient wooing and warning. Our Lord is so tender in His discipline. He leads us gently along if we are willing to repent. Over and over again, Jesus invites us to turn from sin, to flee from fallen flesh, to be forgiven, to be healed. If that grace is spurned over and over again, the Lord has no recourse but to break us, and that breaking can be final if we greet God's severity with the same foolish hard heart with which we refused His kindness. In observing others misfortune or reflecting on our own plight, we can be sure that any violent correction of God is only unleashed after relentless and repeated attempts that were oh so kind and gentle. We do not presume that all misfortune is God's judgment, but when it is, it is still mercy (albeit severe) triumphing over and through judgment.

29.2

Right and righteous leadership actions bring long-term joy even if they necessitate short-term pain. That joy is experienced in radiating circles and has a ripple effect of good. Conversely, wicked leadership decisions are easier to make in the short term and more damaging in the long term; they are short-term joy resulting in long-term pain. What judges a decision as right or wicked is its long-term effect, and it takes great courageous fortitude to continually make decisions that hurt in the short term while blessing in the long term. Leadership in this sense then is pain, for a good leader must often make a decision that costs him and those around him for the good of those far away. Wicked leaders make decisions that are easy for themselves and their associates to the groaning pain of those far away both in relationship, time, and space.

29.3

Wisdom is stewarded and stored. Wisdom hidden and hoarded is actually foolishness, for what is good was intended by God the giver to be disbursed abroad. The selfish retention of truth or resources has a contaminating effect on that which was holy in origin. Only by passing on the gifts of God do we really retain and enjoy them. Therefore, those who share the gospel, the good news about the character of God, make their heavenly Father happy. Those who hoard the gospel waste it. Those who hide the gospel warp it. Those who live among the lost in glee without gladly proclaiming God's truth waste the wealth of heaven to their shame and their Father's fury.

29.4

Stability, for children and countries, comes through the restricting "no" just as often as it comes through the releasing "yes." We do our families and our followers no favors if we remove all constraints. In fact, by doing so we leave them unguarded which over time makes them unstable. The loving authority is the one who says no to what is corrupt as well as no to what will corrupt his own, even when they plead for it with tears. Bribes can be crude and open, or they can be delicate and subtle—the tears or pleadings of those we love for a desire that will be detrimental to them. Wise leadership allows no corruption in the sphere of his authority and influence, neither the manipulative greed from without nor the misguided lust from within.

29.5

Flattery is one of the more sinister weapons of darkness, for it does the opposite of what it pretends. Flattery pretends good while planning evil, even if that evil is simply getting one's own way. When others flatter us, we should beware, for no lasting good will come of it, neither for us nor them. When we flatter others, we likewise sin and need to examine our hearts to see why we feel the need to lie and deceive. The God of truth does not flatter, though He does encourage. Flattery (false praise) is easier to produce than the legitimate, more life-giving exhortation (true praise). Flattery is the devil's lingo and should never be allowed to fall from our lips or drip into our ears.

29.6

When Jesus rescues us from temptation, we should make some noise about it. The undeniable result of sin is sorrow, and we know all too well the burden of disobedience which results from giving in to temptation. Unfortunately, we do not celebrate as often or as exuberantly as we should when God helps us deny the flesh while obeying the Spirit. Accountability with brothers and sisters does not usually rise to the realm of praise as we have become so accustomed to confessing failure. Accountability is intended to lift us from the dusty plains of vulnerability to soar in the skies of victory with glad rejoicing in how the Spirit has empowered us to live free and fully. By all means let us confess when we have slipped into ourselves but let us also with just as much discipline confess when God has glorified Himself through our mortal bodies and minds.

29.7

Evil power consolidates wealth and strength for self-interest, while righteous power ever gives it away. John Wesley told people that if at his death he had more than ten pounds in his possession, they could call him robber. Dictators and tycoons have billions of dollars in the bank, a ridiculous redundancy. When asked how much money is enough, John D. Rockefeller said, "Just a little bit more!" The litmus test for righteous power brokers (whether wealth or authority) is how much they give away. Godly leaders give away to those poor in power and privilege, and they begin when they have little to share. It is folly to think that generosity grows with wealth. Greed must be defeated when it is an infant, for when it grows into its giant form, it is almost impossible to overcome.

29.8

The wise have the discipline to let their spirits rule their emotions. As holistic humans we are emotional beings, and in their pure forms anger, zeal, passion, and hate are not intrinsically wrong. There are some evils (slavery, human trafficking, child abuse, etc.) we should be *so* against that we are willing to take action to destroy them, for even God hates sin and is angry at the wicked every day. God has emotions, but even in the Godhead, decisions are not made emotionally. This is because emotions unruled by the spirit only make conflicts worse. Fools allow their emotions to lead them astray and in so doing damage others. The wise do not deny or repress their emotions. They allow their emotions to inform their decisions; they don't let their emotions drive their decisions. In this way our emotions help us heal and calm, not inflame and confuse.

29.9

A wise man cannot win an argument of words with a fool because the fool cannot be won by logic, only by love or lash. Fools can be the most self-intelligent persons in the world; their very independence condemning them to blindness. It is a mistake to conflate folly with stupidity, for often the most simple-minded have the humility to say, "I don't know" and "I need help." The essence of folly is to say, "I am" or "I know" or "I can do it by myself." Those fools are either angered that you presume to inform them or amused that you could provide any insight they have not already considered. It is their pride that rages and ridicules. And only love (kindness) and lash (misfortune) can penetrate those hard heads and hearts. Only when a fool has been brutally confronted with the reality that they are not, know not, and cannot but are loved anyway, do they have the humility to listen.

29.10

Our fallen natures love to attack others; thus, we seek to find a blemish which justifies our aggression. This search for wrong in others, which in our brokenness makes us feel better about ourselves, is rooted in insecurity, which is another face of pride. Fault finding is wicked sin, demonic in essence and far from the heart of God. Rather, the humility of Christ seeks what is good and godly in others and broadcasts that widely. The wise are not blind to the flaws and follies of others, but neither do they spend energy looking for them. This is because the wise know the greatest fulfilment comes in building others up, not tearing others down. There is a God-ordained pleasure attached to work that is nobly done for the good of others. We rise no higher when we pull others down, yet when we stoop to serve, we conquer.

29.11

God gave us our temper and our temperament. In His loving wisdom He did not make us emotionless robots; rather He made us in His image with the capacity and the expectation that we would both love and hate, rest and rage. It is foolish to say that anger is always wrong and rage always misguided, for God Himself is recorded in Scripture as a consuming fire. He is also a controlled fire, as we should be. Folly is demonstrated and most damaging when fury is not harnessed and channeled. Like fire, we were created by a good and holy God to burn for what is right and against what is wrong. That burning unguarded takes a powerful tool for right and twists it into an unfortunate weapon for evil. A wise person then leans on and learns from a holy God as to when and how to let the fire within burn for good without.

29.12

Leadership that listens to lies creates liars. Leadership that coerces creates tyrants. Leadership that is defensive creates insecure viceroys. What leaders do in moderation their followers do in excess including lying, coercing, blaming, intimidating, aggrandizing, posturing, ignoring, despising, and neglecting. Wise leaders stay further than necessary from any immoral lines, from any mean-spirited actions. Wise leaders know that to be on the safe side of wrong is not wise enough, for if we are even near it, our followers will cross it. Wise leaders concentrate on grace and truth, for if they don't, those who follow them will err on the side of law and lies.

29.13

God's common grace is completely unbiased. The unrepentant and rebellious against God take great pleasure in sunsets, good food, firm friends, precious family, and spring rains. Beauty and art, hiking and camping, travel and history, science and industry are appreciated and enjoyed by the spiritually lost as much as by the spiritually found. Robert Murray M'Cheyne wrote to a prodigal: "I know that I was very happy when I was unforgiven. I know that I had great pleasure in many sins.... Many a delightful walk I have had—speaking my own words, thinking my own thoughts and seeking my own pleasure...I fancy few boys were ever happier in an unconverted state than I was.... But ah! Is not this just the saddest thing of all, that you should be happy whilst still a child of wrath—that you should smile, and eat, and drink, and be merry, and sleep sound, when this very night you may be in hell? Happy while unforgiven! A terrible happiness.... When you look back from hell, you will say, it was a miserable kind of happiness.... Do you not think it would give you more happiness to be forgiven—to be able to put on Jesus and say: 'God's anger is turned away?'"[8]

29.14

Royal behavior is determined by how we treat the poor and helpless. The uncompassionate are rascals, rebels, and renegades no matter their earthly power. What makes us regal is how we treat those who cannot harm or help us, those who cannot ban or bless us, those powerless to do us good or grant us gain. When we take compassion on those who cannot reward us, we enter into the nature of God and delight Him fully. The reality of God is that every moment He gives good to those who have nothing that He needs. God is constantly granting favor either by the mercy He gives or by the wrath He withholds. When we in lovingkindness mercy others, we act in that moment as our King never ceases to function. We are never more like Jesus than when we take mercy on souls, souls that can offer us nothing in return for our giving.

29.15

Granting those you disciple and parent their unfettered own way is a damaging act of cruelty to them. A spoiled child is a ruined adult. An unreproved disciple is a ruined discipler. Love cares enough to cause pain to the objects of their affection, pain that is not necessarily earned by error. Our sinless Christ learned obedience by the things that He suffered. He learned to trust by being denied His own way. Not even God in the flesh received a "yes" to every heartfelt petition. If Father God said "no" on occasion to His beloved begotten Son, should we not also deny those we love for their greater good? Wise leadership not only denies what is harmful, but it also sees clearly enough into the future to deny a temporary good, for the prize of the long-term great.

29.16

Justice is always on the side of the righteous. The wise are ever patient, saddened yet unalarmed by the increase of iniquity. The surest sign of the fall of the wicked is their increase in wickedness and their increased power. The wise realize that the nature of evil is self-destructive. The lot of Satan is that he is so filled with hate that he destroys his own in his fallen intelligence. The devil is his own worst enemy. He can but eventually lash out at any threat, at anyone, and the more powerful the evil he raises up, the more certain it is he will turn on his own creation to devour and destroy it. This is why abortion and betrayal are signatures of Satan; any twisted destruction of your own is a mimicry of the devil's nature. When the wicked grow in power, the godly wise lament even for them, for their doom draws nigh. Evil always turns on itself. In the end only the righteous are left standing.

29.17

The spirits and hearts of children and followers cry out to be corrected. Their wills and flesh and mouth pretend to value autonomy over accountability, but this charade is easily seen through by the wise. Do not listen to the voices and tears and blame of those you correct, for their mouth does not represent their spirit and their actions do not speak for their need. The best thing you can do for the future of your followers is to correct them. If we correct quickly, kindly, faithfully, and lovingly, we will bring comfort in the short term and safety over time, for we will develop those who are wise and kind enough to correct (and comfort) us when inevitably we falter or fall.

29.18

When we do not provide clear, simple, and unified vision for those we lead, they come up with their own. The lack of clear, simple, and unified vision leads to a book of Judges-like confusion where everyone comes up with their own vision. The result is unrestrained confusion, complexity, and division. Wise leadership does not neglect the constant articulation of vision, providing the riverbanks for strong currents and personalities to flow. Foolish leaders abdicate the formation of vision and are swept along or aside by irresponsible and contrary tides.

29.19

If we as leaders do not model, we lose moral authority. No matter how experienced we are, nor how articulate, the moment we stop living what we espouse, we begin to lose transformative power. The goal of teaching and preaching is not to inspire, but to transform, and transformation at the spiritual and moral level can only be instigated and maintained if the speaker is authentic. We cannot call others to abide if we do not abide, to holiness if we are not holy, to sacrifice if we do not sacrifice, to evangelism if we do not evangelize, or to Jesus if we are not with Him ourselves. As humans we need more than understanding. We need conviction, and we are convicted when we see the speaker live out her words. The steady legitimacy of our deeds prove the worth of our words. We demonstrate our words are worthy by living them.

29.20

Haste at best fools the wise and at worst makes them foolish, while prudence wises the fool. We can be decisive without being hasty. In fact, a mark of the wise is that they are calm under pressure, they do not overreact, they are not impulsive, yet neither do they stall. The best athletes talk about being in a "zone" where the game slows down for them and they are able to read the field in an instant, making the right move to the right place at the right time. Wisdom does this for us as well. It slows down the emergencies of life so that in the moment we see the wider scenario and decide what is best for the long term in that instant. Folly speeds us up and wisdom slows us down, even when events accelerate all around us.

29.21

Our greatest inheritance is kindness. What our future needs more than money, more than food, and more than shelter is love. We need to be the recipients of lovingkindness from others. We receive kindness when we become weak if we liberally dispense it when we are strong. God, the reservoir of all goodness, delights when we represent Him who abounds in love and in His impeccable memory, He takes note. He will ensure that we reap what we sow. It is foolish to fixate on building up a large retirement portfolio if we neglect to make daily deposits of kindness. Godlike kindness has higher interest rates, and that is the kindness that is merciful and gracious to those who cannot or will not be kind to us in return.

29.22

Anger is a flammable neutral. We know that anger is not always bad, for God is often angry, and in His wrath, He destroys what is wicked. The danger is that anger is often linked to the urge to destroy, and humans can hardly be trusted with that desire. Controlled and purified anger is deferred anger. We should not, we must not remove anger from the catalogue of gifts God has given us, but we also must recognize that for God and for us it is a latter utility. It is only employed after much patience, prayer, and consideration. God is slow to anger, as we must be. Anger differentiates the wise from the foolish. Fools are quick to anger, and the wise very slow.

29.23

Pride is so vain. It has no efficacy. It just doesn't work. The irony of pride is that it drives us to the opposite of our intention. Pride desires praise and glory, and in its delusion hires attention to be the means. That attention is a transient lifting which betrays us by serving only to give momentum and force to our fall. The prouder we are, the more we are eventually criticized. Attention proves a traitorous medium, for we employ it to be praised but it always ends up being used to castigate us. The wise fear attention, knowing that there is only One worthy of praise and only One with the purity to handle attention. The humble are happy enough to receive only the honor they can handle, seeking it not, dispensed by the only One wise enough to know the perfect dosage.

29.24

Sins never come in the singular; they always travel in gangs. You cannot steal without hating and you cannot hate without having a murderous heart. Fools think that sin is isolated and in vain they hope that consequences can be escaped. The wise ever remember that sin is plural, always escalates, always is discovered, and always increases in complexity and damage. The wise refuse small sins, for they see the invisible, inevitable connection to egregious sins. David's choice not to go to war led to a walk he should not have taken, a sight he should not have seen, a lust he should not have harbored, an invitation he should not have offered, an act he should not have contemplated, a lie he should not have considered, a murder he should not have ordered, and sons killing sons, then citizens killing one another. When tempted with a small sin, wisdom looks past it and sees all the connected, escalated consequences, shudders, and goes to war.

29.25

The wise have room in their heart for only one fear: the fear of the Lord. Fear is a cruel prison, a prison of our own devising. Fools lock themselves up for years, the bars imaginary but effective all the same. The wise live fear free when it comes to man and thus deal with far fewer restrictions. The fearless see more, experience more, laugh more, travel more, attempt more, and fail more, but their failures tend to make them happy not sad, wiser for the effort, equipped to try again with greater knowledge. Because God knows no fear, He has a special affinity for the fearless. Because God doesn't care what man thinks about Him, He loves it when He sees that freedom in others—and He rewards it. It is the Father, not fortune, that favors the bold.

29.26

It is wise to seek the favor of the most powerful in the land. It is foolish to think that that power resides in a human or an institution. Prayer is powerful and effective because it totally bypasses all human bureaucracy. Prayer doesn't have to stand in line. Prayer doesn't have to fill out a form. Prayer doesn't have to have a human intermediary. Prayer doesn't have to pay money, dues, or penance. Prayer skips all these and boldly approaches the throne. Prayer doesn't have to be polished or professional, and it doesn't have to be approved or edited by a censor. Prayer is the privilege of the believer, the direct appeal to Daddy who, conveniently for His children, also happens to be omnipotent. Foolish children go to Daddy last, while wise children go there first.

29.27

The righteous and the wicked abominate each other. They are mutually exclusive, sharing only one thing in common: their mutual disgust. The righteous are despised for what they don't do as much as for what they do, for who they are as much as for who they are not. To be wise you must recognize that you must be unpopular and come to terms with that ever-present status. In fact, if you are universally liked and all speak well of you, woe, as Jesus said, for there is evidently some folly still resident in your action or inaction. When we do not master our craving for all to like us, we end up acting foolishly. We can only be consistently wise when we are at peace with being constantly disliked.

PROVERBS
Chapter 30

30.1

Wisdom is refined in community. It is not the proprietary possession of any one individual, including Solomon. Wisdom, like praise, must be articulated to be verified. It must be lived out or spoken out; it cannot just be internal musing or meditation. Wisdom is proved and justified by her children, by visible demonstration that passes the test of time and critique. We are not wise until our thoughts and our actions have proven themselves in community by adding life, by doing long-term good, and by fighting what is evil. Brilliance is theoretical, while wisdom is eminently practical, fleshed out in family, with friends, and in the world.

30.2

Humility has more to do with grace than with sin. We tend to equate humility with the humiliation of being caught doing something wrong, the embarrassment of being less, worse, last, broken, or errant. While our deficiencies, errors, and sins do humble us, they do not make us humble by nature; only God's grace can do that. When we acknowledge that we are stupid, fallen, and devoid of understanding, yet loved by God past, present, and future anyway, this is true humility. Jesus was humble without being sinful or wrong. True humility walks on the legs of grace and truth.

30.3

Humanism breeds the spirits of "I know," "I can," and "I am." Humility says, "I can do nothing without my heavenly Father." It is astounding that God in the flesh, Jesus the perfect man, was the holiest and the humblest *because* He was acutely aware that He could do nothing apart from His Father. Even fools cry out to God when they are overwhelmed. We are wisest when we remember we need God's help for everything, for every small thing, for every breath, every thought, every decision, and every obedience. If Jesus was so wise to know that He could do nothing without the Father, let us not be so foolish that we think we can do so much without Him. To need God *before* we need Him is the heart of both humility and wisdom.

30.4

Wisdom exalts the Lord and spends more time in adoration than intercession. It is foolish to ask more frequently than we praise. There is only One who ascends to and descends from heaven, only One who gathers wind and subdues waves, only One who establishes the earth. If God is sovereign over history and nature, He certainly can handle whatever my little day and small, short life contain. Foolishly we worry when we focus on our very minor problems (by comparison) rather than on the enormity of God's power in creation, time, space, and redemption history. If God can defeat sin and death, He can certainly triumph over my day.

30.5

We stand on the promises of God, and His promises are not theoretical. God's promises are a tested shield and refuge; they have been proved true by millions before us. God's promises are personalized but not unique to us. I know God can save me because He has saved millions before and around me. I know God can heal me because He has been faithful to heal before I was born. I know God can comfort me because He cried at Lazarus' tomb. I know God can deliver me to my heavenly home, for there waiting for me are a heavenly host from as far away as Adam to as near as my grandparents. Every word of God has been tested by millions before me, and His promises are proven in time and preciously new.

30.6

It is incredibly arrogant to try to improve on God's thoughts and speech. It is folly indeed to censor the Almighty God by diluting or distorting His word. How presumptuous the preacher or prophet who thinks that he is wiser or more temperate than God or that Jehovah needs an editor. God is both kinder and harsher than man, and so He should be, for we are all corrupt in opposite directions. We have not the reservoir of love that He has; thus, we ever fall short in compassion. We have not the purity of justice that is His nature; thus, we fall short in truth. If we are wise, when we open our mouth to say, "Thus says the Lord," we quote Him exactly and we let Him translate Himself.

30.7

Ironically, there are some privileges that life on fallen earth allows which will not be possible in the re-creation. In heaven, we will not be able to praise during pain, trust during trial, and triumph over temptation. There is an elegant beauty when God's people praise Him from prison, gravesides, hospital beds, poverty, and tears of agony. There is sweet incense when we trust God to be for us when all are against us. There is simple joy when we choose to say "yes" to His still small voice and "no" to the very loud call of the flesh. None of these delights will be possible in heaven; the wise will enjoy them fully here on fallen earth.

30.8

Wealth and poverty are both a form of deception. When Jesus comes in glory, we will live in a redeemed community where the lies of the rich and the poor do not exist. Wealth is a lie, for it indicates we have the resources and power to solve eternal problems—and we don't. Poverty is a lie, for it indicates eternal problems can't be solved—and they can. Wealth whispers that we are God and poverty shouts that He does not exist. On that wonderful day when God wisely abolishes both wealth and poverty, there will be no comparison, no lack, no injustice, no imbalance, and no more lies. We will all be fed our portion and we will all be satisfied. It is wise for us to live in that satisfaction now, even if by faith.

30.9

Both physical fullness and physical emptiness lead us away from a pure view of the Lord. When we are full, we deny that we need Him, and when we are empty, we resort to means that dishonor Him. The beauty and the safety of heaven is that we will neither be full nor empty of any of the physical realities. In eternal life we will enjoy the perfect blend of being satisfied. Our physical contentment will be led (as is always the case) by our spiritual peace.

There will be this perfect blend of complete satisfaction in Jesus *and* an eagerness for more of Him. Satisfaction doesn't mean the end of capacity; it simply means there is space for more *and* complete joy in what we have.

30.10

Slander is perhaps one of the most foolish behaviors of fallen man. Slander ultimately invokes wrath from all directions. The one you lie about is offended, the one you lie to is offended, the ones who hear you lie about another are offended, and all parties lose trust in you. The lie in slander is that you will look better to others by making someone else look worse. This is sheer lunacy, for whenever you make another appear worse than they are in a vain effort to make yourself more respected, you merely dishonor yourself and lose the respect others held for you. Wisdom tells the truth and errs on the side of compassionate, merciful kindness. Compassionate truth is the tide that lifts all boats, while slander is the folly that takes everyone down.

30.11

Sin has the untiring capacity to destroy the sinner. The deception of sin is in its transient joy. What seems like fun is actually poison, what seems entertaining is actually dulling, and what seems like pleasure is actually pain. It is with the fool who curses his parentage or his heritage, for all he is doing is cursing himself. We cannot criticize our family without indicting ourselves. The wise realize that we carry the same faults within as our forebearers (whether they be biological or spiritual) and rather than blaming or condemning others take responsibility and seek freedom through repentant tears. We are not bound to the sins of our fathers, but neither are we naturally free from them. Despite the faults of our predecessors, we bless them, for in their spiritual blessing there is ongoing hope even for us.

30.12

Purity is not a self-awarded status, simply because no man or woman has the capacity to be ruthlessly honest with themselves. Most underestimate their own depravity, and those who overstate it do so in a twisted manner which is itself false and depraved. Only God is pure, and our purity, whether imputed and imparted, is sourced in Him alone. We are never the source of our own purity. How foolish and dangerous to not know we are naturally filthy. How wise to rely daily on the purity of God. "Jesus, thy blood and righteousness, my beauty are, my glorious dress; midst flaming worlds, in these arrayed, with joy shall I lift up my head."[9]

30.13

There are kinds of men and women that God has no tolerance for, and chief among those are the arrogant. Arrogance is as ugly as humility is beautiful. Arrogance mars as surely as humility adorns. The folly in man is drawn to what disfigures him, while the wisdom of God calls us to that which glorifies us. The glory of man is to live in the image of God, and what makes God beautiful in part is His lowliness. The incarnation is beautiful. The cross is beautiful. The resurrected Lord making breakfast for His wobbly disciples is beautiful. Humility beautifies. Arrogance just makes us ugly.

30.14

Violence weakens the one who uses it selfishly. The folly in humans deludes us to think we are more powerful if we can coerce others to our way of worship. Wisdom drives us to meekly woo others to the worship of God. Godless humans use violence to attract attention and cultivate the fear of men. Godly humans use love to win peace and attract men to the goodness of Christ. The stronger we are, the more we will swallow offenses and resort to patient mercy. The weaker we are, the quicker we resort to anger and the forceful establishment of our destructive will. The wise ever remember that love is stronger than violence, that love never fails.

30.15

Receiving does not have the requisite ability to satisfy. Giving does. It is wonderful to receive, but it is more wonderful to give. As all beautiful things are, this principle is sourced in the character of God. God loves to receive: our worship, our praise, our trust, our hope, our thanks, our lives, our obedience. But He loves even more to give: His life, His love, His light, His joy, His grace, His truth, His mercy, His kindness, His presence, and so much more. God is incredibly satisfied when He gives—as are we. To give to the Lord, to give to His people, to give to His world satisfies so much more than whatever we receive. God wants us to be givers so that we look, act, and feel like Him.

30.16

An indication of evil and wickedness is dissatisfaction. The righteous are satisfied with little to nothing of the practical, physical comforts of life. The righteous can be poor and unknown, unrecognized and weak. The wicked are never satisfied with the wealth, power, recognition, or pleasure they have. Yet, when it comes to the Spirit, it is the opposite. The righteous are satisfied with Jesus even as they hunger for more. The wicked want less and less to do with the Lord of heaven and earth; they run from and rebel against the only One who can deeply satisfy. The first step towards evil is when we stop hungering for good, for God. A dissatisfaction with having few practical goods and a satisfaction with only having little or nothing of God are dangerously related.

30.17

Jesus has very little tolerance for those who dishonor their authorities. Whether it be parents who give us life, officials that give us order, or leaders that set our limits, Jesus expects us to honor and obey. There is shockingly little qualification in Scripture regarding obeying and honoring limited, flawed, broken, weak, incompetent, even corrupt leaders. Jesus, fully God, was and is fully submitted to the Father, and He brokers no rebellion and no mocking of authority. The link between Satan's pride and his rebellion is so fine as to be practically indistinguishable. The wise do not tolerate any mocking, rebellion, undermining, disrespect, or gossip about their leaders and authorities. If we really believe the God of Daniel appoints whoever He chooses over men, we will honor whoever God chooses over us (however unlikely he or she seems).

30.18

Wonder is never intended to be overcome. Rather, it exists to master us. Part of the joy of our being is the capacity to wonder. Animals can be afraid and surprised. They can feel pain and can romp in joy, but they cannot wonder. To lose wonder is to lose part of being human; to lose wonder is to pretend to be divine. We were created to take joy in what is wonderful. The beauty of heaven is not only that we will go from glory to glory, but from wonder to wonder. The wisdom of God will eternally have something new of Himself, for Himself, from Himself to marvel at. We will enjoy wonder forever, which is a wonder in and of itself.

30.19

Flying, sliding, sailing, and romancing all have their own unique and beautiful movements. God made everything beautiful in its time and in being itself. We are most beautiful and most glorifying to our Creator when we have the confidence to be ourselves. We spend so much of life and energy trying to be like others, thinking then we will be accepted. But we are most beautiful when we act, move, talk, think, interact, worship, and feel like the unique creatures we are. Some of us fly, some of us slide, some of us sail, some of us run, some of us amble, some of us dance, and some of us march, but all of us are loved uniquely and should live uniquely. Folly forever limits itself by imitation. Wisdom is free to be unique, and in that freedom, it is both beautifully fulfilled and uniquely magnificent.

30.20

The most shameful sins have the effect over time of making us shameless. Sin starts as secret rebellion but is not satisfied to be perverse quietly. Sin by nature is selfish, and selfishness has this innate need to boast and broadcast itself and its follies. Sin and self cry out, "Look at me!" Holiness and righteousness cry out, "Look at Jesus!" When we start to sin, we do it secretly, for we know that it's wrong and it disfigures everyone involved. If we continue in sin, we willingly enter into the deception that sin makes us desirable, enviable, respected for our audacity or courage in defying God. This is sheer folly. Sin makes us ugly, and shameless sin makes us hideous.

30.21

Though the curse has affected nature, the whole creation still knows the Creator and groans for liberation from the curse. The earth and elements, while not rational, have order and a spiritual component that recognizes their designer and longs for their redemption. This is not pantheism. This is the reality that under some things the earth quakes, under other influences it shakes, and in the end, it obeys and glorifies its Creator. In Revelation 12:14–16, the wilderness nourishes the woman and then the earth helps her. The earth is not neutral in the cosmic war between good and evil; it is on the side of those loyal to the King and against the usurping rebels. We do not worship nature, but nature joins us in worshiping our mutual Creator. And interestingly, one day God will destroy those who destroy the earth (Rev. 11:18).

30.22

Because nature was created by God with such ingenious order, it does not function nor flourish under disorder. Thus, natural law is violated in human disorder, especially when that action involves rebellion. Authority, order, structure, process, organization, stewardship, ethics, and integrity, these are all good things no matter how often they are twisted by man or questioned by demons. Nature was also intended to grow, to multiply, to expand, to never be static or lazy. Therefore, nature itself is offended by lazy humans. Not that nature is a person or has a personality, but merely that nature was created to be stewarded by organized, purposeful humans, and when we default our responsibility, the earth shudders.

30.23

Pretense does more injury than rejection. In fact, pretense is a long, constant, inescapable rejection. Upfront, concise rejection is easier to manage, for the pain is acute and confined even if its memory endures. Pretense is unending pain, pain of a sort that penetrates every fiber of our being. The rejection of a moment allows the rejected one to move on and begin healing as the wounds form scars, not scabs. Pretense binds the rejected one to the rejector, resulting in a constantly reopened wound which is never allowed time and space to heal. Pretense may seem like the easy way out of difficult situations, but it is the most unloving, unmerciful, and cowardly of all courses. Pretense should be anathema to the people of God, for it is the signature of the serpent, the liar, not of the One who is gracious truth.

30.24

Wisdom is like faith; small mustard seed size doses can work wonders. Though wisdom is usually found in increasing measure in the older and experienced, occasionally a child does lead us. Ironically, wisdom and intelligence or wisdom and formal education tend to have little in common. The illiterate African elder and the simple Nebraska farmer can often have more wisdom than the scientists and scholars of famous global institutions. The poor are often wiser than the rich; the trappings of power and isolation of position often make it harder for humans to be wise than easier. The wise then look for wisdom among the simple and small.

30.25

Preparation defeats strength, and diligence overcomes ability. The reality that work ethic and heart desire overcome natural resources is seen both in engineering and athletics. An army of laborers can slowly build a road up a sheer cliff. In professional sports, every competitor is a world-class performer (all are fit, fast, and strong), so champions are delineated by their mind, will, and heart, not by their body. Wisdom then is not daunted by overwhelming challenges but rather goes to work, prepares, and grinds away. Wisdom takes a million small manageable steps and lives out faith for the impossible through consistent, quiet obedience. Folly attempts great, idealistic leaps neglecting to do the hidden, constant work. Such courage is but stupidity.

30.26

Behind every great, vocal leader is a humble, quiet spouse, parent, friend, or team. Humans foolishly love to make heroes of other humans, and in doing so curse them to loneliness and failure. For every great and grand enterprise, kingdom, business, or ministry, a very few will garner the attention and be viewed by the simplistic public as the mountain conquerors. The reality is, the mountain is shared with innumerable little people (not little because they are less valuable, but because they have little fame). It is these unknowns who have done the bulk of the work and who tend to be more solid than the viewed visionary. It is a collection of the non-mighty who create the mighty legends. Wise leaders never forget that it takes an army to climb a mountain. Foolish leaders despise the very vast throng that elevated them to prominence.

30.27

The smaller the egos, the larger the community effort. Locusts have no egos, so millions of them can work together. Humans have so much pride that we constantly find ways to divide, compete, duplicate, and replicate work, which is terribly inefficient. It is indeed amazing how much can be accomplished if we don't care who gets the credit, if we don't care who leads, or if we don't care who is lauded at the end of the day. Can you imagine the efficiency of heaven? The marvels? The magnitude of the projects accomplished and wonders achieved? Millions of egoless brothers and sisters who love one another, encourage one another, and relish service. The wise remember that our accomplishments will be as grand as our egos are small.

30.28

Humility grants you the access that pride denies. It's hard to sneak a big ego into the halls of power, but geckos frolic on palace walls. God is not impressed with those who are impressed with themselves. They rarely get a hearing before the omnipotent throne, but the little ones, their angels always see the face of the Father in heaven (Matt. 18:10). Humility is attractive to all, not just to Him who sees all. Humility makes others want to help us, while pride makes them want us to hurt. When we share our struggles and vulnerabilities in lowliness, we make friends. When we loftily share our victories and strengths, we tend to either build walls or create idolaters and rivals.

30.29

How we live is as important as what we live. We can walk down a prison corridor in a stately manner and down a palace hall in servile scamper. The wise remember that we are children of the high King and ambassadors of the Most High, and that we are ever being watched, even if just by the great cloud of witnesses. As God's foreign diplomats we hold our heads high and walk into slums, markets, neighbor's houses, and government offices, remembering who we represent and whose authority we steward. The wise know that stateliness is not a posture or a position; it is a responsibility and inheritance. Fools think that offices and titles give them dignity, yet power without honor only magnifies our flaw.

30.30

There is something inspiring about confidence. During the 2012 Arab Spring two rival factions in Cairo, Egypt faced off outside our apartment building. Each side brandished weapons, everything from AK-47s to street lights plucked from the highway median. There were butcher knives and swords, planks and posts, and everything in between. Each faction numbered in the hundreds but neither side had the courage to attack, so a respectful 100 meters separated the two. Until one teenage boy did his best young David impersonation. He separated from his pack and with only one pistol that he fired somewhat randomly charged the opposition. Bullets splattered around his feet, but he charged on. To my surprise the hundreds opposing him turned and ran. One skinny teenager conquered a mob of hundreds. It is always inspiring to watch the lion-hearted. One lion can scatter all kinds of hyenas.

30.31

Godly confidence doesn't strut or prance, but it does march forward in resolute and impressive manner. Godly confidence doesn't talk much, nor does it call much attention to itself. Much of the talk and actions that draw attention are not the hallmarks of the confident but the arrogant and the anxious. The surer you are of yourself, the less you talk of yourself and the less you need to be praised. Those certain of who they are and who they serve do not have time for bragging. They obtain more satisfaction from conquest than from chatter, more joy from obedience than posturing. Wise men talk little and act purposefully; they shut up and do their duty. Foolish men talk much and procrastinate; they prater and meander, drawn to the attention more than to the achievement.

30.32

Self-exaltation is foolish. First, it attracts those who would do you harm, and second, it then repels those you would do you good. When we talk about ourselves, we draw those who would attack us and drive away those who would defend us. The best way to reduce enemies and increase friends is to clap our hand over our mouth's tendency to brag. If we use our mouth to encourage and praise others, including our critics and our enemies, we reduce our critics and gain their respect if not their agreement. The more we talk about ourselves positively, the more negatively we will be viewed. The more we talk about others positively, the more our enemies will rise to our defense.

30.33

Anger inevitably produces strife. Unless you are God, anger never ends a battle; only mercy and grace can do that. Anger just leads to conflict and war. This is why the Bible says that the wrath of man cannot produce the righteousness of God (James 1:20). While there are times holy anger should be employed, we should act in anger sparingly, counting the cost. Jesus hotly cleansed the Temple, and that act inflamed, not quieted, the fury of His enemies, contributing to His death. Wisdom does not deny wrath its calamitous place, but it employs wrath very selectively, fully aware there will be consequences. Fools are quick to anger and to cause emotional bloodbaths, unnecessary conflicts, and profligate war.

PROVERBS
Chapter 31

31.1

Mothers are the disciplers of kings. It is both true that men and women are made in the image of God *and* that God is Spirit; thus, both male and female qualities are sourced in Him. Further, God determines gender, not our inclinations, experiences, or preferences. God determined to come to earth as a man, and He determined to do so through a young woman. In the circle of godly life, there is both order and inter-dependence. God made husbands the spiritual head of the home (whose job description includes laying down his life for his wife), and He made mothers spiritually influential over their sons, even as they submit to and respect their husbands. It's not confusing to God; we are the ones who muddle and mess with gender. God created a beautiful harmony, a reality where mothers raise and influence our leaders and kings.

31.2

The story of Hannah and Samuel reminds us that children are a loan, that we steward them, we don't own them. Children are the sons and daughters of both a mother's womb *and* her promises—promises to raise children to love their heavenly Father more than they do their earthly mother. The best mothers release their children pre-birth into the hands of the Lord, knowing that He is a much better parent than any human could ever be. Possessive, controlling, fearful, self-serving parenting is the least pleasing to the Lord, the least obedient, the least reflective of His parenting style, and the least fulfilling to the parent. It is in releasing our children to the Lord, in trusting Him to parent through us, and in trusting our children in increasing measure as they grow, that we most have them. When parents are "clutchy" and needy, they lose their children. When parents give their children to Jesus gladly and often, they have them forever.

31.3

Men who chase multiple women lose strength at a multiplied rate. What the world calls virile, the Lord sees as sterile, wasted strength. Wisdom focuses and concentrates energy. We are not called to all things everywhere, and men can only be true to all women if they are faithful to one. Godly men are devoted to one woman all the days of their mutual lives, and in that singular devotion bless and are blessed by all women everywhere. Foolish men chase many women and lose all, blessing none and honored nowhere. Leadership, power, vigor, and authority make men attractive to women, but that attraction is a trap, a poison, and a mirage. When a man in leadership becomes enamored with the attention lavished on him due to his status, or even his character, he enters the path of destruction.

31.4

Leaders must live committed lives in order that nothing in them clouds their judgment or brings dishonor to God and man. There are good things that can be bad for the soul, particularly when one holds a position of leadership. While the Bible condemns drunkenness and not alcohol, it also tends to cast a skeptical eye on even the moderate consumption of alcohol. Most of the references or stories in the Bible to alcohol are negative and cautionary, not all, but most. The wise will then steer clear of anything, even good things, that have proved over history to often be used for bad. The Bible is quite clear on a higher standard for leaders: It is not for kings to drink wine. Alcohol is, unfortunately, most often good for bad.

31.5

Self-indulgence leads to sin indulgence. The unrestrained pleasing of self leads to the abuse of others. Wise leaders never take a holiday from sacrifice or dying to self. Leaders of the highest caliber and character do not see self-denial only as part of their job description, a uniform to wear at work and a jacket to be discarded at home or on holiday. Godly leaders continually prefer others over themselves, put the good of others ahead of their own comfort and ease, and never stop carrying their cross. The moment we start living selfishly, we start dying. The moment we start focusing on self-pleasure, we commence perverting. When self-denial becomes a joy and not just a chore, the effect is also immediate and nuclear as justice both reigns and expands.

31.6

Leadership cost is to be embraced, not evaded. If you desire leadership, you must commit to embracing pain, meeting it head on, and dealing with it both honestly and expeditiously. Leadership lives in reality and dies in escapist idealism. While the dying and embittered can medicate life pain with physical drugs, spiritual leaders cannot. They must find solace in a person, not a prescription. Leaders deal with pain by regulating it to measured daily doses and by passing to Jesus (not to those who follow) what cannot be swallowed. No one can handle the compiled brokenness of yesterdays, not our own or those of others. We survive pain by leaving yesterday's pain with Jesus, starting each day fresh, sipping the little limit of our capacity, and passing the cup to Christ.

31.7

Leadership requires us to be the voice of God and in turn the voice for others. Leadership is the platform for prayer and prophecy, never for our own opinions. Leaders are not allowed to self-medicate and focus on personal woes or suffering while losing sight of the big picture and what God is doing in the world over time. Forgetfulness is the luxury of the followers. Folly forgets, while wisdom remembers. Leadership must remember the past if it is to inform the future. Leaders must look honestly at the brokenness of the world, confront misery head on, and hold out hope that one day our King will come. Wisdom remembers that though we are miserable, through the Lord's great mercies we are not consumed. Wisdom remembers that "though this world, with devils filled, should threaten to undo us, we will not fear, for God hath willed His truth to triumph through us."[10]

31.8

The mouth is most honorably employed when it is opened for others. The tongue is such a mischievous member, for it most often wags in favor of its owner. Most of our words are vain, even if they're cloaked in humility. Vanity both exalts and condemns self, as insecurity is but another face of pride. The only way to overcome the insurrection and falsity of our tongues is by the sheer discipline of using them to praise others truthfully, starting with the Lord and continuing on to all His creatures. We must intentionally use our words to praise Jesus and affirm others, and that intention must include the determination that our praise will be genuine, not fabricated. Nothing stinks quite as much as sweet flattery. Great silent wrestling of the heart and will must precede the expulsion of noise from our mouths.

31.9

Leadership words both judge (attack) and plead (defend). Leadership involves apostolic shepherding—both attack and defense. We both protect, nurture, comfort, and shelter those we love, *and* we commission them out into the dangerous, uncomfortable world to take great risks for God. The poor and needy of the world are primarily those rushing toward eternal hell with precious little understandable warning. Leaders must have enough love in their hearts for the lost to commission the safely found to dangerous rescue missions. We cannot purely love those close to home if we are not willing to commission them to the perishing far away. For to not send our beloved to die for the world is to turn our heart from that of Father God, and a heart counter to Him can never be good for the rest of the family.

31.10

Wisdom lets God choose our wife or husband for us—or lets Him choose for us not to have one. God's choices are virtuous; they are all forms of excellence. Worry and haste lead us to choices we later regret, choices so fraught with complexity that they cause more problems than they solve. Trusting Jesus with our marital status is the highest wisdom, for He alone makes determinations that bring no sorrow with them. Godly marriages have plenty of sparks (for we are all fallen), but they bring no sorrow. Godly marriages at their core are simple and uncomplicated. Marriages arranged out of human desperation are complex, and time will simply twist them further. Loneliness and longing can make us shortsighted and spur us to choices we regret. Jesus knows our every weakness. If we will trust Him to choose for us, He will spare us great sorrow.

31.11

Trust, both given and earned, is the bedrock of marriage. Not knowing all things, we must live in good faith with one another, believing the best, reading the best possible interpretation into any word or act. Suspicion, doubt, human jealousy, overprotectiveness, and fear-based controlling tendencies are not virtues but vices, and they poison a marriage. Faithfulness enriches both parties. When one spouse is faithful, the other is strengthened. Faithful and unfaithful behaviors are not equal, for one act of betrayal can undermine a lifetime of good. The heart of the spouse who can trust their beloved (with money, with men or women, with motive) is truly free and empowered. The heart of the trustworthy are just as free and likewise empowered. Real power couples are those that are mutually trusted and trusting all the days of their life. There is no union so formidable anywhere on earth.

31.12

Lifelong, mutual good is God's intention for marriage. Marriage is to make us holy by making the other happy. A truth that marriage reveals is that holiness is happiness, that purity is joyful and glad, not prudish. There is no more joyful being in the universe than God Himself (who is also the holiest). If it's dour, it's not holy. True joy is holy joy, pleasure unsullied by crudity or selfishness, joy derived from selflessness and purified by being God-centered and others-focused. Doing good to others has the byproduct of doing good to our own soul. Our joy is bound up in and multiplied by the joy we give others. The happiest are the holiest, and the most giving of good are the most receiving of joy.

31.13

Work is from God. It brings joy. God worked before the Fall, as did Adam; thus, we will work and labor in heaven and revel in it. We will find it good. Willing work is fulfilling work; coerced work is slavery. When we work for Jesus willingly, there is no sorrow added to it. When we slave away for evil, there may be pleasure, but there is no lasting fulfilment, no enduring joy. Menial work is glorious work when done for the glory of God. Majestic work is servile when done vainly or cruelly. Work done willingly and joyfully for the good of others and as unto the Lord is its own reward. We labor as God did, we look like Him, and He smiles upon us. It is the posture of our heart that dignifies our work, regardless of the nature of the work itself.

31.14

Long-term planning is a skill we learn from God. It is His character to defer self-pleasure for the long-term common good. God, in His omniscience, sees the good that will result from patient endurance and thus, He calmly waits. We in our limited vision panic and rush. Wisdom hastens good by rushing less, by finding comfort in process, by resting in God's sovereign promises. We don't have to see results if we focus our eyes on the God who does not hasten or rest. Seeing that He is ever calm while ever working gives us the peace to plod faithfully on unhurried and unworried.

31.15

Sustained generosity requires a strong work ethic. The lazy cannot be continuously generous. Provision for others is not magical; it is methodical and measured, working humbly and quietly over time in order to provide the means for rest and renewal. Giving is not automatically helpful, for planning in our giving to do good labor is required. Indiscriminate giving does more harm than good. If we want our giving to be grace-laced, then we must labor to ensure the gift is timely, appropriate, measured, empowering, and dignifying. Lazy giving cripples and embitters rather than strengthens and advances. The best gifts have hidden work behind them.

31.16

God intends expansion and growth, blessings that multiply. He wants us to have a holy dissatisfaction with a static life. We should always be dynamically seeking more of Him, so that we have more to bless others. To be satisfied with how much we have of Jesus is suspect. Because He is infinite, we are to infinitely want more of Him, and wonderfully we have an infinite capacity to receive more of Him. That ever-expanding capacity is for the singular reason of growing in our channeling of God's blessing to others. How extraordinary heaven will be, everyone expanding in their capacity to receive more of God so they can be more of a blessing to others. Goodness unfathomable and eternally increasing.

31.17

Wisdom takes responsibility for its own increased strength and invests the profits. The wise realize that the current of life ceaselessly pulls us towards folly and that wisdom is not a status effortlessly maintained. We are only wise if we grow in wisdom, if we daily work at getting wiser. Wisdom is a muscle to be exercised daily; otherwise, it atrophies. My friend Dr. Jim Bradford reminds us that "no one can do your growing for you!" We do not gain wisdom or integrity by observation or association. It must be appropriated by action, by repeated decisions to do as we have observed wise mentors do, to obey for ourselves what has been commanded in Scripture and by the Spirit.

31.18

We are to hold the ground we gain before rushing on to the next best thing before our advances are consolidated and secured. God is ever concerned about quality, and quantity is never expected or desired if it is inferior. Godly growth consolidates goodness, steadily expanding its health like the rings of a tree trunk, rather than rushing up like rootless, sickly weeds. Both qualitative and quantitative growth is the work of all seasons, a slow relentless march that will not be denied. Seen or unseen, hidden or on display, recognized or overlooked, punched or praised, the wise soul doggedly advances. Night and day pressing toward Christlike character, while others sleep.

31.19

We are to embrace the routine, the repetitive daily grind, and find glory in the simple things that we do over and again. G. K. Chesterton in his book *Orthodoxy* wrote: "Because children have abounding vitality, because they are in spirit fierce and free, therefore they want things repeated and unchanged. They always say, 'Do it again'; and the grown-up person does it again until he is nearly dead. For grown-up people are not strong enough to exult in monotony. But perhaps God is strong enough to exult in monotony. It is possible that God says every morning, 'Do it again' to the sun; and every evening, 'Do it again' to the moon. It may not be automatic necessity that makes all daisies alike; it may be that God makes every daisy separately, but has never got tired of making them. It may be that He has the eternal appetite of infancy; for we have sinned and grown old, and our Father is younger than we."[11]

31.20

Generosity begins before you are wealthy. The truly rich are those who learned generosity while still poor. Wealth tends to make you stingy, not generous. The mark of the truly Godlike giver is that we give more than we can afford, we give both sacrificially and gladly. In fact, there is a giddy joy, a wondrous pleasure in giving more than is rational, more than you are "supposed to." God giving His only Son, the Just for the unjust, is ridiculously sublime after all. When we give something so precious it hurts us in order to heal and help others, there is a matchless expansion of our soul—we have less but become more. True sacrifice has both a measure of sadness and a divine, satisfied joy.

31.21

Fear is overcome by preparation, and preparation is buttressed by prayer. When we prepare by praying, we need not worry or fret. There are other valuable preparatory measures—we read, study, research, rehearse, work, store up, think, strategize, imagine, anticipate, etc.—but all these practical exercises are invigorated through prayer. In fact, to not pray as we plan is to sin, for we scorn the wisdom offered by the Spirit and we miss out on the peace and power that He alone can add to the process. Strategic processes that ignore or pay token attention to the Spirit are sinful and suspect. Prayer is the best insurance we can offer for those we love, prayer for them before their day of trial or testing. Certainly, we pray our friends and family through the storm, but let us not neglect to pave their storm passage ahead of time through prayer.

31.22

Self-respect is the foundation of dignity, both for yourself and for others. Those disrespectful of themselves are the most undignified, demeaning themselves and thus ultimately injuring their friends and family. We best take care of others when we are judicious about self-care. We only pour our lives out for others well over time if we have taken care of our own bodies and souls well in time. The lesson of the five wise virgins is that some oil (our intimate time with Jesus, His care, and our care for ourselves) is not to be shared. Folly neglects soul care and leaves us empty, powerless to effectively serve others. We only have resources to constantly give out if we have been diligent to constantly receive in. It is foolish, false humility and indeed long-term selfishness when we neglect to guard and replenish our own oil.

31.23

We are most glorified when we make others valued and valuable. This is true with both God and man. Worship of the Holy glorifies the unholy in that our praise of Jesus adorns us. We are more beautiful and more valuable the more we value and beautify Jesus who is invaluable. One of the most beautiful things a spouse or friend, a follower or leader can do for others is to beautify them, to praise them behind their backs, to value them to others, to speak life and blessing, to cherish, to honor, to loyally defend. The beauty in beautification is that the beautifier is also adorned. We shine best when we beam light on others. We are most beautiful when we glorify others, and we are divinely beautiful when we glorify Jesus. The converse is also true—we are ugliest when we slander and scorn.

31.24

God loves industry and initiative. Wise leadership empowers others to help, to contribute, to own, to belong, to take responsibility. We best help ourselves by helping others. God ever intends His people to be channels of blessing, to be interconnected segments of life-giving flow. God loves hard workers, and He especially loves it when hard workers unite for the greatest good. Sadly and ironically, many hard workers, especially those from individualistic cultures, do not work well with others. This independence is often laced with pride, as collective work results in collective praise and all too often the industrious are unwilling to share credit. The pride of life can drive us both to work hard and hoard glory. Pride then always limits the spread of good; humility always expands it.

31.25

Hope is based in hard work. Peace is formed through patient perseverance. The joys of tomorrow are determined by the calmly steadfast obedience of today. Deferred gratification stewards the strength and honor of today towards the gladness and wholeness of tomorrow. When work is seen as a means to an end, we long to be free from it. When work is seen as dignified and rewarding in itself (as it was for God), then we relish it over time. Our eternal state will be joy—joy in activity, industry, exploits, adventure, discovery, and advance. Hudson Taylor famously said: "There are three stages to every great work of God: first it is impossible, then it is difficult, then it is done." And what reward there is in seeing the difficult done! Which is why heaven will yet have difficult work for us, for delight is not only found in passive ease, but further found in active challenge.

31.26

A prominent mark of true teaching is kindness. Arrogance, no matter how articulate, is laced with folly. If we are cruel, we are not truly wise, for cruelty tears down and destroys. Cruel intelligence puffs up self while kind intelligence builds up others. Only those who use their intelligence to edify are enduringly wise, their wisdom enhanced and enriched by their kindness. Those whose intelligence is cruel are undermined by it and self-destruct, neglecting the eternal law which cautions that any damage to others is ultimately damage to themselves. Satanic wisdom is mean and only ends up hurting him, his minions, and his slaves. Christlike wisdom is kind and always ultimately does radiating good to others and then to self.

31.27

Character is forged by consistent care for others. After all, we are the keepers of both our brothers and sisters. This keeping is not odious, as self and Satan would have us believe. Sin turns us, bends us, and twists us to see that which is life-giving as life-taking. Satan thought worship was demeaning when in reality it is what ultimately fulfils the creation. Sin thinks that serving others is boring and beneath us, and Jesus reminds us it is glorious and noble. When we gladly and willingly care for others, we look like Jesus and represent Him well in the world. He smiles upon us and surges His joy through our very being. The more we act like Jesus, the happier we are. Wisdom resists and exposes the lies of sin, self, and Satan, and spends itself on the good of others, reaping the benefit of godly character, which has its own intrinsic joy.

31.28

Praise from those closest to us (who are unafraid) is the most genuine. Praise from those we domineer or threaten is flattery at best and lies at worst. Praise from those who have seen us at our worst, seen us unguarded, seen us unfiltered, seen us in pain, seen us in loss, seen us in defeat, and seen us under pressure is the most legitimate. No prize or praise from the outside can match that of those who know us best. Folly strives for laud by those far away by exposing only its strengths; wisdom revels in pleasing those who see our weaknesses. To be praised by those who are near is much, much harder than to be praised by those who are far. To be praised by those who are near and know us fully is much,

much more valuable than the praise of those who only know us in part.

31.29

The most noble woman in the world, the most excellent woman of all, is the hardworking wife and mother or the single lady who lays down her life for others. Greater love hath no woman like this. It is the foolishness of the world that fixates first on the fading façade of women, consigning them to neurosis as they age, for they can only decline in beauty. It is the wisdom of the ages that sees the character of godly women and calls them beautiful, for that beauty only increases in time. The most excellent woman of all is the one whose internal beauty constantly grows casting its light from the inside out. The woman most to be pitied is she who is dark on the inside while her external light quickly and constantly fades.

31.30

The God-fearing woman is breathtakingly gorgeous. Charm lingers a little longer than natural beauty but unsupported by spiritual character ultimately fades away. Youth and charm in both men and women that is unsupported by Christlike character decays over time and exposes the ugly heart beneath the external beauty. Inward charm and the beauty of character grow with time, and the decay and aging of the body reveal what is pure, good, and praiseworthy. External beauty garners short-term praise, a premature crescendo that disappears with shocking speed. Internal beauty is not quickly noticed, but it grows with time and once discovered cannot go unseen or unpraised.

31.31

God will publicly reward the hardworking who labor daily in obscurity. He will honor them with soul-bursting joy and satisfaction. Wise men will praise godly women, revering and cherishing them to the mutual good of family, society, and the earth. Wise acts will be their own reward, lavishing upon those who do them lasting respect and honor. At the end of the day, at the end of all things, a central component of wisdom is the law of reaping and sowing. Whatever we plant in the dark we will harvest in the light. Wise men and women diligently plant good secretly, softly, silently, and sacredly, and they harvest glory sweetly, satisfyingly, celebrated, and at rest.

Endnotes

1. Men and women of faith and wisdom from years gone by.

2. From the hymn "I'm Pressing on the Upward Way" by Johnson Oatman Jr.

3. From the hymn "Lead on, O King Eternal" by Ernest W. Shurtleff.

4. From *Marriage to a Difficult Man: The Uncommon Union of Jonathan & Sarah Edwards* by Elisabeth D. Dodds (Auduborn Press, 2005).

5. From Mark Antony's speech in Shakespeare's *Julius Caesar:*
   "Friends, Romans, countrymen, lend me your ears;
   I come to bury Caesar, not to praise him.
   The evil that men do lives after them;
   The good is oft interred with their bones;
   So let it be with Caesar. The noble Brutus
   Hath told you Caesar was ambitious:
   If it were so, it was a grievous fault,
   And grievously hath Caesar answer'd it.

Here, under leave of Brutus and the rest—
For Brutus is an honourable man..."

6. From the hymn "A Mighty Fortress Is Our God" by Martin Luther.

7. The actual line "The evil that men do lives after them; The good is oft interred with their bones" is from William Shakespeare's play *Julius Caesar*.

8. From *Memoir and Remains of the Rev. Robert Murray M'Cheyne, Minister of St. Peter's Church, Dundee* by Andrew Bonar (Miami: HardPress, 2017).

9. From the hymn "Jesus, Thy Blood and Righteousness" by Nikolaus von Zinzendorf.

10. From the hymn "A Mighty Fortress Is Our God" by Martin Luther.

11. From *Orthodoxy* by G. K. Chesterton (New York: John Lane Co., 1909).

Also available from

LIVE | DEAD

The Live Dead Journal

Live Dead The Journey

Live Dead The Story

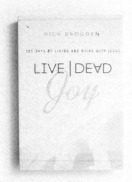
Live Dead Joy

The Live Dead Journal:
Her Heart Speaks

Diario: Vivir Muerto

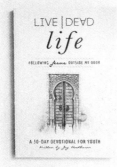
Live Dead Life

Live Dead India:
The Common Table

This Gospel

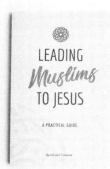
Leading Muslims to Jesus

Live Dead Together

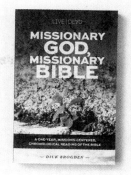
Missionary God, Missionary Bible

Cannibal Island

Hunter and Hunted

Indomitable

Check out our full line of Live Dead books at
www.abidepublishers.com which include:

Individual and group devotionals
Graphic novel biographies of missionaries
Challenging and inspiring stories from work among unreached people